T0293046

Python

AND

Math Essentials for Machine Learning

A BEGINNER'S GUIDE

Anthony Mauro

Python and Math Essentials for Machine Learning

A Beginner's Guide

Anthony Mauro

ISBN 979-8-35096-062-4

To Mom
December 11, 1941 - December 23, 2023

TABLE OF CONTENTS

FORWARD

Intelligence has long been *the* defining characteristic of what makes us human. Yet we, as archetypes of intelligent behavior, have never been given a user manual for the human brain. Nevertheless, a typical child can stand upright (a balancing task) by age 1, speak (a language task) by age 3, and play with balls (a spatio-temporal prediction task) by kindergarten age. These tasks might seem trivial to a human yet they are, in fact, extraordinarily difficult to teach a machine. As Prof. Marvin Minsky would find out when he launched the Artificial Intelligence program in 1959 at the Lincoln Lab at MIT, the simple task of putting one toy block on top of another—a minimally intelligent behavior—is actually a complex task for a machine to learn! This "summer project" would expand into decades-long efforts and eventually evolve into the world's first laboratory dedicated to Artificial Intelligence whose work laid the groundwork for future AI research and education.

Since then, time has progressed and, likewise, AI has progressed as well. Gone are the days in the 70s and 80s when Artificial Intelligence was nothing more than "Artificial Stupidity". No longer do AI programs exhibit *intelligence* by performing simplistic operations quickly, such as an exhaustive search of a game tree. Now, with the advent of Large Language Models, Transformers, and Generative AI, the once insurmountable Turing Test is fast becoming just an afterthought from a bygone era.

Today, we live in a special time in human history–an inflection point if you will–when intelligence is no longer the exclusive domain of *homo sapiens*. In fact, all indications point to the perhaps uncomfortable reality that we may even be the *last* generation of humans to possess an intelligence level superior to machines!

So where are we heading? Will AI lead to a Utopian world where countries no longer see the need to invade another? Where the transformative benefits of AI are universally accessible across national, racial, and religious boundaries leading to world peace. Or will it be a Dystopian existence under the tyranny of an omni-intelligent, rogue computer network named "Skynet"? Where humans barely find their relevance as a sprocket in the ever-expanding universe of immortal intelligent machines.

Imagine just two years ago, only a select few experts and researchers knew of the existence of ChatGPT. Yet today, ChatGPT has become a household name, an innovative tool for anyone with internet access. As such, our collective future is still being shaped every day. This is exactly what makes living in this period of human history uniquely exciting. However, the truth is, it is often the outliers that push forward the frontiers of society. This was true during the Italian Renaissance by the likes of Da Vinci and Galileo. This was true during the Age of Discovery with Columbus and Cook. This was the case again during the Industrial Revolutions by Tesla, Edison, and the Wright brothers.

For AI educators, it is not a hyperbole that they also play a key role in shaping the future of humanity. Through this book, Tony Mauro aims to empower AI educators in the task of equipping the next generation of young minds and future outliers with instruction and insights into artificial intelligence and how it should be used for the maximum benevolence of mankind. It is hardly an overstatement of the immense opportunity and responsibility that an AI education can impart to the future good of society. Let us each take part in the newest revolution to face mankind: the age of AI.

Victor H. Chan
Founder and CEO, Machyna, Inc.
Del Mar, California
March, 2024

INTRODUCTION

When considering the vast landscape of technological evolution, one force has emerged as a true game-changer, reshaping the way we live, work, and interact with the world around us - Artificial Intelligence (AI). AI encompasses the development of systems or machines capable of performing tasks that typically require human intelligence. It aims to create machines that can reason, learn, perceive their environment, and make decisions.

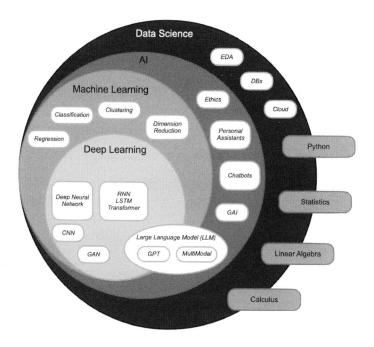

In the broad field of Data Science, Machine Learning is a specialized subset of AI that focuses on developing algorithms enabling systems to learn and improve from experience. In essence, machine learning is the engine that drives AI, providing the ability for machines to automatically learn and adapt without explicit programming. While AI encompasses a broader goal of mimicking human intelligence, machine learning acts as the practical application, enabling systems to autonomously acquire knowledge and enhance their performance over time.

Thus, machine learning, the force behind self-driving cars, intuitive personal assistants, intelligent product recommendations, human-like robots, and the seamless magic of web searches, is not just a subject of academic curiosity; it is the very heartbeat of innovation in our society. It is the engine driving unprecedented progress, redefining industries, and, quite literally, shaping the way we experience the world.

Picture a world where your car learns to anticipate your needs and navigates through the bustling streets with an uncanny sense of intuition. Imagine personal assistants that not only respond to your queries but understand the nuances of your preferences, adapting and learning from each interaction. Envision a shopping experience where recommendations are not just products but reflections of your unique taste, intelligently curated through the lens of machine learning.

From healthcare diagnostics that predict illnesses in their infancy to financial systems that analyze intricate patterns in real-time, machine learning is not merely a tool; it is the foundation of intelligent systems that augment human capabilities and redefine what is possible.

In the book series, "Machine Learning: A Beginner's Guide", we will unravel the intricacies of machine learning, demystifying its power and potential. The adventure begins with the first book in the series "Python and Math Essentials for Machine Learning: A Beginner's Guide" as Python becomes your linguistic companion, opening doors to the world of data structures, recursion, object-oriented-programming, and advanced functions through a literate programming approach. Then, layered on top of Python are the bread-and-butter libraries of NumPy, Pandas, and Matplotlib which provide the tools and functions used to pre-process, vectorize, and visualize your data. Finally, the essential mathematics required to implement and analyze machine learning algorithms is then covered, including key concepts in Statistics, Linear Algebra, and Calculus.

The subsequent books in the series, "Machine Learning Algorithms: A Beginner's Guide" and "Artificial Neural Networks: A Beginner's Guide" journey through the application of the foundational concepts covered in the first book to traditional machine learning algorithm implementations.

In "Machine Learning Algorithms: A Beginner's Guide," Regression, Classification, Clustering, and Dimension Reduction are explored, then validation methods are covered to assist with choosing which algorithms to use and how to evaluate them.

In "Artificial Neural Networks: A Beginner's Guide," you will uncover the principles that govern Artificial Neural Networks (ANNs) and explore the vast terrains of Deep Neural Nets (DNNs), Convolutional Neural Networks (CNNs), and introductions to the foundational elements behind Natural Language Processing (NLP) and Large Language Models (LLMs).

SECTION 1:

Python Programming for Machine Learning

In this section we will cover the fundamental concepts supported in the standard Python programming language.

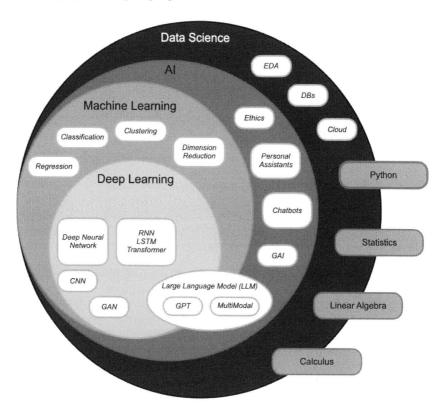

LEARNING OBJECTIVES

By the end of this section, you will be able to do the following:

- Create a working Python script in the Google Colaboratory Environment
- Identify the Python built-in primitive and non-primitive data types
- Write a Python conditional statement (all forms)
- Write a Python function utilizing positional, arbitrary, and keyword arguments
- Write a Python script implementing Lists, Dictionaries, Tuples, Sets, Stacks, and Queues
- Write a Python script implementing NumPy and Pandas data structures and visualizing data with Matplotlib

CHAPTER 1:
PYTHON FUNDAMENTALS

INTRODUCTION

In this chapter we focus on Python Fundamentals. This starts from the beginning, describing the code development environment we will use for this course as well as the basics of Python. The topics described in this Module include:

- Google Colaboratory Integrated Development Environment (IDE), Variables, Data types, Printing
- Boolean operations, Conditional Statements, Loops
- Functions
- Test and Debug

LEARNING OBJECTIVES

By the end of this chapter, you will be able to do the following:

- Create a working Python script in the Google Colaboratory Integrated Development Environment
- Identify several Python built-in data types
- Write a Python conditional statement (all forms)
- Write a Python function utilizing positional, arbitrary, and keyword arguments
- Test and debug your Python programs

1.1:

GOOGLE COLABORATORY INTEGRATED DEVELOPMENT ENVIRONMENT (IDE)

Examples	Recent	Google Drive	GitHub	Upload

Filter notebooks

Title	First opened	Last opened	
CO Welcome To Colaboratory	8 days ago	0 minutes ago	
CO first_steps_with_tensor_flow.ipynb	3 days ago	3 days ago	
O mandelbrot.ipynb	3 days ago	3 days ago	
CO tensorflow_programming_concepts.ipynb	3 days ago	3 days ago	
CO intro_to_pandas.ipynb	3 days ago	3 days ago	

NEW PYTHON 3 NOTEBOOK ▾   CANCEL

The first thing we'll need to write our code is a development environment. There are several Integrated Development Environments, or IDEs available. In this course series we'll use the Google Colaboratory, or 'Colab' environment but you could also use Jupyter notebooks, as the code format and execution is compatible in both these IDEs. The code examples and reference templates including embedded test scripts provided in this course series will all be Colab files, so it is recommended that this IDE or Jupyter notebooks be used as you develop your code.

The Colab IDE is cloud-based, and you'll need a Google account to create and save your code and data files. To set up the Colab environment, point your browser to https://colab.research.google.com/.

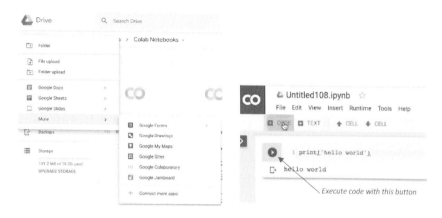

Execute code with this button

One of the powerful features of Colab is that no local development environment installation is needed, which is useful if you have processing or memory limitations in your computer. It also minimizes the headaches involved in managing library installation and keeping track of which library versions you currently have installed - these are easily changed in the Colab environment.

Creating a Colab notebook is quite simple if you are familiar with the Google suite of tools, such as Docs, Slides, or Sheets. Given that we'll be working in the cloud, your files will be saved automatically and accessible from any machine with a browser and internet connection. There are also Python packages that are available and example code that we will access during this course.

Now, the notebook is comprised of editable cells, and that's where you will write your Python code. You can execute either a single line or a multiple line program, which we'll refer to as a 'script' in each cell. Additionally, Python libraries and packages can be imported and installed. The cells in a Colab file are either code-based or text-based, where the text-based cells are primarily used for documentation purposes and the code-based cells for the executable scripts.

Each cell contains a small Play button graphic located in the upper left corner of the cell, and to execute the code, simply press Play and Colab will launch the code and output any of your results, including text or graphics on the console located directly beneath the code cell.

Documenting your work in text cells will be required in the courses in this series for the Colab notebooks that you'll be creating. The text boxes have simple editing tools available to support your formatting preferences. You can also add math equations using LaTeX, which is a coding scheme that allows inserting standard mathematical symbols directly into the text stream.

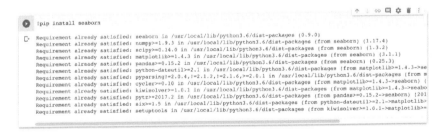

Finally, you can install Python packages that are not already available via the import command using Pip, which stands for "Package Installer for Python"]. Pip is the defacto standard package installer for all versions of Python. If you use pip on your local machine, you can install the version you need or just specify it in the code cell in Colab.

1.2:

DATA TYPES

Now let's look at some of the introductory concepts in Python, including data types, variables, printing, and how to comment code.

Python supports several data types which we'll cover in detail in future chapters. The most familiar are *Numerics*, which are the numbers that we are used to working with, such as whole or integer numbers, decimal or floating-point numbers, and complex numbers. Another familiar data type are "Strings". Strings are a collection of single characters which may form words, spaces, special characters, or a combination of these and are defined in Python with either a single or double quote around them. The *Boolean* data type includes binary values which take on the values of either True or False. Another data type includes collections of multiple items stored in an organized fashion, and those are called *Sequences*. Sequences include *Lists*, *Tuples* and *Range* types where each element in the collection is indexed by a number. Sequences can be either mutable, which means you can change them, or immutable, which means you cannot. There are some benefits to data being immutable. For example, immutable sequences are faster to access, which is an important consideration when training a machine learning model. Finally, *Dictionaries* are a collection of items that are indexed, not by numbers as with Sequences, but with keys, forming what are called a key-value pairs. We'll see that Dictionaries are also very applicable in the implementation of many machine learning algorithms.

```
1    #Data type examples
2    #Numerics
3    myInt = 5
4    myFloat = 3.478
5
6    #String
7    myString = 'Hello World'
8
9    #Lists
10   myList1 = [1,2,3,4]
11   myList2 = ['Cat','Dog','Horse']
12   my_list3 = [1.3,4.35,7.1,9.0]
13
14   #Boolean
15   my_boolean_1 = True
16   my_boolean_2 = False
17
18   #Dictionaries
19   my_dict1 = {1:'Tom', 2:'Kate', 3:'Jim'}
20   my_dict2 = {'Key1':'Hello','Key2': 'My','Key3':'World' }
21
22   print('Hello World')
23   print('Numeric Integer:', myInt)
24   print('Numeric Float:', myFloat)
25   print('String:', myString)
26   print('List1:', myList1)
27   print('List2:', myList2)
28   print('List3:', my_list3)
29   print('Boolean1:', my_boolean_1)
30   print('Boolean2:', my_boolean_2)
31   print('Dictionary1:', my_dict1)
32   print('Dictionary2:', my_dict2)
```

Now one of the nice things about Python is that it will automatically sense the data type when you assign it to a variable in your code, as opposed to other programming languages which require you to declare the data type first. So, for each of the data types just described, a variable declaration and assignment was done simply by creating a name and assigning it a value. Standard programming convention is to define descriptive variable names either using "camel case" or "snake case" formatting. In camel case, we start the variable name with a lower-case letter and use upper case letters to delimit separation between different words in the variable name, while in snake case, the delimiter is an underscore. For example, if we wanted to assign a variable to the string "my string," we could either name it *myString* (camel case) or *my_string* (snake case).

To print out either text or text mixed with the contents of the variables, we simply use the print command with the contents of what we want to print with open and closed parentheses. If using a mix of text and variables, you will need to delimit them in the print statement with a comma. The Python print statement displays its output in the console then moves to the next line. The output of the code example above is shown here.

```
Hello World
Numeric Integer: 5
Numeric Float: 3.478
String: Hello World
List1: [1, 2, 3, 4]
List2: ['Cat', 'Dog', 'Horse']
List3: [1.3, 4.35, 7.1, 9.0]
Boolean1: True
Boolean2: False
Dictionary1: {1: 'Tom', 2: 'Kate', 3: 'Jim'}
Dictionary2: {'Key1': 'Hello', 'Key2': 'My', 'Key3': 'World'}
```

Python is not pre-compiled like some other programming languages; it is an interpreted language which means that the execution runs line by line. Python is also dynamically typed. So, when defining a variable, you do not have to tell the processor its datatype – Python will automatically detect that and assign it the proper memory allocation.

Commenting your code is always highly recommended and good programmers take the time to make sure their code is properly documented through comments. If you want to insert block comments or single-line comments, use triple quotes or the hashtag symbol respectively. For block comments, use three single quotes to delimit the beginning and the end of the block as shown in the code example.

We can create nicer looking output from our code using formatted print statements and type casting. Type casting is a mechanism to convert or "cast" the data type of a variable to another data type. For example, the output of a Numeric variable can be converted to a String then that String can in turn be concatenated to another String using the "+" symbol, and this converts the printed output into one contiguous String. Note that we do not use the comma in the print statement when concatenating strings together in our output as opposed to what was shown in the previous print example.

To format numeric types, we can use the percentage symbol to define the number of digits that get printed. For example, we can print out text and embed numeric formatting within a string as shown in the following example.

```
1   #This is a single line comment
2   ''' This is a block
3   comment (3 single quotes)'''
4
5   # Type casting
6   x_new = 3.425
7   x_list = [7, 3, 8, 2, 0]
8   print ('Printout a float: '+ str(x_new))
9   print ('Size of x_list: ' + str(len(x_list)))
10
11  # Formatted print statements
12  boys = 120
13  totalStudents = 240
14  k = 7
15  user_id = 3
16  print('Output1 : %03d, Output2 : %5.2f' %(14, 5.333))
17  print('Total students : %3d, Boys : %02d' %(totalStudents, boys))
18  print('%1.4E' %(356.08977))
19  print('{0} most similar users for User {1}:\n'.format(k, user_id))
20  print('x_new reformatted %1.1f' %(x_new))
```

In this example the %02d prints a leading 0 followed by the first output, where the 'd' indicates an integer number format, that is no decimal point is printed in the output. The %5.2f in the example refers to the second output and has 5 spots allocated to the integer part of the output and 2 spots allocated to the fractional part. The f in the format indicates the output is floating point, that is it has a decimal point. Note that we can print out actual numbers, or the contents of variables in our formatted print statements. We can also output our numbers in exponential notation using the E designator in our formatting. In this case our output has 1 spot allocated to the integer and 4 allocated to the fractional part, where the output is rounded to fit within the number of digits allocated, and the E in the output represents the power of 10 that the number is multiplied by.

```
Printout a float: 3.425
Size of x_list: 5
Total Students : 240, Boys : 120
Output1 : 014, Output2 : 5.33
Total students : 240, Boys : 120
3.5609E+02
7 most similar users for User 3:
```

Shown in the next code block are some examples of basic math operations that can be performed in Python. The usual symbols are used for addition, subtraction, multiplication, and division. Exponents in Python are implemented using double asterisk symbols. The *floor* operations is implemented using the double forward slash. Recall *floor* performs standard division but truncates the fractional part, without rounding, so that only the integer is remaining. Python version three and onward will automatically convert integers to floats for the division operation. If you would like to perform a floating-point truncation operation in Python, like how it is done in Java by declaring two variables as integers and performing division which truncates off the fractional part, you must use the floor operation.

Finally, the 'modulus' operator is implemented with the percentage symbol. This operation performs division and returns the remainder. For example, 6 mod 5 would be computed as 6 divided by 5 which is 1 with a remainder of 1, so would return the remainder value of 1.

For complicated equations, the order of precedence follows the acronym PEMDAS (parenthesis, exponents, multiplication, division, addition, subtraction). If you are in doubt, use parentheses to define operations that should be grouped together and their order of execution, with the innermost parentheses defining operations executing first and the outer most executing last.

```
1    # Basic math
2
3    V = 4.5
4    W = 7.1
5    X = 5
6    Y = 4
7    Z = 6
8
9    print('Addition: ', X+Y)
10   print('Subtraction: ', X-Y)
11   print('Multiplication: ', X*Y)
12   print('Division (integer): ', Y//X) #use floor operator
13   print('Division: ', Y/X) #integer divide yields float
14   print('Division: ', V/W) #float divide yields float
15   print('Exponent: ', X**Y)
16   print('Modulus: ', Z%X)
17
18   print('mod of a negative number -5mod8: ', -5%8
```

Finally, we can format what are called escape sequences within our print statements. The /n escape sequence forces a line feed in the output. The /t escape sequence inserts a tab in the output. The single slash escape sequence will allow the next character to be printed if it is a control character such as a single quote. Recall a single quote is used to delimit a string so if we want to have that symbol printed, we need to precede it with a single slash.

The individual characters in a string can be accessed using the standard zero-based array indexing scheme used in other programming languages. Zero based means the first character in the string is accessed using the index 0, the fourth character, is indexed using 3 and so on. If the index is a negative number, the reference point from which the character is indexed is from the last character. So, in the example of the following code block, the negative represents the second character from the end of the string.

Some useful String functions include *upper* which prints out the characters of a string in upper case, *lower* which prints out the characters of a string in lower case, and *len* which returns the length in number of characters of a string. And as we showed previously, we can concatenate strings using the plus symbol.

We show several examples in the following code block along with the output.

```
1   #Strings
2
3   myString = 'This is MY string.'
4   myString2= 'I\'m tired!'
5   pi = 3.14159
6
7   print(myString2)
8   print(myString[0])
9   print(myString[3])
10  print(myString[-2])
11  print('Length of string: ', len(myString))
12  print('Upper case: ', myString.upper())
13  print('Lower case: ', myString.lower())
14  print('Concatenated string: ', myString + '\t' + myString2 )
15  print('Printing a float: ', pi
```

```
I'm tired!
T
s
g
Length of string: 18
Upper case: THIS IS MY STRING.
Lower case: this is my string.
Concatenated string: This is MY string.        I'm tired!
Printing a float: 3.14159
```

1.3:

CONDITIONAL STATEMENTS

All programming languages include the ability to implement conditional statements, and the way they do this is by evaluating statements using comparators which evaluate to either true or false, then taking some kind of action based on the comparison. In Python the comparators we use are defined in the following table. Each operation is intuitive, and we will show their use in some examples later.

Function	Operator
Equal	==
Not equal	!=
Less than	<
Less than or equal	<=
Greater than	>
Greater than or equal	>=

One important note of caution, though, is with the "==" comparator function. Note that checking if a variable is equal to another is done using the double equal operator. A common mistake that causes many bugs to go initially unnoticed is to use a single equal instead of double equal in a comparison statement. Using single equals will simply make an assignment and will return a True even if performed within an if statement. In other words,

var_a == var_b	Checks if var_a is equal to var_b and returns "True" if so
var_a = var_b	Assigns var_a to the value of var_b

We also can condense our code a bit by using compound comparators as shown in the following table.

Logic Function evaluates True	Python Operator	Operator in other languages
All inputs True —> True	and	&&
One input True —> True	or	||
True —> False False —> True	not	!

The three basic functions include: *and*, *or*, and *not*. Each of these operators implement a Boolean logical function. The *and* operator requires all input conditions to be True for the output to be True. The *or* operator requires at least one, but not all, of the input conditions to be True for the output to be True. And the *not* operator simply takes the opposite Boolean state of an input condition. In other words, an input that is True would evaluate False and vice-versa if using the *not* operator. The following code block provide several conditional statements which evaluate and print out either True or False.

```
1    #Booleans
2    X = 5
3    Y = 4
4    Z = 6
5
6    print('Compound boolean 1:', 1 < 2 and 4 != 4)
7    print('Compound boolean 2:', -(-(-(-3))) == 3 and 4 >= 16**0.5)
8    print('Compound boolean 3:', 19 % 4 == 300/10/10 and True)
9    print('Compound boolean 4:', -(1**2) < 2**0 and 10%10 <= 20-10*2)
10   print('Compound boolean 5:', True and False)
11   print('Compound boolean 6:', X > Y+Z )
12   print('Compound boolean 7:', X == (Z-Y)/2*5 )
13   print('Compound boolean 8:', 'hello' == 'Hello' )
14   print('Compound boolean 8:', 'Hello' == 'Hello' )
15   print('Output is: ', X**2 < 25 or Y**2 <= 16)
```

```
Compound boolean 1: False
Compound boolean 2: True
Compound boolean 3: True
Compound boolean 4: True
Compound boolean 5: False
Compound boolean 6: False
Compound boolean 7: True
Compound boolean 8: False
Compound boolean 8: True
Output is: True
```

Now we're going to put the Boolean comparator evaluations together with some conditional statements, but before we do that, we'll discuss the specific Python syntax and scope for these statements. The comparison structures in Python use the keywords *if, elif* and *else.*

The code syntax of the *if* and *elif* statements is to surround the evaluated condition with parentheses and end the line with a colon. The *else* statement is just terminated with a colon, no condition is evaluated because this is the catch-all state, in other words, the else is used if all the other *if's* and *elif's* evaluate to False. Also note the indentation of each of the print statements under each of the *if, elif,* and *else* statements. Python defines what is called its scope with indentation. For example, all lines that are indented and under line 4 in the example would be executed if the conditional statement evaluated to True. This is different from other languages such as java and C which use brackets to define their scopes. So be careful when writing your Python code to use proper indentation.

Now let's check out a few examples, shown in the following code block, to illustrate each of the *if, elif,* and *else* statements. Note that Python does not require braces or brackets to define scope in the code, where scope refers to the code that will execute when the conditional statement evaluates to True. Instead, scope is defined in Python by indentation rules. We will show several examples on how this works but any code block that would run, say under a conditional statement, in a loop, or in a function, is delimited by an indentation scheme.

In Example 1, we evaluate an assigned integer variable X against several values and print out a message based on which comparison is evaluated as True.

Since 15 is greater than 10 the first *if* statement evaluates to False so we skip the code indented underneath it and proceed to the next conditional. In the second *if* statement, 15 is greater than or equal to 10 so we print out the message "greater than or equal to 10" and proceed to the next *if* statement. Here 15 is greater than or equal to 15 (it is equal in this case) so we print out the message "greater than or equal to 15" and proceed to the next *if* statement. Here 15 is not greater than or equal to 20 so we do not execute its print statement. Note that in this example, all the conditional statements were executed since they were formed as independent *if* statements; that is, they have no *elif* or *else* statements in the code block.

In Example 2 and 3, we evaluate an assigned integer variable *Y* against several values and print out a message based on which comparison is evaluated as True. In Example 2, the first conditional statement evaluates to True because 15 is less than 18, so we print the message 'under 18' then jump to the bottom of the *if-elif-else* code block because the *elif* and *else* statements are only executed if the previous statements evaluate to False. In other words, since the previous *if* statement in the block evaluated to True, we do not execute any of the following *elif*'s or *else* statements.

In the Example 3, we evaluate the first conditional statement to False since 28 is greater than 18 so the program jumps to the following *elif* statement, which again evaluates to False since 28 is greater than 20. The program then jumps to the following *elif* statement which evaluates to True since 28 is less than 30 so we print the message '20 or over, but under 30' then jump to the end of the *if-elif-else* code block in the program.

```
1    #Conditionals
2
3    #Example 1
4    X = 15
5    if(X < 10):
6        print('less than 10')
7    if(X >= 10):
8        print('greater than or equal to 10')
9    if(X >= 15):
10       print('greater than or equal to 15')
11   if(X >= 20):
12       print('greater than or equal to 20')

14   #Example 2
15   Y = 15
16   if(Y < 18):
17       print('under 18')
18   elif(Y < 20):
19       print('18 or over, but under 20')
20   elif(Y < 30):
21       print('20 or over, but under 30')
22   else:
23       print('30 or over')

14   #Example 3
15   Y = 28
16   if(Y < 18):
17       print('under 18')
18   elif(Y < 20):
19       print('18 or over, but under 20')
20   elif(Y < 30):
21       print('20 or over, but under 30')
22   else:
23       print('30 or over')
```

These examples illustrate simple comparator operators inside the if statements but note that we could have implemented compound conditional statements as described previously with the same results.

Additionally, we can implement multiple *if* statements by nesting them together in our code as shown in the following code block. The nesting operation works like a compound statement. We will explain it with a couple examples here. Can you see why the two conditional statements in the following code produce the same output? If we consider X equals 15 in the example, we will evaluate the conditional statement on line 27 as True since 15 is both greater than 10 and less than 20.

```
27    if(X > 10 and X < 20):
28        print('greater than 10 but less than 20')
29
30
31    if(X > 10):
32        if(X < 20):
33            print('greater than 10 but less than 20')
```

Now the conditional statement on line 31 would evaluate as True so would proceed to the code under it that is indented, and in this case the second conditional would also evaluate as True so we would proceed to the code under it and print the message.

Python programmers need to be careful with how they pair up their *elif* and *else* statements with the corresponding *if* statements when nesting. For example, what would be printed in the following code block if X were equal to 4? Here we see that this conditional would evaluate to False since 4 is less than 10, but if we look at the *elif* statement we see 4 is greater than 2, so should it print the message at line 41? In this case the answer is no since this *elif* is paired with the if statement on line 38 by noting its indentation, and therefore this *elif* statement is not evaluated since we never executed past the first conditional statement on line 37.

```
36    X = 14
37    if(X > 10):
38        if(X > 20):
39            print('greater than 10 but less than 20')
40        elif(X > 2):
41            print('which if do I belong to??')
```

Now what if X were equal 14, what would be the output then? In this case we would evaluate the first conditional on line 37 to True and because of that we would proceed to evaluate if X is greater than 20 on line 38. Since this would evaluate as False, then we would proceed to the *elif* in line 40 and since this would evaluate as True, that is 14 is greater than 2, we would print out the message "which if do I belong to??" on line 41.

1.4:

LOOPS

Loops are a fundamental programming structure that is supported in all programming languages. In fact, the traditional programming model is primarily
built upon both conditional statements and loops, so it is particularly important
to become familiar with them and more specifically how they work with the
Python language.

A loop simply repeats or "iterates" through a sequence of instructions until
some condition is met. There are two basic types of loops that we will consider, the
for loop and the *while* loop. Now, why do we need to know loops? Besides being
a common structure that you will use in most of your programs, loops make code
more efficient, flexible, and readable.

A diagram of a *for* and *while* loop is shown below.

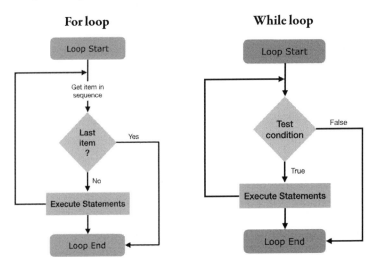

For loops execute program statements over a determined number of iterations. The loop iterates over values in a sequence, which may be a range of numbers or items in a collection. In Python, the syntax includes the keyword *for*, and a representation of the sequence which the loop will be iterated over followed by a colon. The sequence may be defined by a range of integers which establishes how often the loop is executed, and this range is tracked by a variable called an iterator. The for-loop terminates when the iterator cycles through all the items in the sequence. The interval conditions are set at the beginning of the loop usually by initializing the iterator to an integer or reference to a collection of items and then it is checked every cycle through the loop. If the iterator does not meet the termination condition, the program executes the statements indented underneath it. The interval condition is then updated and cycled back to the beginning of the loop. If the termination condition is met, for example all numbers in a range or elements in a list have been cycled through then the loop ends and the program proceeds to the statements outside the scope of the loop (the next statement that is not indented under the loop), otherwise the indented sequence of instructions underneath it are executed again, and this is cycle is repeated until the termination condition is met.

Let's go through some examples. The following code block demonstrates several different versions of the Python for-loop structure. The for-loop on line 26 iterates through all the keys in a dictionary called *inventory1*. in a structure known as a "for each" loop. Now don't worry if you do not know what a Python dictionary is, we will cover that soon. The next loop on line 29 iterates through all the characters in the string *myString*. The example on line 32 iterates through all integers in the range from 0 up to but not including 6. Note that we set the range parameter to 6 here which tells the for-loop to execute 6 times. The iterator, however, assumes zero-based indexing, so the count would start at 0 and end at 5. The next example on line 35 iterates through the integers over the interval starting from the first range parameter, in this case 1, up to but not including the second parameter, 5. The example in line 38 iterates through the integers in the interval from the first range parameter up to but not including the second parameter in steps of the 3rd parameter. So, in this case the loop would iterate starting from 1, up to but not including 10 in steps of 2 resulting in a range of 1,3,5,7, and 9. The final example on line 41 iterates through a range in reverse order, decrementing the interval variable each cycle. So, in this example, the iterator would take on values 100, 80, 60, 40, 20.

		Output
20	#For loops	Coat
21	inventory1 = {'Coat': 1000,	Shirt
22	'Shirt': 2000,	Slacks
23	'Slacks':3000,	Shoes
24	'Shoes': 4000}	m
25		y
26	for item in inventory1:	S
27	print(item)	t
28		r
29	for i in 'myString':	i
30	print(i)	n
31		g
32	for i in range(6): #iterates [0-6) i.e. 0-5	0
33	print(i)	1
34		2
35	for i in range(1,5): #iterates [1-5) i.e. 1-4	3
36	print(i)	4
37		5
38	for i in range(1,10,2): #iterates [1-10) with +2 increment	1
39	print (i)	2
40		3
41	for i in range(100,10,-20): #iterates [100-10) with -20 increment	4
42	print (i)	1
		3
		5
		7
		9
		100
		80
		60
		40
		20

In a *while* loop, we repeat a sequence of instructions if an evaluated condition is true. In Python, the syntax includes the keyword *while*, then the evaluated statement followed by a colon. The evaluated statement is checked at the beginning of the loop and if it is true, the program executes the statements indented underneath it. If the evaluated statement is false, then the program proceeds to the statements outside the scope of the loop.

Let's go through another example. The following code block prompts a user to guess a number that is randomly generated by the computer. The user has 4 tries to guess the number. In addition to the initial setup and input of the user's guess, we initialize a "trial counter" variable in line 8. The while-loop checks a compound condition in line 9, in this case the code is looking to see if the user guessed the random number or if the trial counter is greater than or equal to 4. If not, meaning the user did not guess the number and the trial counter is less than 4, then the code under the while-loop is executed. The code prints out a message and prompts the user for another guess in line 10, then increments the trial counter by 1. Note the short-cut syntax of the code in line 11, here we are incrementing the variable *trialCount* by 1. Then the code returns to the top of the loop to evaluate the conditions again, and if the compound condition is still true then it executes the code underneath it. Now, if the user fails to guess the random number within 4 trials, the variable *trialCount* will be equal to 4 and when that happens, the evaluated condition statement will fail, and the program will fall out of the loop. A couple trial runs of the output are shown.

```
1   #While loops
2
3   from random import randint
4
5   number = randint(1,10) #random int from 1-10
6   userInput = int(input('Try to guess the number (1-10) in less that 4 tries:'))
7
8   trialCount = 1
9   while userInput != number and trialCount <4:
10      userInput = int(input('Wrong - try again:'))
11      trialCount += 1
12
13  if(userInput==number and trialCount<=4):
14      print('You guessed it!!', number)
15  else:
16      print('Sorry you lost :(')
```

```
Try to guess the number (1-10) in less that 4 tries:1
Wrong - try again:2
You guessed it!! 2
```

```
Try to guess the number (1-10) in less that 4 tries:1
Wrong - try again:2
Wrong - try again:3
Wrong - try again:4
Sorry you lost :(
```

One common error that programmers make with while-loops is to improperly form or evaluate the conditional statement. In some cases, the while-loop will always evaluate the condition to True and thus will never exit the loop resulting in "hanging" the program.

For example, if the *trialCount* variable in the previous code block was missing or failed to increment properly within the scope of the loop, the condition statement would never evaluate to False and thus would execute the loop forever. This is called an infinite loop.

Now we will describe a simple application that utilizes a loop. One of the common introductory coding problems that can utilize a loop is the generation of the numbers that follow a Fibonacci sequence. Fibonacci was an Italian mathematician who was born in the 12th century. He studied the growth of a population of rabbits and came up with his famous sequence where the current number is computed as the sum of the previous two numbers, with the exception that the first two numbers are initialized to 0 and 1 respectively. The sequence has impacts today in the areas of computer search algorithms and parallel distributed systems, as well as producing some interesting geometrical patterns. It also can be used to do a rough translation between miles and kilometers where for two consecutive numbers in the sequence the smaller number represents miles and the larger kilometers!

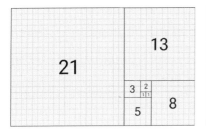 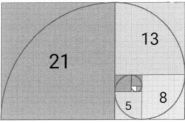

Attribution for images: Wikipedia Creative Commons
https://creativecommons.org/licenses/by/2.5 *by Romain - Own work*

Let's look at some code that will generate the sequence.

		Output
61	count = 0	
62	n1, n2 = 0, 1	
63	NumOfFibTerms = 5 #must be > 1	⮞ 0
64	while count < NumOfFibTerms:	1
65	print(n1)	1
66	next = n1 + n2	2
67	n1 = n2	3
68	n2 = next	
69	count += 1	

We initialize the variables in lines 61 and 62 including a counter for the number of terms we are computing and the first two numbers in the sequence. Then we enter a while-loop, where the number of terms desired is evaluated against a running counter. If the count is smaller than the number of desired terms, then the program executes the statements defined by the scope of the loop; that is, the indented code statements underneath the *while* statement. Inside the loop the sequence number is printed, then the next term is computed in line 66, and the previous two terms are updated with the current terms. Finally, the counter is incremented by 1 in line 69 and the loop cycles back to evaluate the termination condition again.

Another common use of the while-loop is shown in the following example. In this example we show a way that you can implement an infinite loop using a while statement. The while-loop condition, "True" in this case, evaluates whether True is "True", and since it is, the loop would execute forever. The only way the loop could be terminated would be to break out of is using what is called a *break* statement, which we will cover next. But in this example, the string "Python" would be printed on subsequent lines forever.

```
1   while True:
2       print('Python')
```

The final structure we will cover before leaving Python loops is the *break* and *continue* statements. Both these statements allow for modification of the execution sequence in a loop. Now programmers should try to avoid using break and continue statements in their code, mainly because they are not as efficient or "clean" for the processor to manage and could introduce hard-to-find bugs or create security vulnerabilities, but many times they reduce the computational complexity by allowing a program to terminate a loop before the termination condition has been met or to skip ahead in the loop iteration sequence, so they do exist and are frequently used. We show a couple code examples and corresponding outputs showing how you can modify a loop cycle with a break or continue statement.

		Output
1	#Example 1	
2	hello = "Hello World"	
3	print("First word:")	First word:
4	for c in hello:	H
5	if c == " ":	e
6	break	l
7	print(c)	l
8		o
9	#Example 2	No vowels:
10	print("\nNo vowels:")	H
11	for c in hello:	l
12	if (c == 'a' or c == 'e' or c == 'i' or c == 'o' or c == 'u'):	l
13	continue	W
14	print(c)	r
		l
		d

In the Example 1, the break statement on line 6 will cause the for-loop to terminate as soon as the space in the string "Hello World" is encountered, which will occur on the 6th iteration. In Example 2, the *continue* statement will skip all the following code in a block that follows that statement for the current iteration and cause the program to immediately jump back to the beginning of the for-loop. In this case, the print(c) statement would be skipped when a vowel in the input string is encountered. If you have a nested loop, you could modify the sequence in whichever loop the program is currently executing in with a *break* or *continue* statement. The *break* statement would terminate the current loop, and the *continue* statement would skip all the code in a block that follows that statement for the current iteration.

Finally, we'll conclude with some comments about how conditional statements are used in machine learning. The figure depicts a high-level interface diagram of a Traditional Programming versus machine learning model. The traditional programming model shows how conditional statements are built into it whereby a set of rules are implemented, then data is applied to those rules, and based on a set of evaluated conditions between the rules and the data, the answers are generated.

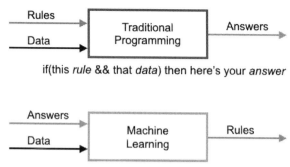

if(this *rule* && that *data*) then here's your *answer*

if(this *answer* && that *data*) then here's your *rule*

Now, even though a machine learning model shows a different ordering of the inputs and outputs, conditional statements are still relied upon. For example, a comparison between the answers, also known as labels, and the model's predicted output may be evaluated and if the difference exceeds a threshold, the parameters in the model may be updated. This is known in machine learning as "training the model". The machine learning model is trained to update its parameters and determine the rules that then can later be deployed in what's called prediction or inference. So even though machine learning has a different way of implementing the programming paradigm, conditional statements are still used throughout.

1.5:

FUNCTIONS

If you have some programming experience, you know that a function is essentially a container for, or reference to a body of code that is grouped together to accomplish a task. Functions are used primarily to help organize code and decompose it into smaller pieces, which results in less memory required to store a program if a sequence of instructions are executed many times, as well as reduces the number of bugs that could arise if the same block of code is copied in several locations in the program. Coding with functions also results in the added benefit that they could be distributed to a team to promote more efficient software development in an organization. A block diagram of the anatomy of a Python function is shown below.

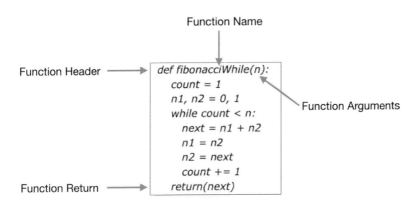

Like conditional statements and loops, all programming languages support functions, which are also known as methods when defined inside an object-oriented programming "class" structure. The main ideas to grasp with Python functions are the syntax of the declaration code, or "header" and the definition of the input and output parameters that can be passed to or returned from it, respectively. In Python, a function header starts with the keyword *def* which stands for "define", followed by the function name, which is used to execute or "call" it in our main program. This is followed with parentheses and arguments inside the parentheses. The arguments are the parameters that are passed in, and there are several different options that can be used when defining them which we will cover in detail. Finally, the header definition ends like a conditional statement or loop, with a colon, which is the standard Python syntax to define the indented block of code underneath it which belongs to the function.

def function_name(args):
   #code
	def function_name(args):
	   #code
	   return x

def function_name(args):
   #code
   return
	def function_name(args):
	   #code
	   return x, y, ...

The return statement in Python is optional, and if not included, or is included without any parameters following it means the function returns nothing. This is called a "void" function. If a return statement is included, it must be the last statement in the function, and it will typically return the result of a calculation containing numerics, collections, sequences, and objects. This is known as a "fruitful" function.

Now that we have defined the function header, we can describe the different argument options that we have with Python. The first option, and this is the most common, contains what are called "positional" arguments. The arguments passed to the function may include none, meaning you would have the function header with the arguments blank, so you just have an open and closed parenthesis, or one or multiple parameters which would be comma separated, in any order, in your parameter list. We do not have to define a datatype for our function parameter list because Python is automatically typed, so we just list the arguments themselves each separated with commas. Now, the reason positional arguments are called "positional" is because when we call the function in our main program, we need to maintain the order of the parameters that we pass in corresponding to the order in which they are listed in the function header. The following code blocks show several examples of functions with positional arguments. The no arguments case is denoted with simply an open and closed parenthesis.

```
41   def fibonacciNoInputArgs():
42       count = 1
43       n1,n2 = 0,1
44       num_of_terms=10
45       while count < num_of_terms:
46           next = n1 + n2
47           n1 = n2
48           n2 = next
49           count += 1
50       return(next)
51
52   print(fibonacciNoInputArgs()
```

A single parameter positional argument example is shown in the following code block, where n is the number of Fibonacci terms to generate.

```
54   def fibonacciWhile(n):
55       count = 1
56       n1,n2 = 0,1
57       while count < n:
58           next = n1 + n2
59           n1 = n2
60           n2 = next
61           count += 1
62       return(next)
63
64   print(fibonacciWhile(7))
```

A multiple parameter positional argument example is shown in the following code block. Note that the order of the arguments in the code that calls the function must be consistent with that defined in the header.

```
66   def fibonacci_while_pos(in_str, n):
67       print(in_str, 'at position', n)
68       count = 1
69       n1,n2 = 0,1
70       while count < n:
71           next = n1 + n2
72           n1 = n2
73           n2 = next
74           count += 1
75       return(next)
76
77   print(fibonacci_while_pos('Fibonacci Term:', 7)
```

The second type of function arguments are called "arbitrary" arguments. In this case, we pass iterable parameters which are identified using the asterisk immediately preceding the parameter variable name.

The example in the following code block returns a concatenated string from the list of characters that are passed in. Here we show a couple of different runs of the function. In the first run, identified by the variable *word_1*, we call the function and pass in several individual characters, each separated with a comma. Then, in the second run, we pass in a string, which is a simply a list of individual characters. The string would then be split apart in each iteration of the loop, character by character then concatenated to *out_word* and finally returned.

```
1    def create_word (*letters):
2        out_word = ''
3        for letter in letters:
4            out_word+=letter
5        return out_word
6
7    #Runner
8    word_1 = create_word('h', 'e', 'l', 'l', 'o')
9    letter_list = 'world' #strings are list of characters
10   word_2 = create_word(letter_list)
11   print(word_1, word_2)
```

⮐ hello world

The third type of arguments are called "keyword" arguments, and they are identified with a double asterisk in front of the input parameter. The function implementation typically performs a conditional check on the parameters that comprise the keyword argument. So, in the example that we show in the following code block, we have defined a keyword argument called *dimensions*, and the two parameters that comprise the dimensions are the keywords called *width* and *length*. The conditional check is performed inside the function, and if they exist as part of the function call, then we proceed in doing the calculation. Note in this function we return multiple parameters. Multiple parameters returned in a function are called tuples, which will be covered when we discuss data structures in more detail.

```
1   def calc_rect_perimeter_and_area (**dimensions):
2       perimeter = 0
3       if 'width' in dimensions and 'length' in dimensions:
4           perimeter = 2* (dimensions['width'] + dimensions['length'])
5           area = dimensions['width'] * dimensions['length']
6       return perimeter, area
7
8   #Runner
9   rect_perimeter, rect_area = calc_rect_perimeter_and_area(width = 4, length = 5)
10  print('Perimeter: ', rect_perimeter)
11  print('Area: ', rect_area)
```

```
Perimeter: 18
Area: 20
```

Finally, Python supports default arguments in our function headers. This provides fixed assignments to one or more arguments that are set in the function header itself. If no arguments are passed in the function call, then default values are used. In the example shown in the following code block, we have a function called *train* with several arguments defined, one of which is *error*. If we were to call the function without a parameter defined for the *error* then the default "binary_cross_entropy" would be assigned. Conversely, if we were to provide an argument for *error*, then that would take precedence over the default value listed in the header.

```
1   def train(X, Y, learning_rate, error='binary_cross_entropy'):
2
3       # Extract number of examples from the shape of Y.
4       m = Y.shape[1]
5
6       # Compute AL by running forward propagation.
7       # call feedforward and pass in the training data
8       AL = feedforward(X)
9
10      # Compute the cost
11      if error == 'mean_square_error':
12          cost = np.mean(np.power(Y - AL, 2))
13      else: #binary_cross_entropy
14          cost = (- 1 / m) * (np.sum(Y*np.log(AL) + (1 - Y)*(np.log(1 - AL))))
15          cost = np.squeeze(cost)
```

1.6:

TEST AND DEBUG

Next, we'll describe methods of test and debug that can be used with the Python language and the Colab IDE. We will cover two different debugging strategies, the first is through what's called "in-place" debugging and that is via assertions, exceptions and the Python debugger called *pbd*, and the second uses a post-processing technique with a module called doctest. The intention here is just to provide exposure to each of these methods and leave it to the programmer to decide which is the best to implement for their particular needs, but in general we should always have the ability to thoroughly test our code and provide mechanisms to gracefully exit in case of some condition that could result in the program crashing.

DOCTEST

First, we'll describe the post-processing technique using the module *doctest*. A link to the Wikipedia reference is shown here, https://en.wikipedia.org/wiki/Doctest, but this is basically a library which allows you to generate different testing scenarios or test vectors (test vectors are test inputs that generate known outputs) for your functions. We need to read in the *doctest* library using the Python *import* statement. Python *import* statements provide access to the methods and libraries, such as *testmod*, that have been previously developed and presumably already tested. We will use the *testmod* function from the *doctest* library to execute our doctests. The tests results are generated and output from the standard Python interpreter and then copied and pasted into what are called *docstrings*. An example is shown in the following code block.

```
1    import doctest
2
3    """
4    #Test the following functions:
5    #helloStudent(name), helloStudents(name1, name2)
6       >>> helloStudent('Jim')
7       Hello Jim
8       >>> helloStudents('Jim', 'Jane')
9       Hello Jim and Jane
10   """
11
12   doctest.testmod()
```

All *doctest* modules are delimited using triple quotes so as shown in the example, we construct our *doctest* with a triple quote, then the test code followed by another triple quote. The functions that are tested are placed after three right-angled brackets; that is, three ">>>" symbols and the expected output is then placed underneath it directly under the column containing the first right-angled bracket. Code comments may also be included, and this can be done using the single line comment, or hashtag, symbol. When the *testmod* function is called after the closing quotes, via *doctest.testmod( )*, a message will be printed on the console indicating whether your test output matched the expected value or values listed in the test, basically whether your test has passed or failed.

The following code block shows a couple examples of how to use doctest with the Fibonacci function that we created previously. The *fibonacciWhile(n)* function is shown in the first code block followed by the doctest in the second code block, which is used to verify the function.

```
1    def fibonacciWhile(n):
2        count = 1
3        n1,n2 = 0,1
4        while count < n:
5            next = n1 + n2
6            n1 = n2
7            n2 = next
8            count += 1
9        return(next)
```

In this example, we execute a call to the *fibonacciWhile(n)* function within a print statement such that the returned value that normally would be printed out on the console is instead passed to the Python standard output in the form of a "docstring". The docstring is then compared to the expected value listed immediately underneath the test (under the >>>). In this example, we called the *fibonacciWhile(n)* function twice, the first call passing a 6 and expecting a return value of 8, and a second call passing a 10 and expecting a 55. When the *testmod* function is executed, we see the results displayed in the "TestResults" message output to the console, which indicates how many test we attempted and how many failed, where the message "failed=0" indicates all tests passed.

```
1    import doctest
2
3    """
4    #Test the fibonacci function
5        >>> print(fibonacciWhile(6))
6        8
7        >>> print(fibonacciWhile(10))
8        55
9    """
10
11   doctest.testmod()
```

TestResults(failed=0, attempted=2)

In the second example, we create a second fibonacci function with a bug introduced, called *fibonacciWhile2(n)* as shown in the following code block. After running *doctest.testmod* on both *fibonacciWhile(n)* and *fibonacciWhile2(n)* (note, we can call multiple functions from within the same doctest), we see a console message indicating which test failed, what the expected output was according to the doctest, and what the code actually returned.

```
1   def fibonacciWhile2(n):
2       count = 1
3       n1,n2 = 0,1
4       while count < n:
5           next = n1 + n2
6           n1 = n2
7           #n2 = next       #remove correct code
8           n2 = n1          #bug introduced
9           count += 1
10      return(next)
```

```
1   import doctest
2   """
3   #Test the fibonacci function
4       >>> print(fibonacciWhile(6))
5       8
6       >>> print(fibonacciWhile2(10))
7       55
8   """
9
10  doctest.testmod()
```

```
****************************************************************
File "__main__", line 6, in __main__
Failed example:
    print(fibonacciWhile2(10))
Expected:
    55
Got:
    2
****************************************************************
1 items had failures:
    1 of 2 in __main__
***Test Failed*** 1 failures.
TestResults(failed=1, attempted=2)
```

One note to be aware of is that the *testmod* function is extremely picky about the formatting of your doctest. The column position of the right-angled brackets and the expected results is very important to maintain as shown in the example. Additionally, any extra spaces (whitespace) following the expected output will also produce a failed result, even if the non-whitespace characters are correct.

PYTHON DEBUGGER (*PDB*)

Now, what if we want to debug our code, in place as it is executing. In other words, we want to set a breakpoint in our code, then execute and run to the breakpoint, stop the code and then check the contents of our variables. Some IDEs allow for doing this with an integrated graphical user interface, but in Colab, we can perform in place debugging with a library called the Python Debugger or *pdb*. A reference to the documentation is shown in the link here https://docs.python. org/3/library/pdb.html. With this tool, we use a function called *set_trace* to place a breakpoint on a specific line in our code. Now this method is not the cleanest solution in that it requires placing the *set_trace* function call in your code, but for now, we need to insert the *set_trace* line then when the code is run, it will stop execution at the line containing the *set_trace* call and open an interactive dialog box from which the user can enter debug commands. The 'help' command will provide a list of supported debug functions that can be used. We will describe a few of the most useful commands next.

```
  1 import pdb
  2 a = 12
▸ 3 pdb.set_trace()
  4 print(a)

  --NORMAL--

  --Return--
  None
  > <ipython-input-3-b2953aad80e9>(3)<cell line: 3>()
        1 import pdb
        2 a = 12
  ----> 3 pdb.set_trace()
        4 print(a)

  ipdb> help

  Documented commands (type help <topic>):
  ========================================
  EOF      commands    enable     ll        pp        s               until
  a        condition   exit       longlist  psource   skip_hidden     up
  alias    cont        h          n         q         skip_predicates w
  args     context     help       next      quit      source          whatis
  b        continue    ignore     p         r         step            where
  break    d           interact   pdef      restart   tbreak
  bt       debug       j          pdoc      return    u
  c        disable     jump       pfile     retval    unalias
  cl       display     l          pinfo     run       undisplay
  clear    down        list       pinfo2    rv        unt

  Miscellaneous help topics:
  ==========================
  exec   pdb

  ipdb>
```

In this example, we walk through a typical debugging session. First, we need to import the pdb library. Then we set a breakpoint by inserting the *set_trace* method as the first instruction inside the for-loop. When we run the code the *set_trace* method will launch the debugger dialog in the console and wait for the user to enter a command. We can see from the code listing, line 6, that the code has been paused at this position in the execution (shown with a small triangle to the left of the line number).

```
1 import pdb
2 a = 12
3
4 for i in range(12):
5     pdb.set_trace()   ### insert breakpoint here ###
▶ 6     a -= 1
7     a *= 2
8
9 print(a)

--NORMAL--

None
> <ipython-input-4-e1e1fba651c2>(6)<cell line: 4>()
      4 for i in range(12):
      5     pdb.set_trace()   ### insert breakpoint here ###
----> 6     a -= 1
      7     a *= 2
      8

ipdb>
```

We can then view the current contents of variables using the Python *print* command (note that this is not a *pdb* command but we can view variables this way). We can also single step through the code one line at a time using the *next* command, and execute multiple lines to the next *set_trace* breakpoint using the *continue* command as shown in the example output.

```
> <ipython-input-2-e1e1fba651c2>(6)<module>()
-> a -= 1
(Pdb) print(a)
12
(Pdb) next
> <ipython-input-2-e1e1fba651c2>(7)<module>()
-> a *= 2
(Pdb) print(a)
11
(Pdb) next
> <ipython-input-2-e1e1fba651c2>(4)<module>()
-> for i in range(12):
(Pdb) print(a)
22
(Pdb) continue

> <ipython-input-2-e1e1fba651c2>(6)<module>()
-> a -= 1
(Pdb) print(a)
22
(Pdb) next
> <ipython-input-2-e1e1fba651c2>(7)<module>()
-> a *= 2
(Pdb) print(a)
21
(Pdb) next
> <ipython-input-2-e1e1fba651c2>(4)<module>()
-> for i in range(12):
(Pdb) continue
> <ipython-input-2-e1e1fba651c2>(6)<module>()
-> a -= 1
(Pdb) continue
> <ipython-input-2-e1e1fba651c2>(5)<module>()
-> pdb.set_trace()  ### insert breakpoint here ###
(Pdb) next
> <ipython-input-2-e1e1fba651c2>(6)<module>()
-> a -= 1
(Pdb) print(a)
82
(Pdb) [               ]
```

This technique is a common approach if you have bugs in your code and you wanted to for example check the contents of variables after each iteration of a loop and to see if some may be going astray.

EXCEPTIONS

An exception is an event that alters the normal flow of an executing program. We use the term "throws an exception" when this normal flow is disrupted, and we call the response, "exception handling". We incorporate exception handling as a sort-of safety net to ensure our programs do not crash the system they are running on due to anomalous behavior that may have occurred such as if unanticipated combinations of inputs or outputs are introduced into the system. There are many distinct types of exceptions and most programming languages have mechanisms to detect and respond to them. Python supports at least 29 different standard exceptions.

Let's look at some example structures that we would use when coding exception handling in a Python program.

```
try:
    program statements/operations here
except Exception1:
    if an exception is raised, execute program statements here
else:
    if no exception is raised, execute program statements here
```

The first example shows the most basic structure incorporating a *try, except,* and *else* clause. We use the keyword *try* to tell Python that we want to try executing a piece of code, but if that code results in behavior defined by *Exception1,* then we would like to catch that, and we invoke it with the *except* keyword. In other words, if we execute the program statement under the *try* label and it results in an exception then the code under the *except* label will run. In that case we would want to have some type of error message displayed to the user and execute some code to gracefully recover the program or exit it without crashing the user's device. If the code under the *try* label does not throw an exception; that is, it does not result in a system error, then the code under the *else* label will execute.

```
try:
    program statements/operations here
except Exception 1:
    if an exception is raised, execute program statements here
except Exception 2:
    if an exception is raised, execute program statements here
else:
    if no exception is raised, execute program statements here
```

Now, we can construct our program to catch multiple exceptions (*Exception* 1 and *Exception* 2 in this case), and run different code for each of them by stacking up the exception types in our code as shown in this example. We can place as many exceptions as needed to provide a robust error handling capability in our programs.

```
try:
    program statements/operations here
except Exception1 as Argument:
    if an exception is raised, execute program statements here
    and printout the actual error that occurred
finally:
    Execute always (regardless of whether an exception is raised)
```

We can also catch our exception and store it in an argument using the *as Argument* clause as shown in the third example. In this case the type of exception that was thrown would be saved as a string, for example "divide by zero". This allows the programmer to use the stored argument, for example to print it out in a message. We can also force execution of a piece of code whether the exception is thrown or not by using the *finally* label.

Exception Name	#	Description
StandardError	4	Base for all built-in exceptions
ArithmeticError	5	Base for all errors involving numeric calculations
ZeroDivisionError	8	Raised when divide-by-zero or modulus-by-zero occurs
AssertionError	9	Raised in case of failure of the Assert statement (more on this later)
EOFError	11	Raised when no input is available via raw_input() or input() and end-of-file is reached
IndexError	15	Raised when an index is not found in a sequence
KeyError	16	Raised when specified key is not found in a dictionary
IOError	20	Raised when input/output (e.g. print or open()) fails

Of the 29 exception types that exist in Python, the table shows some of the more common ones that programmers use to implement exception handling. A full listing of the exceptions supported in Python can be found at the link here. https://docs.python.org/3/library/exceptions.html. The table lists the exceptions in order from generic to specific errors. Next, we look at some specific examples.

In the following code block, we see two versions of code implementing a simple calculation of a fractional value where the denominator is input by the user.

In the first code listing and corresponding console output, we see no exception handling, and if the program is run with an input of zero, it results in a crash of the program when the attempt to divide by zero is made.

```
1   #Error handling.
2
3   #Divide by zero (no exception handling)
4   a = 7
5   b = int(input('Input a fraction denominator: '))
6   c = a/b
7   print('c = ', c)
```

```
Input a fraction denominator: 0
-----------------------------------------------------------------------
ZeroDivisionError                        Traceback (most recent call last)
<ipython-input-3-cd546f9d3e5a> in <cell line: 6>()
      4 a = 7
      5 b = int(input('Input a fraction denominator: '))
---> 6 c = a/b
      7 print('c = ', c)
      8

ZeroDivisionError: division by zero
```

Alternatively, in the following code block we implement exception handling with the same code. The first run shows the output when the user inputs a non-zero number for the denominator, and in this case the code executed the print statement in the else clause. The second run shows the output when the user inputs 0 for the denominator. In this case the code caught the exception then printed the message. Note that no crash of the program occurred when the exception occurred.

```
1    #Divide by zero (with exception handling)
2
3    a = 7
4    b = int(input('Input a fraction denominator: '))
5    try:
6        c = a/b
7    except ZeroDivisionError:
8        print('Divide by zero!!!')
9    else:
10       print('c = ', c)
```

Input a fraction denominator: 7
c = 1.0

Input a fraction denominator: 0
Divide by zero!!!

The next code block shows use of the Argument parameter and the *finally* clause.

This is the same code as the divide by zero exception example shown earlier so refer to that case for the output without exception handling. For the handler case we catch the exception on line 6 and store the message as an Argument, then output it in the print statement. Additionally, we incorporate the *finally* label on line 10 which will get executed regardless of whether we throw an exception or if the else clause is executed indicating no exception was encountered.

```
1    #Divide by zero with Argument and Finally (with exception handling)
2
3    a = 7
4    b = int(input('Input a fraction denominator: '))
5    try:
6        c = a/b
7    except ZeroDivisionError as Argument:
8        print('Exception raised!!!', Argument)
9    else:
10       print('c = ', c)
11   finally:
12       print('Always execute this....')
```

Input a fraction denominator: 0
Exception raised!!! division by zero
Always execute this....

Input a fraction denominator: 5
c = 1.4
Always execute this....

ASSERTIONS

Assertions are Boolean expressions that will check a condition, and if that condition passes, meaning the condition evaluates to True, then nothing will happen but if it fails then an "Assertion Error" exception will be raised. What we want to do in our code is to place what are called assertion statements at strategic points which would catch conditions that will not or should not occur. Now, we do not want to replace exception handling with Assertion statements since the exceptions themselves are more applicable for errors that are more likely to happen, such as files not present when we are trying to access them or when trying to execute illegal mathematical operations such as divide by zero as was shown previously. Therefore, we want to wrap the assertion statements inside exception handling, and that will allow us to perform a graceful exit of our code if we generate one of these conditions.

The first example shows how an assert statement can be implemented in code using the keyword *assert*. Here we force the assert statement to evaluate the *myVar* conditional statement to True, and when the code is executed, it runs as expected and prints the message.

```
1  #Assertions
2
3  myVar = 1
4  assert myVar==1, 'myVar should be 1'
5
6  #Continue on with code
7  print('Hello world')
```

Hello world

In the second example we force the assert statement to evaluate the *myVar* conditional statement to False, and when this code is executed, it will throw an Assertion Error exception, print out the message and stop execution.

```
1  #Assertions
2
3  myVar = 2
4  assert myVar==1, 'myVar should be 1'
5
6  #Continue on with code
7  print('Hello world')
```

```
        ----------------------------------------------------------------
⇥       AssertionError                      Traceback (most recent call last)
        <ipython-input-6-7179126e5a2c> in <cell line: 3>()
              1 #Assertions
              2 myVar = 2
        ----> 3 assert myVar==1, 'myVar should be 1'
              4
              5 #Continue on with code

        AssertionError: myVar should be 1
```

CHAPTER 2:
PYTHON DATA STRUCTURES

In this chapter we will cover Python Data Structures including Lists, Dictionaries, Tuples Sets, Stacks and Queues.

LEARNING OBJECTIVES

By the end of this chapter, you will be able to do the following:

- Learning Objectives
- By the end of this chapter, you will be able to do the following:
- Identify several primitive and non-primitive Python data structures
- Create and use one-dimensional and multi-dimensional Lists in Python scripts
- Write a List comprehension
- Create and use flat and hierarchical dictionaries in Python scripts
- Create and use Tuples and Sets in Python scripts
- Compare the pros and cons of using Lists, Arrays and Tuples
- Create and use Stacks and Queues in Python scripts

2.1:

Data Structures - Introduction

In the next several units of this chapter we are going to cover Python data structures, which are also known as collections. The diagram shown breaks down the Python data structures into its Primitive and non-primitive elements.

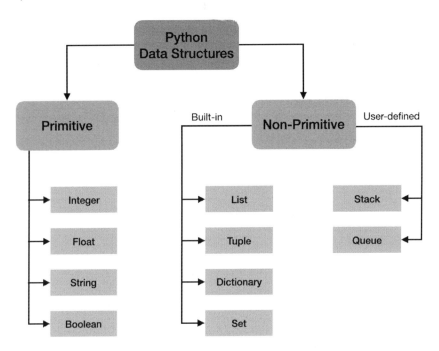

Now we've already discussed the primitives, so we'll next cover non-primitive, built-in data structures including *Lists*, *Dictionaries*, *Tuples*, *Sets*, and then those which are user-defined that we could build from either the built-in data structures or from imported libraries, and those include the *Stack* and the *Queue*.

Collection Types	Description
List	Ordered.
	Changeable.
	Allows duplicate members.
Tuple	Ordered.
	Not Changeable.
	Allows duplicated members.
	Faster access than List
Dictionary	Ordered (as of Python version 3.7)
	Changeable.
	Indexed.
	No duplicate members.
Set	Not ordered.
	Not indexed.
	No duplicate members.
Stack	Implementation via List,
	collections.deque, queue.LifoQueue
Queue	Implementation via List,
	collections.deque, queue.Queue

2.2:
DATA STRUCTURES - LISTS

A List is simply an ordered collection of items. The items may be accessed individually using what is called an index, which is an incrementing integer starting from zero for the first item, one for the second item, up to n, where n is the length of the *list-1*. This is commonly known as "zero based indexing". The official Python List Application Programming Interface (API) is shown here: https://docs.python.org/3/library/stdtypes.html#list

Collection Types	Description
List	Ordered. Changeable. Allows duplicate members.
Tuple	Ordered. Not Changeable. Allows duplicated members. Faster access than List
Dictionary	Ordered (as of Python version 3.7) Changeable. Indexed. No duplicate members.
Set	Not ordered. Not indexed. No duplicate members.
Stack	Implementation via List, collections.deque, queue.LifoQueue
Queue	Implementation via List, collections.deque, queue.Queue

The list items may be any data type including strings, numbers, variables, as well as objects and even lists themselves. An example of a list is shown in the following code block. A list assignment uses an equal sign, just like we use when assigning a primitive to a variable, but the syntax of this data structure uses square brackets to delimit the beginning and end of the list and separates each item in the list with a comma. We see in the example that lists may include items which are strings, integers, or a mix with variable elements too.

```
1  test_string = 'test_string'
2  car_brands = ['Porsche', 'Lamborghini', 'Bugatti', 'Alfa-Romeo', 'Mercedes-Benz']
3  numbers_list = [0, 1, 0, 1, 1, 2, 1, 2, 0, 2, 1]
4  random_list = ['Words and stuff', 12345, test_string]
```

Several useful operations are shown in the following table. We will show how to use these operations in the following examples, but a brief description of some of the common commands is shown:

- x in s (x not in s): searches the list s and looks for the item x. It returns the Boolean True (False) if the item is found (not found).
- s + t: concatenates two lists, in other words it will append the list t to the list s.
- s * n: multiplies all elements in s by a number n, in other words it will add the list s to itself n times.
- s[i]: accesses the element at the index i. Note that the indices are zero-based, that is index 0 is the first element, index 1 is the second element, and so on.
- s[i : j]: accesses what is called a slice or subset of the list from element i up to but not including element j
- s[i : j : k]: accesses a slice but skips elements defined by the step parameter k
- len(s): returns the length of the list. This is useful in loops.
- min(s) and max(s): returns the minimum and maximum value in s respectively.
- s.index(n): returns the index from the list s that contains item n.
- s.count(n): returns the number of occurrences of item n in list s.

Operation	Result
x in s	True if an item of s is equal to x, else False
x not in s	False if an item of s is equal to x, else True
s + t	Concatenation of s and t
s * n	Add s to itself n times
s[i]	Access ith item of s with 0-based indexing
s[i:j]	Access slice of s from i to j
s[i:j:k]	Access slice of s from i to j in steps of k
len(s)	Number of elements in s, or length of s
min(s)	Minimum value in s
max(s)	Maximum value in s
s.index(n)	Index of n in s
s.count(x)	Total number of occurrences of x in s

LIST INDEXING - SLICING

List slicing is a powerful and commonly used feature that is not only supported in the standard Python library but also in machine learning libraries such as NumPy. Given its power and flexibility, list slicing can get a little complicated, so we will go through several examples to demonstrate its functionality.

Let's first consider the Python List called *car_brands* as shown in the following code block. We can print the entire list simply by passing the variable name to the print method.

```
1  car_brands = ['Porsche', 'Lamborghini', 'Bugatti', 'Alfa-Romeo', 'Mercedes-Benz']
2  print(car_brands) # print all elements in car_brands
```

→ ['Porsche', 'Lamborghini', 'Bugatti', 'Alfa-Romeo', 'Mercedes-Benz']

Accessing and modifying individual cars contained in the car brands list can be done using their zero-based indices as shown in the following code block.

```
1  car_brands = ['Porsche', 'Lamborghini', 'Bugatti', 'Alfa-Romeo', 'Mercedes-Benz']
2
3  print(car_brands[0]) # print the first element (zeroth index) in car_brands
4  car_brands[0] = 'Tesla' # change the first value of car brands
5  print(car_brands) # the rest of the elements stay the same
6  print(car_brands[0]) # now the first element in car_brands says 'Tesla
```

⊡→ Porsche
    ['Tesla', 'Lamborghini', 'Bugatti', 'Alfa-Romeo', 'Mercedes-Benz']
    Tesla

List slicing allows you to access multiple items from the list within a specified range and returns those items as a new list. We show several examples in the following code block.

```
1  # List slicing - returns a portion of a list
2
3  car_brands = ['Porsche', 'Lamborghini', 'Bugatti', 'Alfa-Romeo', 'Mercedes-Benz']
4  print(car_brands) #Prints all elements in car_brands
5  print(car_brands[1]) #Prints the 2nd element of car_brands
6  print(car_brands[1:3]) #Prints the 2nd element up to (but not including) the 4th
7  print(car_brands[0:5:3]) #Print every third element from index 0 to index 4
8  print(car_brands[::2]) #Print every other element from index 0 to index length-1
9  print(car_brands[2:]) #Prints all elements starting from index 2
```

⊡→ ['Porsche', 'Lamborghini', 'Bugatti', 'Alfa-Romeo', 'Mercedes-Benz']
    Lamborghini
    ['Lamborghini', 'Bugatti']
    ['Porsche', 'Alfa-Romeo']
    ['Porsche', 'Bugatti', 'Mercedes-Benz']
    ['Porsche', 'Bugatti', 'Mercedes-Benz']
    ['Bugatti', 'Alfa-Romeo', 'Mercedes-Benz']

Note the syntax of the slice commands which start from the first index and includes up to but not including the second index. In other words, we identify the first index, then place a colon to mark that we are going to take a slice, where 0 is the minimum index, and the list length -1 as the maximum index.

Therefore, the example on line 6 in the above code block prints the slice of *car_brands* from index 1 up to but not including index 3; that is, it prints the elements from index 1, "Lamborghini" and index 2, "Bugatti". In this example, index 3 is actually the fourth item on the list, but we do not print the element from that index because the last index you specify in the slice is not included.

We can define a step in the slice as shown on line 7 in the code block, by placing a second colon after the max index then a step size which indicates the number of indices to step while slicing. Now, the default condition, when no step is inserted in the slice, results in accessing each element, one at a time from the list. A step of 2 means it will access every other item, and a step of 3 means it will access every third item. In the example on line 7, we step from the first item in the range of the slice at index 0, "Porsche", to three items past it at index 3, "Alfa-Romeo". Note that we technically access up to but not including the stop index 5, but since the next step after accessing index 3 would be index 6, we terminate the slice with the previous stepped index.

Python is also able to fill in some gaps for us as shown in line 8 of the code block. In this example, we could have written the slice as [0 : 5: 2], but [: : 2] works too because Python will assume, when no start index is specified, that the slice will start at the beginning index in the list; that is index 0, and similarly if no index is given for the end (remember, if we provide an index, the slice will access up to but not including the last index), then the whole list to the length - 1 will be accessed. Therefore, in the example on line 8, the slice will access every other element in the list from index 0 to the list length - 1.

Finally, if we wanted to access the last n items in this list, we could use [n :] since the colon assumes the end index will be the last element in the list. Therefore, in the example on line 9 of the code block, the slice will access from index 2 to the end of the list and use a step size of 1, printing the last 3 car brands "Bugatti", "Alfa-Romeo", "Mercedes-Benz".

LIST NEGATIVE INDEXING

Now, if the previous examples were not confusing enough, Python allows us to use negative numbers for indexes. The examples shown thus far used positive indexing, which means we referenced the beginning of the list at index 0.

Negative indexes are like positive numbered indexes, except that they start at the end of the list and move backwards from there.

Several examples are shown in the following code block. For example, if we want the last item in the *car_brand* list, "Mercedes-Benz", we could use the −1st (negative first) index. Accessing the last item using the −1st index is a quite common trick. Similarly, if we wanted the second from the last item in the list,

"Alfa-Romeo", we could use the index −2, and if we wanted the first item in the list, "Porsche", we could use the -5th index, which is the fifth item counting backward from the last item.

```
1   #Negative indexing
2
3   car_brands = ['Porsche', 'Lamborghini', 'Bugatti', 'Alfa-Romeo', 'Mercedes-Benz']
4   print(car_brands[-1]) # Prints the last element
5   print(car_brands[-2]) # Prints the second to last element
6   print(car_brands[-5]) # Prints the first item (5th from the end)
7   print(car_brands[::-1]) # Prints the whole list indexing it in reverse order
8   print(car_brands[-3::-2]) # Prints from index −3 in reverse order in steps of 2
```

```
⌐→  Mercedes-Benz
    Alfa-Romeo
    Porsche
    ['Mercedes-Benz', 'Alfa-Romeo', 'Bugatti', 'Lamborghini', 'Porsche']
    ['Bugatti', 'Porsche']
```

We can also implement list slicing with negative indexing. Line 7 in the above code block shows how we can use negative indexes with list slicing, using a step of −1. This will access each item in the list in reverse order, returning a reversed version of the original list, which is another common trick that can be used to reverse the elements in a list. Other than using a negative step, negative indexes work similarly with slicing as do positive indexes. For example, line 8 shows how we can access the 3rd item from the end of the list in reverse order with a step size of 2.

USEFUL LIST FUNCTIONS AND OPERATORS

Lists support many functions that you will become familiar with as you gain Python coding experience. We will focus on a few of the most common functions here.

As was previously described, accessing and editing parts of a list can be performed by directly indexing into the list, however dynamically adding elements to a list cannot be done with simple indexing. Instead, items can be added using the *append* and *insert* functions. The append function lets us add an item to the end of the list as shown in the following example. The following code block shows how an element can be added (appended) to the end of the list.

```
1   # Append
2
3   car_brands = ['Porsche', 'Lamborghini', 'Bugatti', 'Alfa-Romeo', 'Mercedes-Benz']
4   car_brands.append('BMW')
5   print(car_brands)
```

→ ['Porsche', 'Lamborghini', 'Bugatti', 'Alfa-Romeo', 'Mercedes-Benz', 'BMW']

The insert function allows for adding elements into the middle of a list at a specified index. In the following code block, the element, "BMW", is added to the list at index 2.

```
1   # Insert
2
3   car_brands = ['Tesla', 'Lamborghini', 'Bugatti', 'Alfa-Romeo', 'Mercedes-Benz']
4   car_brands.insert(2, 'BMW')
5   print(car_brands)
```

→ ['Tesla', 'Lamborghini', 'BMW', 'Bugatti', 'Alfa-Romeo', 'Mercedes-Benz']

The *pop* function can be used to extract and return an item from a list as shown in the following code block. For example, you could assign a variable to a popped value and remove it from a list. When using *pop*, the last element in the list is removed if an index is not provided, or optionally an indexed element can be removed which results in the index of every other element following the popped one in the list being reduced by 1.

```
1   # Pop from end of list
2
3   car_brands = ['Tesla', 'Lamborghini', 'Bugatti', 'Alfa-Romeo', 'Mercedes-Benz']
4   removed_item = car_brands.pop() #Remove last item from list end and store it to var
5   print(removed_item)
6   print(car_brands)
```

→ Mercedes-Benz
['Tesla', 'Lamborghini', 'Bugatti', 'Alfa-Romeo']

```
1   # Pop from middle of list
2
3   car_brands = ['Tesla', 'Lamborghini', 'Bugatti', 'Alfa-Romeo', 'Mercedes-Benz']
4   removed_item = car_brands.pop(2) #Remove indexed item from list end and store it to var
5   print(removed_item)
6   print(car_brands)
```

 Bugatti
['Tesla', 'Lamborghini', 'Alfa-Romeo', 'Mercedes-Benz']

The *len* function provides a count of the number of elements that exist in a list. If your code adds or removes elements with the append, insert, or pop functions as previously described, it may be necessary to determine the size of the list during run-time, and this can be done with the *len* function. We will see next how *len* can be used in loop implementations to iterate through the elements of a list.

A couple useful list operators implement concatenation and initialization. To concatenate multiple lists, simply use the "+" operator. An example is shown in the following code block.

```
1   # Concatenate lists
2
3   car_brands = ['Tesla', 'Lamborghini']
4   truck_brands = ['Ford', 'General Motors']
5   auto_inventory = car_brands + truck_brands
6   print(auto_inventory)
```

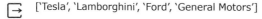 ['Tesla', 'Lamborghini', 'Ford', 'General Motors']

Initializing the elements of a list may also be required by your algorithm if you are updating the elements using "accumulation" which adds or subtracts a computed value from the previous value. An example is shown in the following code block. On line 4 we are initializing the elements of a list with zeros, where the size of the list has been predetermined in this example ($SIZE=10$), but could also be set dynamically, for example as an input parameter to a function.

```
1  #Initialize elements of a list
2
3  SIZE = 10
4  my_list = [0]*SIZE #init with 0's
5  print(my_list)
```

→ [0, 0, 0, 0, 0, 0, 0, 0, 0, 0]

MULTIDIMENSIONAL LISTS

Processing data with multidimensional lists, either through standard Python libraries or with machine learning libraries such as NumPy or Pandas is extremely important since most data is comprised of multiple features or independent variables.

We can also construct a 2-dimensional list as shown in the following code block. Here we show how to create a 3x3 list (matrix) of integers, and how to print the complete matrix, a specific row, and an individual element. The outer square brackets in the initialization shown in line 2 define the whole matrix with each row being delimited by a comma separated, square bracket pair. Note that we use zero-based indexing, so in line 5, the row identified by index 2 is the 3rd row. Also, Python uses what is called "row-major" indexing, which means the row is indexed first and the column second as shown in line 6; that is, the element in the 2nd row and first column would be indexed as [1][0].

0	1	2
3	4	5
6	7	8

```
1  #2D Lists (matrices)
2
3  myMatrix1 = [[0,1,2],[3,4,5],[6,7,8]]
4  print(myMatrix1)
5  print(myMatrix1[2])
6  print(myMatrix1[1][0])
```

→ [[0, 1, 2], [3, 4, 5], [6, 7, 8]]
  [6, 7, 8]
  3

The syntax of defining a 3-dimensional list of integers is shown in the following code block. Note that the bracket structure is like 2-dimensional lists where the outer-most brackets delimit the complete 3-D list, the next inner brackets define row, then column, then run. A diagram of the 3-D list created in the example code follows. Therefore, to access an element in a 3-D list, the row is indexed first, then the column then the run. Note in the commented line 6, an attempt to access row 3 is shown which does not exist as shown in the visual representation (this would generate a run time error).

```
1   #3D Lists
2
3   my3Dlist1 = [[[10,11,12,13],[20,21,22,23],[30,31,32,33]],[[40,41,42,43],[50,
    51,52,53],[60,61,62,63]]]
4   print(my3Dlist1[1][1][2])
5   print(my3Dlist1[1][2][3])
6   #print(my3Dlist1[3][2][1])
```

```
52
63
```

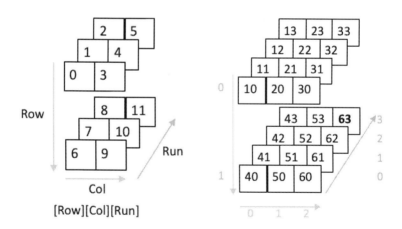

[Row][Col][Run]

LIST LOOPING

As discussed previously, the Python *for* and *while* looping structures can take on many forms to implement repeated processing. Specifically, a for-loop can be written to efficiently iterate through the elements of a list using the for-each or "range object"; that is, for-in-range, structures along with the list *len* function. A couple examples are shown in the following code blocks.

In the first example, we use a for-each loop to extract and print each of the list *brands* in the *car_brands* list.

```
1   # Looping over a list
2
3   car_brands = ['Porsche', 'Lamborghini', 'Bugatti', 'Alfa-Romeo', 'Mercedes-Benz']
4   for brand in car_brands: # Iterates over each car brand in car_brands
5       print(brand)
```

```
Porsche
Lamborghini
Bugatti
Alfa-Romeo
Mercedes-Benz
```

In the second example, the *car_brands* list is iterated using a for-in-range loop. In this case the iterator, itakes on each of the indices from 0 up to but not including the length of the *car_brands* list.

```
1   # Looping over a list
2   car_brands = ['Porsche', 'Lamborghini', 'Bugatti', 'Alfa-Romeo', 'Mercedes-Benz']
3
4   # Iterates over the numbers in the range of 0 to the length of car_brands
5   for i in range(len(car_brands)):
6       print('Car_brand index:', i)
7       print(car_brands[i])
```

```
Car_brand index: 0
Porsche
Car_brand index: 1
Lamborghini
Car_brand index: 2
Bugatti
Car_brand index: 3
Alfa-Romeo
Car_brand index: 4
Mercedes-Benz
```

Looping over multidimensional lists can be implemented similarly to single dimension loops as shown in the following code blocks. In the first example shown we use a range object type loop to print one of the dimensions, and in the second example, a nested loop to access individual elements.

```
1   # Looping over a 2D list – range object
2
3   two_d_list = [ [0,1,2,3],
4                  [4,5,6,7],
5                  [8,9,10,11] ]
6
7   for row in two_d_list:
8       print(row)
```

⊡→
```
[0, 1, 2, 3]
[4, 5, 6, 7]
[8, 9, 10, 11]
```

In the first example, the outer loop, x, on line 7 accesses each row in the list, while the inner loop iterator, y, accesses each column element in the row accessed by the outer loop iterator.

```
1   # Looping over a 2D list - nested range object
2
3   two_d_list = [ [0,1,2,3],
4                  [4,5,6,7],
5                  [8,9,10,11] ]
6
7   for x in two_d_list:
8       for y in x:
9           print(y)
```

The second example shows how we can index an individual element in a 2-dimensional list using nested loops with the *len* function. In the outer loop, x iterates from 0 up to but not including the the length of the outer list, which represents the total number of rows, while the inner loop accesses each of the column elements in the row currently accessed by the outer loop iterator.

```
1    # Looping over a 2D list - nested indexing
2
3    two_d_list = [ [0,1,2,3],
4                   [4,5,6,7],
5                   [8,9,10,11] ]
6
7    for x in range(len(two_d_list)):
8        for y in range(len(two_d_list[x])):
9            print(two_d_list[x][y])
```

Both examples produce the following output.

⤷ 0
   1
   2
   3
   4
   5
   6
   7
   8
   9
   10
   11

LISTS VERSUS ARRAYS

Most programming languages implement the basic Python List functionality described using arrays. The two data structures are similar, but arrays are not an official Python data structure. Python supports arrays through a library called *array* which must be imported to be used in your code. While Python programmers almost always use Lists instead of arrays, there may be an occasion when arrays may be preferable. The following table summarizes the main differences.

Category	Lists	Arrays
Data types	Can be heterogenous (multiple types in a list)	Must be homogeneous (same data type)
Declaration	No	Yes - import array
Speed		Faster since homogeneous data
Flexibility	Easier to add, delete elements Easier to print	
Memory		More compact
Item Notation	[ ]	( )

As seen in the table, Arrays are more restrictive in the data types they can contain; that is, arrays must contain homogeneous data whereas Lists can mix any data type and are more flexible to add and delete elements. Lists are Python built-in non-primitive data type, whereas Arrays must have the *array* library imported to use the functions. The primary advantage of using an Array over a List comes if your program requires fast access or has memory constraints; in this case, an Array is more efficient than a List.

LIST COMPREHENSION

Finally, you may encounter what is called "comprehension" in reading some Python reference code, or you may want to use it as a more compact way of implementing loop iterations. List comprehension is not required to use in your programs, but you should be able to recognize and interpret it if you encounter it in reference code. The following code blocks show how to implement list comprehension in loops. The first example iterates through a list and extracts all the even elements. We first show a common method using a traditional loop, then refactor the code using a single line of code as shown on line 14. With comprehension, we iterate through all the elements in the list using the iterator, x, check if it is even using the modulus operator, then append it to the resultant list.

```
1    #List comprehension
2    #Extract even integers from list
3
4    #Using loop
5    res_1 = []
6    my_list = [1, 3, 2, 5, 8, 4, 10, 50, 2, -3]
7    for x in my_list:
8        if (x%2 == 0):
9            res_1.append(x)
10   print('Loop extract evens:', res_1)
11
12   #Using comprehension
13   res_2 = []
14   [res_2.append(x) for x in my_list if x%2==0]
15   print('Comprehension: extract evens:', res_2)
```

⤷   Loop extract evens: [2, 8, 4, 10, 50, 2]
      Comprehension: extract evens: [2, 8, 4, 10, 50, 2]

The second example shows how to perform a more complex function using comprehension. In this example, we are provided a list of x and y coordinates. The code shows how to implement both a standard loop and comprehension to extract and print the coordinates which lie above the diagonal in a matrix, assuming the coordinates are the element indices in the matrix. Again, here we see that comprehension can collapse a multi-line nested loop into a single line.

```
1   #List comprehension
2
3   #Create coordinates not on a matrix diagonal
4   x_list = [1,2,3,4]
5   y_list = [3,4,5,6]
6
7   #Using nested loops
8   z1 = []
9   for x in x_list:
10      for y in y_list:
11         if x != y:
12           z1.append([x,y])
13  print('Nested Loop to create coord not on diagonal:\n', z1)
14
15  #Using comprehension
16  z2 = []
17  [z2.append([x,y]) for x in x_list for y in y_list if x!=y]
18  print('\nComprehension: coord not on diagonal:\n', z2)
19
20  #Remove coordinates above the diagonal
21  remove = []
22  [remove.append([x,y]) for x in x_list for y in y_list if x!=y and y<x]
23  print('\nComprehension: coord not on or above diagonal', remove)
```

Nested Loop to create coord not on diagonal: [[1, 3], [1, 4], [1, 5], [1, 6], [2, 3], [2, 4], [2, 5], [2, 6], [3, 4], [3, 5], [3, 6], [4, 3], [4, 5], [4, 6]]
Comprehension: coord not on diagonal: [[1, 3], [1, 4], [1, 5], [1, 6], [2, 3], [2, 4], [2, 5], [2, 6], [3, 4], [3, 5], [3, 6], [4, 3], [4, 5], [4, 6]]
Comprehension: coord not on or above diagonal [[4, 3]]

2.3:
DATA STRUCTURES
- DICTIONARIES

A Python Dictionary is another useful data structure like a List, but it extends the concept to include a collection of "key-value" pairs stored in memory.

The official Python Dictionaries Application Programming Interface (API) is shown here: https://docs.python.org/3/library/stdtypes.html#dict

Collection Types	Description
List	Ordered. Changeable. Allows duplicate members.
Tuple	Ordered. Not Changeable. Allows duplicated members. Faster access than List
Dictionary	Ordered (as of Python version 3.7) Changeable. Indexed. No duplicate members.
Set	Not ordered. Not indexed. No duplicate members.
Stack	Implementation via List, collections.deque, queue.LifoQueue
Queue	Implementation via List, collections.deque, queue.Queue

Python Dictionaries were changed to be "insertion-ordered" as of version 3.7. This was done to improve efficiency for applications such as in search algorithms, and basically means that Python maintains the order in which the items were added. A key in a dictionary can be a string, a number, tuple, or an object; in other words, any data type that is immutable (not changeable), and this restriction exists because no duplicate keys are allowed, which could be violated if the key could be changed. So, what this means is that a List or a Dictionary itself cannot be a key. The value, however, can be any of the datatypes including Lists and Dictionaries. The notation for a Dictionary is to delimit it with an open and closed curly brace, with each entry as a comma separated key-value pair where each key is followed by a colon then the value. An example Dictionary is shown in the following code block. Note that the keys in may be a mix between integers and strings as shown in *random_dict* on line 5.

```
1   #Dictionary creation
2   car_dict = {'brand': 'Porsche', 'year': 2016, 'model': '911'}
3   print(car_dict)
4
5   random_dict = {0: 'one', 'two': 3, 4: 'five'}
6   print(random_dict
7   print(car_dict.get('model'))
```

```
{'brand': 'Porsche', 'year': 2016, 'model': '911'}
{0: 'one', 'two': 3, 4: 'five'}
```

To access an item from a Dictionary, we simply reference the key and the value will be returned. An example is shown on lines 7-8 of the following code block. To modify an existing item in a Dictionary, we reference the key and set it equal to a new value. We can also add a new item to the end of the Dictionary by creating a new key and then setting it equal to a value, or by using the *update* function as shown on lines 11-12. We can use the *pop* function to extract an item from a dictionary by referencing the key, and this will remove both the key and its associated value from the Dictionary as shown on line 16.

```
1   #Dictionary modifications
2
3   car_dict = {'brand': 'Porsche', 'year': 2016, 'model': '911'}
4   print('car_dict:', car_dict)
5
6   #Get a value using bracket notation or the get function
7   print('Brand:', car_dict['brand'])
8   print('Model:', car_dict.get('model'))
9
10  #Add an item using the update function
11  car_dict['exterior'] = 'blue'
12  car_dict.update({'interior': 'tan'})
13  print('Update after add:', car_dict)
14
15  #Remove an item from a dict using the pop function
16  removed_value = car_dict.pop('exterior')
17  print('Update after remove:',car_dict)
18  print('Removed value:', removed_value)
```

car_dict: {'brand': 'Porsche', 'year': 2016, 'model': '911'}
Brand: Porsche
Model: 911
Update after add: {'brand': 'Porsche', 'year': 2016, 'model': '911', 'exterior': 'blue', 'interior': 'tan'}
Update after remove: {'brand': 'Porsche', 'year': 2016, 'model': '911', 'interior': 'tan'}
Removed value: blue

DICTIONARY LOOPING

Accessing elements in a Dictionary can be done with loops using the same structure that we used for Lists. The following code blocks show examples of a couple of methods that can be used to loop through a Dictionary. The first example on line 5 uses the for-in structure which iterates through all the keys in the Dictionary then prints the value corresponding to that key. The second method shown in line 8 uses the Python *enumerate* function. The enumerate function is convenient for looping over Dictionaries in that it provides two parameters, the current index of the key-value pair (*index*) and the key at that index (*key*) as shown on line 8. Here we see that of the returned parameters from enumerate, *index* is a zero-based index like in a List, and *key* is the Dictionary key. The Dictionary value can then be obtained by indexing the Dictionary directly with the key as is shown on line 9.

```
1    #Dictionary Looping
2
3    car_dict = {'brand': 'Porsche', 'year': 2016, 'model': '911'}
4
5    for key in car_dict:
6        print(key, ':', car_dict[key])
7
8    for index, key in enumerate(car_dict):
9        print(index, ':', key, ':', car_dict[key])
```

```
brand : Porsche
year : 2016
model : 911
0 : brand : Porsche
1 : year : 2016
2 : model : 911
```

Like lists, we can implement comprehension on Dictionaries, which again is a more efficient way to implement looping. In this example, we have a couple of Lists that are created, and we want to assemble them into a Dictionary. We can iterate through each of the items in the list simultaneously using the Python *zip* function. The *zip* function allows us to combine two or more iterable items, such as the Lists we have in this example, and index them using two variables. You can then see on line 6 how we can iterate through each of the items in the individual Lists, and then assemble them into the *car_dict* Dictionary on a single line. We will cover the *zip* function in more detail when discussing advanced functions.

```
1    #Dictionary Comprehension
2
3    key_list = ['brand', 'year', 'model']
4    value_list = ['Porsche', 2016, '911']
5
6    car_dict = { k:v for (k,v) in zip(key_list, value_list)}
7    print(car_dict)
```

```
{'brand': 'Porsche', 'year': 2016, 'model': '911'}
```

Next, we will show an example application using a Python Dictionary. Let's say we want to create an inventory of items in a clothing store using a Python data structure. The store offers the following categories: Coats, Shirts, and Shoes, and each has several specific items available. The coats category includes 3 types: Raincoats, Windbreakers, and Pullovers. The store also includes the following types of Shirts: 2 types of T-shirts including V-necks and Crew styles, as well as Button-downs, and Sweaters. And finally, the store offers Dress shoes, Boots, and Cross-fit shoes, where the dress shoes category includes both Wingtips and Loafers. We would like to store this inventory using a Python Dictionary for both the clothing items (keys) and their prices (values). A diagram of the data structures comprising our inventory design follows.

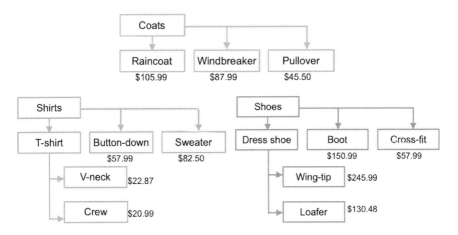

We can implement our Dictionary as shown in the following code example. We define the variable *coatPrices* as a Dictionary with keys assigned to the coat types and their values as the prices. For the shirts, we create a Dictionary for the *shirtPrices* with the button-down and sweater and their corresponding prices as key-value pairs, but we also define the t-shirt category as a key with the value set to the Dictionary *tshirtPrices*.

For the shoes, we create a similar structure as with the shirts with *Boots* and *Crossfit* as keys and their prices as values, then the dress shoe category is defined with a value set to the Dictionary *dressShoePrices*.

Now, we can create a top-level Dictionary called *inventory* following the diagram with *Coat*, *Shirt*, and *Shoes* as the keys and their values as the price Dictionaries we just defined. Then if we want to print out our entire store inventory, we simply print the top-level dictionary, *inventory* as shown in line 25. Further, we can print out individual categories and items. For example, if we want to see all the *Coat* inventory, we can specify it as shown in line 26. Or if we want to see the price of a specific item in the *Coat* category, say the *Windbreakers*, we can specify it by first indexing the *Coat* key, then the *Windbreaker* key (in that order) as shown in line 27. And finally, if we need to update a price for a specific item in our inventory, we can access it individually using the appropriate key as shown in line 32.

```
1   #Dictionaries example
2
3   coatPrices = {'Raincoat': 105.99,
4                 'Windbreaker': 87.99,
5                 'Pullover': 45.50}
6
7   tShirtPrices = {'CrewNeck': 20.99,
8                   'Vneck': 22.87}
9
10  shirtPrices = {'Tshirt': tShirtPrices,
11                 'ButtonDown': 57.99,
12                 'Sweater': 82.50}
13
14  dressShoePrices = {'WingTip': 245.99,
15                     'Loafer': 130.48}
16
17  shoePrices = {'Boots': 150.99,
18               'CrossFit': 57.99,
19               'Dress': dressShoePrices}
20
21  inventory = {'Coat': coatPrices,
22               'Shirt': shirtPrices,
23               'Shoes': shoePrices}
24
25  print('Total inventory:', inventory)
26  print('All coat inventory:', inventory['Coat'])
27  print('Windbreaker price:', inventory['Coat']['Windbreaker'])
28  print('Dress shoe inventory:', inventory['Shoes']['Dress'])
29  print('Loafer shoe price:', inventory['Shoes']['Dress']['Loafer'])
30
31  #Price change update
32  coatPrices['Pullover'] = 50.99
33  print('All coat inventory(after price change):', inventory['Coat'])
```

Total inventory: {'Coat': {'Raincoat': 105.99, 'Windbreaker': 87.99, 'Pullover': 45.5}, 'Shirt': {'Tshirt': {'CrewNeck': 20.99, 'Vneck': 22.87}, 'ButtonDown': 57.99, 'Sweater': 82.5}, 'Shoes': {'Boots': 150.99, 'CrossFit': 57.99, 'Dress': {'WingTip': 245.99, 'Loafer': 130.48}}}
All coat inventory: {'Raincoat': 105.99, 'Windbreaker': 87.99, 'Pullover': 45.5} Windbreaker price: 87.99
Dress shoe inventory: {'WingTip': 245.99, 'Loafer': 130.48}
Loafer shoe price: 130.48
All coat inventory(after price change): {'Raincoat': 105.99, 'Windbreaker': 87.99, 'Pullover': 50.99}

2.4:
Data Structures - Tuples

A Python Tuple is yet another data structure that is like an array, but instead of requiring an imported library, like the array does, the Tuple is a built-in, non-primitive data structure.

The official Python Tuple Application Programming Interface (API) is shown here: https://docs.python.org/3/c-api/tuple.html

Collection Types	Description
List	Ordered.
	Changeable.
	Allows duplicate members.
Tuple	Ordered.
	Not Changeable.
	Allows duplicated members.
	Faster access than List
Dictionary	Ordered (as of Python version 3.7)
	Changeable.
	Indexed.
	No duplicate members.
Set	Not ordered.
	Not indexed.
	No duplicate members.
Stack	Implementation via List,
	collections.deque, queue.LifoQueue
Queue	Implementation via List,
	collections.deque, queue.Queue

Tuples are an ordered collection of items that are stored in memory, where each of the items is individually referenced and accessed using its index. The main distinction between a Tuple and List or Dictionary is that its data is immutable, meaning it cannot be changed once it has been created. An item can be any of the previously mentioned data types, and they can be mixed, for example, you can store strings with other data types such as integers. However, once created a Tuple cannot be changed, and for this reason, it is common to convert between Lists and Tuples depending on the program's purpose and efficiency requirements. As shown in the following code blocks, the syntax used to create a Tuple is to separate the items with commas, and this can be done with or without parentheses as shown in lines 3-4. We can convert a List to a Tuple as shown in line 5 by simply casting it using the *tuple* constructor. Note that the List created is the parameter passed to the function, and we know this is a List since it is delimited with square brackets. If we want to create a Tuple with a single value, we need to follow it with a comma, and this is because Tuples require comma separated objects versus just the parentheses. So, if the single value on line 6 has the comma omitted, the parentheses will be ignored and the variable will simply store the integer, 1, and then if a subscripted print is performed as in line 11, it will throw an error (called a *TypeError*) since integers are not subscriptable.

We can then print out the whole Tuple, as shown on line 8, or individual slices or elements using the List indexing schemes previously discussed.

```
1    #Tuple creation
2
3    candy_tuple = 'reeses', 'hershey', 'gummies'
4    food_tuple = ('taco', 'pizza', 'sushi', 'spaghetti', 'soup', 'sandwich')
5    mixed_tuple = tuple(['water', candy_tuple, 'lemonade', 5.42])
6    single_item_tuple = (1,)
7    single_item_tuple_error = (1)
8
9    print(candy_tuple)
10   print(food_tuple[ :4])
11   print(mixed_tuple[-1])
12   print(single_item_tuple[0])
13   print(single_item_tuple_error[0])
```

```
('reeses', 'hershey', 'gummies')
('taco', 'pizza', 'sushi', 'spaghetti')
5.42
1
-----------------------------------------------------------------------
TypeError                         Traceback (most recent call last)
<ipython-input-3-dfc6b545c517> in <cell line: 13>()
     11 print(mixed_tuple[-1])
     12 print(single_item_tuple[0])
---> 13 print(single_item_tuple_error[0])

TypeError: 'int' object is not subscriptable
```

Note the error when the code executes line 13. Here the difference is subtle, but tuples must be subscriptable (can be accessed individually), and as a result, we must initialize a single element tuple like is done in line 6 which encapsulates the integer as a subscriptable collection, versus line 7 which does not.

Now, because Tuples are immutable, this lends them to being very fast and efficient in their access. This is one of the main reasons why a programmer might use a Tuple instead of a standard List.

Tuples share many of the common operations as Lists if there is no attempt to change the contents. The following code block shows more examples of Tuple creation and indexing using standard List functions. We also show in line 17 that trying to change an individual item in the Tuple will result in a type error. Thus, if you wanted to update an individual item in a Tuple, you would need to recreate the whole data structure with the modified item.

```
1    #Tuple examples
2
3    test_variable_bool = True
4    test_variable_9 = 'nine'
5    test_tuple = (test_variable_bool, 6, 7, 8, 'nine', 8, 'ten', test_variable_9)
6
7    print('Whole Tuple:', test_tuple)
8    print('4th element:', test_tuple[3])
9    print('Slice:', test_tuple[:3])
10   print('Slice with step:', test_tuple[1:5:2])
11   print('Number of occurances of 8:', test_tuple.count(8))
12   print('Number of occurances of "nine":', test_tuple.count('nine'))
13   print('Boolean whether "hello" exists:', 'hello' in test_tuple)
14   print('Length:', len(test_tuple))
15
16   #Error case - trying to change a Tuple item
17   test_tuple[0] = '7'
18   print(test_tuple)
```

```
Whole Tuple: (True, 6, 7, 8, 'nine', 8, 'ten', 'nine')
4th element: 8
Slice: (True, 6, 7)
Slice with step: (6, 8)
Number of occurances of 8: 2
Number of occurances of "nine": 2
Boolean whether "hello" exists: False
Length: 8
-------------------------------------------------------------------------
TypeError                          Traceback (most recent call last)
<ipython-input-12-0adb1f1ea436> in <cell line: 17>()
      15
      16 #Error case - trying to change a Tuple item
---> 17 test_tuple[0] = '7'
      18 print(test_tuple)

TypeError: 'tuple' object does not support item assignment
```

In the following code block, we show how returning multiple values from a function is done using Tuples. We can see the data type is a Tuple by calling the *type* function as shown on line 6.

```
1    #Tuples returned in function
2
3    def test_function():
4        return 1, 3, 6
5
6    print(type(test_function()))
7    print(test_function())
8
9    var1, var2, var3 = test_function()
10   print(var1, var2, var3)
```

⎆ <class 'tuple'>
   (1, 3, 6)
   1 3 6

TUPLE LOOPING

Finally, iterating over the items in a tuple is done the same as was shown previously with Lists. We can use the for-in (or for-each) technique, to iterate over each of the items in a Tuple. We can also use the range-object loop structure, where we iterate from a start index, which may be 0 or any other index up to the end of the Tuple, and we can use the Python *len* function to provide the last element. The following code block shows looping using the standard zero-based indexing and slicing.

```
1    # Looping over a Tuple is similar to looping over a List
2
3    test_variable_bool = True
4    test_variable_9 = 'nine'
5    test_tuple = (test_variable_bool, 6, 7, 8, 'nine', 8, 'ten', test_variable_9)
6
7    for item in test_tuple:
8        print(item)
9
10   for i in range(len(test_tuple)):
11       print('Test_tuple index, value:', i, test_tuple[i])
```

⊡→ True
6
7
8
nine
8
ten
nine
Test_tuple index, value: 0 True
Test_tuple index, value: 1 6
Test_tuple index, value: 2 7
Test_tuple index, value: 3 8
Test_tuple index, value: 4 nine
Test_tuple index, value: 5 8
Test_tuple index, value: 6 ten
Test_tuple index, value: 7 nine

2.5:
Data Structures - Sets

The next Python data structure we will cover is the Set. Sets are unordered collections of unique elements, meaning they cannot have any duplicate items.

The official Python Set Application Programming Interface (API) is shown here: https://docs.python.org/3/c-api/set.html

Collection Types	Description
List	Ordered. Changeable. Allows duplicate members.
Tuple	Ordered. Not Changeable. Allows duplicated members. Faster access than List
Dictionary	Ordered (as of Python version 3.7) Changeable. Indexed. No duplicate members.
Set	Not ordered. Not indexed. No duplicate members.
Stack	Implementation via List, collections.deque, queue.LifoQueue
Queue	Implementation via List, collections.deque, queue.Queue

As shown in the following code blocks, the syntax used to create a Set is to separate the items with commas and delimit it with curly braces. New single items can be added using the *add* function as shown on line 8. Sets require that all items be unique, so if you try to add an item that is already there as in line 12, the request will not be flagged as an error, but it will be ignored, and no update will be made. Adding an iterable item, such as a List, can also be done using the *update* function as shown on line 16-17. If we try to remove an item that does not exist, Python will generate an exception called a *KeyError*.

```
1    #Sets
2
3    test_set = {'one', 2, True, 2, 2, 2, 2, False, True}
4
5    print('Set creation:', test_set)
6
7    # Add a single item to a set using the add function
8    test_set.add('new item')
9    print('Add an item:', test_set)
10
11   # Attempt to add an item that already exists
12   test_set.add('one')
13   print('Add a duplicate item:', test_set)
14
15   # Add a list using update
16   more_stuff = ['two', 'three', 'four']
17   test_set.update(more_stuff)
18   print('Add an item using "update"', test_set)
19
20   # Remove an item using remove
21   test_set.remove('new item')
22   print('Set with removed item:', test_set)
23
24   # Attempt to remove an item that is not present
25   test_set.remove('new item')
```

```
Set creation: {False, True, 2, 'one'}
Add an item: {False, True, 2, 'new item', 'one'}
Add a duplicate item: {False, True, 2, 'new item', 'one'}
Add an item using "update" {False, True, 2, 'two', 'new item', 'three', 'four', 'one'}
Set with removed item: {False, True, 2, 'two', 'three', 'four', 'one'}
-------------------------------------------------------------------
KeyError                              Traceback (most recent call last)
<ipython-input-17-9eb021abf16c> in <cell line: 25>()
     23
     24 # Attempt to remove an item that is not present
---> 25 test_set.remove('new item')
     26
     27

KeyError: 'new item'
```

Finally, if we want to loop through the items in the set, we must use the "for-in" syntax. We cannot use the range syntax because sets are unordered, and that means that the order of the items that exist is not predictable. Further, since the items are unordered, when you print them, you also cannot predict the order in which they will be printed.

BUILT-IN DATA STRUCTURE SYNTAX SUMMARY

In the following code block, we summarize the syntax to create one of the 4 data structures covered thus far. Note the differences between how a List, Dictionary, Tuple, and Set are initialized.

```
1   #List syntax: comma separated items with square bracket delimiters
2   myList2 = ['Cat','Dog','Horse']
3
4   #Dictionary syntax: comma separated key-value pairs with curly brace delimiters
5   myDictionary = {'Coat': 1000, 'Shirt': 2000, 'Slacks': 3000, 'Shoes': 4000}
6
7   #Tuple syntax: comma separated items with parenthesis delimiters
8   test_tuple = (5, 'seven', True)
9
10  #Set syntax: comma separated items with curly brace delimiters
11  test_set = {'one', 2, True, 2, 2, 2, 2, False, True}
12
13  print(myList2)
14  print(myDictionary)
15  print(test_tuple)
16  print(test_set)
```

['Cat', 'Dog', 'Horse']
{'Coat': 1000, 'Shirt': 2000, 'Slacks': 3000, 'Shoes': 4000}
(5, 'seven', True)
{False, True, 2, 'one'}

2.6:
DATA STRUCTURES - STACKS

The next data structure we will cover is the Stack. The Stack is what is called a user-defined data structure, and that is because it doesn't have a default supported datatype which means, in Python, we must create it.

Collection Types	Description
List	Ordered. Changeable. Allows duplicate members.
Tuple	Ordered. Not Changeable. Allows duplicated members. Faster access than List
Dictionary	Ordered (as of Python version 3.7) Changeable. Indexed. No duplicate members.
Set	Not ordered. Not indexed. No duplicate members.
Stack	Implementation via List, collections.deque, queue.LifoQueue
Queue	Implementation via List, collections.deque, queue.Queue

You can think of this data structure as a pipe where you insert items into the pipe at one end and then extract them out of the pipe from the same end. We call this access method "Last-In-First-Out or a "LIFO" because we are inserting and extracting items from the same location in the pipe. Thus, the two most important functions that we implement with a Stack are so-called *push* (when inserting data) and *pop* (when extracting data). A common application of a Stack is with recursion, where process "activation records" are pushed to a stack during a recursive phase and popped during the unwinding phase. We will discuss the use of Stacks in recursion in more detail later.

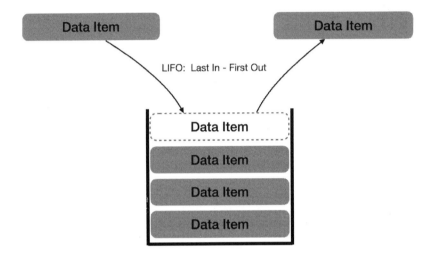

There are several ways to implement a Stack, namely using a standard Python List, the *queue.LifoQueue* class, and the *Collections.deque* class.

The first Stack implementation method we will examine is using standard Python Lists. A list of the common functions used when implementing a Stack from a Python List is shown in the following table. To *push* items onto the Stack, we use the append function. This will add items to the Stack at the top or highest index in the List. To remove items, we use the *pop* function with no input arguments. This will pop the last item added to the Stack, at the highest index or "right" side of the List, and return the popped item. We need to be careful when popping items from a Stack and use exception handling because if we happen to have no items to pop off the Stack, Python will throw an *IndexError* exception. If we want to remove all the items from the Stack, we can clear them using the *clear* function. And if we want to return the number of elements that are equal to some item, we can count them using the *count* function.

Method	Description
append(x)	Add x to right side (top) of stack
pop(i)	Remove item at index i from the list, and return the item. If no i given then remove from right side of list (top of stack). (IndexError) if no elements in stack
clear()	Remove all elements
count(x)	Return number of elements equal to x
insert(i,x)	Insert x into stack at index i (IndexError) if i > len(stack)
remove(value)	Remove first occurrence of value (ValueError) if value not found
index(x)	Return index of first occurrence of x in stack (ValueError) if x not found

Now, if we want to insert an item at a particular position, we can use the insert function. However, this violates the basic notion of the LIFO structure for a Stack in which the items are added and extracted from the same point in the data structure. Additionally, we can remove individual values from the Stack using the remove function, but again, this violates the spirit of the LIFO structure since this function would allow removal of an item from any index in the Stack. If we want to return the index of an item, we can find the position of the first occurrence of the item, or if we want to peek at the value of an item at a specific index we can use List indexing. And recall that with a Python List, we can use negative indexing to access items from the end of the List. For example, accessing the Stack with an index of -1 would return the value at the top of the Stack (which is the insertion and extraction point).

The following code block example initializes the Stack as a Python List, then shows several pushes to the stack using the append function which places the added items at the top (or highest index) of the Stack. The List *pop* method (with no input arguments) is then used to remove items from the top of the Stack, at the highest List index. Line 15 implements a *peek* function to view the value of the current item at the top of the Stack; that is, the next item that will be popped, and this is done by indexing directly into the stack with index set to -1. Finally, the example shows execution of several pop's of the stack which ultimately generates an *IndexError* exception when the first pop is executed on the empty List.

```
1    #Stack implementation using Python List
2
3    stack = ['big', 'hello']
4    print('Print 1:', stack)
5
6    stack.append('from')
7    stack.append('python')
8    stack.append('python')
9    print('Print 2:', stack)
10
11   stack.remove('python')
12   print('Print 3:', stack)
13   print('Print 4:', stack.pop())
14   print('Print 5:', stack)
15   print('Print 6:', stack[-1])
16
17   #Pop stack until empty then try to access
18   stack.pop()
19   stack.pop()
20   stack.pop()
21   stack.pop()
22   stack.pop()
```

Print 1: ['big', 'hello']
Print 2: ['big', 'hello', 'from', 'python', 'python']
Print 3: ['big', 'hello', 'from', 'python']
Print 4: python
Print 5: ['big', 'hello', 'from']
Print 6: from

IndexError   Traceback (most recent call last)
<ipython-input-1-305490e0a533> in <cell line: 21>()
     19 stack.pop()
     20 stack.pop()
---> 21 stack.pop()
     22 stack.pop()

IndexError: pop from empty list

Another Stack implementation can be done with a less commonly used library called the *queue.LifoQueue* class. Though it is the least common Stack implementation option, it will implement a true stack, in that it only supports methods that allow you to push and pop from the top of the stack. This implementation option is used primarily in multi-threaded communication protocols and is slower than using a deque which we will cover next. In addition to the speed issue, another reason LifoQueue is not commonly used, is that it will "block" if you try to insert items onto your Stack past the size you have initialized it to. This will result in your program hanging in an infinite stall until the stack size drops below the initialized limit. So, if using a LifoQueue, you will want to build in error checks, and there exist some methods, such as *qsize*, that can be used to implement error handling. A summary of the important methods that are available in the LifoQueue class is shown in the table.

Method	Description
put(x)	Add x to the end of the queue (i.e. to top of the stack)
get()	Remove item from the end of the queue (from top of stack)
empty()	Returns True if queue is empty
qsize()	Returns the size of the queue
full()	Returns True if queue is full

An example Stack implementation using a *LifoQueue* is shown in the following code block.

```
1   # Stack from LifoQueue
2
3   from queue import LifoQueue
4
5   stack = LifoQueue(maxsize = 5)
6   print('Print 1:', stack.qsize())
7   stack.put('hello')
8   stack.put('python')
9   stack.put('world')
10
11  print('Print 2:', stack.qsize())
12  print('Print 3:', stack.get())
13  print('Print 4:', stack.empty())
14  print('Print 5:', stack.full())
```

```
Print 1: 0
Print 2: 3
Print 3: world
Print 4: False
Print 5: False
```

Finally, the most popular Stack implementation method is from the Python *Collections.deque* class, where "deque" stands for "doubly ended queue". The deque is more efficient than both Python Lists and LifoQueue, and is safe in that it will not block if a program attempts to add items to a full Stack. The programmer can set a size limit, and if that is exceeded, the deque will automatically discard the "oldest" items; that is the items at the end opposite from where the items were added. While this may not be preferred in certain applications, it allows a failsafe mechanism if memory constraints exist in the application. The deque functionality supports more than just a single entry/exit point stack referred to in the LIFO, it will also implement FIFO type operations, or First-In-First-Out, which means we can extract data from both the right side of the Stack and the left side. The deque implementation has the fastest execution time, so is a more efficient way to implement your Stack, and it also supports exceptions, specifically the *IndexError* and *ValueError*. Some of the methods that you can utilize are shown in the table.

Method	Description
ppend(x)	Add x to right side of deque (top of stack
ppendleft(x)	Add x to left side (bottom) of deque
op()	Remove and return item from right side of deque (top of stack/queue) (IndexError) if no elements in deque
opleft()	Remove and return item from left side o deque (bottom of stack/queue) (IndexError) if no elements in deque
lear()	Remove all elements
ount(x)	Return number of elements equal to x
isert(i,x)	Insert x into deque at position i (IndexError) if i > len(deque)
emove(value)	Remove first occurrence of value (ValueError) if value not found
idex(x)	Return position of first occurrence of x i deque (ValueError) if x not found

The following code block shows a Stack implementation example using a deque. First, we need to import the deque library as shown in line 3, then create the Stack by calling the deque constructor as shown on line 5. Then we can append some items, and we show that on lines 6-8. The next lines show various operations that can be performed specifically to add and remove items. As mentioned previously, note that the access flexibility we have with the Stack using deque essentially violates the idea of a LIFO Stack, but we show them here to demonstrate functionality.

```
1    #Stack from deque
2
3    from collections import deque
4
5    stack = deque()
6    stack.append("hello")
7    stack.append("python")
8    stack.append("world")
9    print('Print 1:', stack)
10   print('Print 2:', stack.pop())
11   print('Print 3:', stack)
12   print('Print 4:', len(stack))
13
14   stack.appendleft("big")
15   print('Print 5:', stack)
16
17   stack.append("python")
18   print('Print 5b:', stack)
19   print('Print 6:', stack.count('python'))
20   print('Print 7:', stack.index('python'))
21
22   stack.insert(2,'from')
23   print('Print 7:', stack)
24
25   stack.remove('python')
26   print('Print 8:', stack)
```

```
Print 1: deque(['hello', 'python', 'world'])
Print 2: world
Print 3: deque(['hello', 'python'])
Print 4: 2
Print 5: deque(['big', 'hello', 'python'])
Print 5b: deque(['big', 'hello', 'python', 'python'])
Print 6: 2
Print 7: 2
Print 7: deque(['big', 'hello', 'from', 'python', 'python'])
Print 8: deque(['big', 'hello', 'from', 'python'])
```

2.7:
Data Structures - Queues

We will complete our discussion of Python data structures with Queues. Like Stacks, the Queue is another user-defined data structure because it doesn't have a default supported datatype and so, in Python, we must create it.

Collection Types	Description
List	Ordered.
	Changeable.
	Allows duplicate members.
Tuple	Ordered.
	Not Changeable.
	Allows duplicated members.
	Faster access than List
Dictionary	Ordered (as of Python version 3.7)
	Changeable.
	Indexed.
	No duplicate members.
Set	Not ordered.
	Not indexed.
	No duplicate members.
Stack	Implementation via List,
	collections.deque, queue.LifoQueue
Queue	Implementation via List,
	collections.deque, queue.Queue

This data structure can be thought of as a pipe where you insert items into the pipe at one end and then extract them out of the pipe from the opposite end. This was discussed briefly with the deque class with Stacks, and was called "First-In-First-Out or a "FIFO". Though Queues function differently that stacks, the two most important functions are the same; that is, *push* (when inserting data) and *pop* (when extracting data). The figure shows both how items are added and removed from both a Stack and Queue to highlight the LIFO versus FIFO structures.

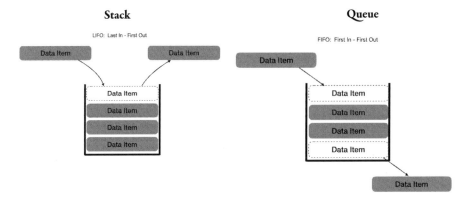

As mentioned, the Queue is like the Stack in that it is user-defined, and similarly there are several ways to implement a Queue, namely using a standard Python List, Collections deque class, and the *queue.Queue* class.

The first Queue implementation method uses standard Python Lists. A list of the common functions used when implementing a Queue from a Python List is the same as was shown in the with Stacks, and is shown again in following table. To push items onto the Queue, we use the *append* function. This will add items to the top of the Queue or highest index in the List. To remove items, we use the *pop* function, but instead of calling *pop* with no input arguments, we call it with an index of 0 which will remove and return the item from the left side of the List, or the bottom of the Queue. Note that the same care needs to be taken when popping items from a Queue to avoid the *IndexError* that was described with Stacks.

Method	Description
append(x)	Add x to right side (top) of stack
pop(i)	Remove item at index i from the list, and return the item. If no i given then remove from right side of list (top of stack). (IndexError) if no elements in stack
clear()	Remove all elements
count(x)	Return number of elements equal to x
insert(i,x)	Insert x into stack at index i (IndexError) if i > len(stack)
remove(value)	Remove first occurrence of value (ValueError) if value not found
index(x)	Return index of first occurrence of x in stack (ValueError) if x not found

The following example code block initializes the Queue as a Python List, then shows several "pushes" to the Queue using the List append function which places the added items at the top (or highest index) of the Queue. The List *pop* method (with input argument set to 0) is then used to remove items from the Queue.

```
1    #Queue from a Python List
2
3    queue = []
4    queue.append('big')
5    queue.append('hello')
6    queue.append('from')
7    queue.append('python')
8    queue.append('python')
9
10   print('Print 1:', queue)
11   print('Print 2:', queue.pop(0))
12   print('Print 3:', queue)
13   print('Print 4:', queue.pop(0))
14   print('Print 5:', queue)
```

Print 1: ['big', 'hello', 'from', 'python', 'python']
Print 2: big
Print 3: ['hello', 'from', 'python', 'python']
Print 4: hello
Print 5: ['from', 'python', 'python']

The next implementation example uses the Python *Collections.deque* class. The table of common functions is again shown in the following table, but is the same as what was used with Stacks.

Method	Description
append(x)	Add x to right side of deque (top of stack)
appendleft(x)	Add x to left side (bottom) of deque
pop()	Remove and return item from right side of deque (top of stack/queue) (IndexError) if no elements in deque
popleft()	Remove and return item from left side of deque (bottom of stack/queue) (IndexError) if no elements in deque
clear()	Remove all elements
count(x)	Return number of elements equal to x
insert(i,x)	Insert x into deque at position i (IndexError) if i > len(deque)
remove(value)	Remove first occurrence of value (ValueError) if value not found
index(x)	Return position of first occurrence of x in deque (ValueError) if x not found

The following code block shows a Queue implementation example using a deque. First, we need to import the *deque* library as shown in line 3, then create the Queue by calling the deque constructor as shown on line 5. Then we can append items, and we show that on lines 6-8. The next lines show various operations that can be performed specifically to pop items from the Queue.

```
1   #Queue from Collections deque
2
3   from collections import deque
4
5   queue = deque()
6   queue.append("hello")
7   queue.append("python")
8   queue.append("world")
9
10  print('Print 1:', queue)
11  print('Print 2:', queue.popleft())
12  print('Print 3:', queue)
```

⊡→ Print 1: deque(['hello', 'python', 'world'])
Print 2: hello
Print 3: deque(['python', 'world'])

Finally, the queue.Queue class comes from the same Python package as the LifoQueue class. As with the Stack implementation using the LifoQueue class, the Queue class implements a true FIFO structure, but also has the same drawbacks in efficiency and blocking concerns as was described with Stacks, and as a result this is not a common implementation option. For completeness though, we show the example in the following code block.

```
1   #Queue from Queue class
2
3   from queue import Queue
4
5   q = Queue(maxsize = 3)
6   print(q.qsize())
7   q.put('hello')
8   q.put('python')
9   q.put('world')
10  print('Print 1:', q.full())
11  print('Print 2:', q.get())
12  print('Print 3:', q.get())
13  print('Print 4:', q.get())
14  print('Print 5:', q.full())
```

⊡→ 0
Print 1: True
Print 2: hello
Print 3: python
Print 4: world
Print 5: False

CHAPTER 3:
Python Recursion, File IO, OOP, and Advanced Functions

In this chapter we will cover Python Recursion, File Input-Output, Object-Oriented Programming, and Advanced Functions.

LEARNING OBJECTIVES

By the end of this chapter, you will be able to do the following:

- Identify and write a recursion function base case and recursive call.
- Define an activation record and its use in a recursive push and pop (unwind) function.
- Create a recursion trace diagram is and how to evaluate a recursive function using one.
- Define and implement memoization with a recursive function.
- Define a data analytics algorithm that uses recursion and how it improves performance.
- Define 2 common data analytics file formats, and write a Python script to read and write file of those types.
- Write a Python class, including constructors and methods.
- Define and Implement an object-oriented programming hierarchy consisting of a parent and child class.
- Write Python scripts which implement map, zip, filter, lambda, and apply the glob library.

3.1:

RECURSION

Recursion is supported in most programming languages and is a process in which a function or a method will call itself repeatedly until a certain condition is met. This is an abstract concept, particularly when we try to analyze code implementations, so before we get into the details, we will provide some background high-level concepts and terminology, and discuss when the use of recursion may be more appropriate than a standard iterative approach. We will also illustrate ways to trace through recursive functions without the help of entering and running code in an integrated development environment.

Sometimes we can model complex problems, especially ones that contain several branches, into smaller repetitive chunks, and if we do that, we can simplify both the coding complexity and amount of code needed by implementing a recursive routine versus a standard iterative, or loop based, approach. For example, recursion is used in the most efficient sort and search routines such as MergeSort and QuickSort. Both algorithms use recursion to efficiently partition a problem into smaller pieces using fairly simple functions which call themselves. The efficiency of these search algorithms is on the order of the log of the number of items that are being sorted, and this is due, in part, to the recursive implementation of the algorithm.

So how does recursion work? A recursive function has two parts, the base case, and the recursive call. The base case is typically implemented using conditional statements where we check for a particular condition that will define a way to terminate the recursive calls, and this is done with what is called the termination condition. The recursive call refers to a function calling itself. When a recursive call is made, the processor will push what are called "activation records" onto the processor hardware stack. One of the benefits of using the processor hardware stack is that we have faster execution speed because stack memory that is dedicated to the processor can be accessed faster than external memory. Once the termination condition is met in the base case, then the activation records are popped from the stack in a process called "unwinding".

For example, we looked at the Fibonacci function previously, and the following code block shows how we can generate one of the values in the sequence using a standard Python while-loop.

1	#Fibonacci calculator – iterative approach
2	
3	def fibonacciWhile(n):
4	count = 1
5	n1,n2 = 0,1
6	while count < n:
7	next = n1 + n2
8	n1 = n2
9	n2 = next
10	count += 1
11	return(next)

Alternatively, the following code block performs the exact same calculation and produces the same output with less lines and more efficient code.

1	#Fibonacci calculator – recursive approach
2	
3	def fibonacci(n):
4	if(n<=1):
5	return n
6	return fibonacci(n-2) + fibonacci(n-1)

To create a recursive function, we first need to define a way to stop it, otherwise the function will call itself continuously until it overruns the computer memory and crashes.

The stop mechanism is executed in the "base case" and is typically implemented with a conditional statement, which when evaluated as true will execute the "termination condition" and start the process of unwinding.

Now every time a recursive function calls itself, a bunch of information is assembled in what is called an "activation record" and saved in a dedicated segment of memory in the computer called the stack, which is a segment of contiguous, or sequentially addressed, memory locations that can be written-to and read-from very quickly by the computer hardware. Recall that a software implementation of the stack was discussed previously. The process of storing the activation record uses what we previously described as "pushing" to the stack. When the termination condition is met in the base case, the recursive function performs what is called "unwinding" and the processor begins the process of popping activation records from the stack.

Let's go through an example. The following code shows a simple recursive routine which prints a decrementing sequence of numbers starting from a start value, 4, and ending at the value passed into the function parameter list, where the input parameter must be less than 4.

```
1    #Recursive routine to print a decrementing sequence
2
3    def recurDecSeq(x):
4        if(x < 4):
5            recurDecSeq(x+1)
6        print(x)
7        return
8
9    recurDecSeq(1)
```

⤷   4
      3
      2
      1

We will walk through the code and show graphically how the information is tracked when a recursive routine calls itself several times. The function is called with an input parameter of "1" from line 9. The input parameter is checked in the function base case, on line 4, against the termination condition, (the value 4 in this case), and since 1 is less than 4, a recursive call is executed from line 5, this time with input parameter x + 1 or 2 in this case. When the recursive call is made, the 1st activation record is pushed to the stack.

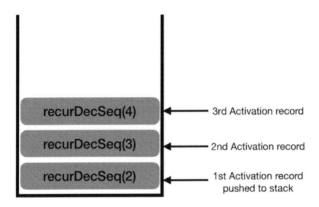

The next call with input, 2, is checked against the termination condition and since 2 is less than 4, it calls the recursive function again with the value, 3, and pushes the 2nd activation record on to the stack. The process is repeated, this time the input, 3, is checked against the termination condition, and since 3 is less than 4, it calls the function with the value, 4, and pushes the 3rd activation record on to the stack.

Now, with the input, 4, we see that the termination condition is activated, meaning 4 is no longer strictly less than 4, so we skip the call to the recursive function, and this starts the "unwinding" process.

We first print the current value of x, which for this call was a 4, then we return to the previous call to the function and pop the 3rd activation record from the stack. Since the next record on the stack has input parameter of "3" (see the block pointed to as the 2nd activation record), we print that value out and pop the 2nd activation record. Next, we print the input parameter for the current record on the stack, which is pointed to as the 1st activation record, and pop the activation record. Finally, we return to the first call of the function with the input, 1, so we print that out and the call sequence is complete.

Now we will look at one of the most common recursive examples; that is, calculating the factorial of an input number, but this time we will trace through the call sequence a bit differently. The recursive function is shown in the following code block, and we see that the output if we call the function with an input, 4, the output is 24.

```
1    #Factorial using recursion
2
3    def factorial(n):
4        if(n == 1):
5            return 1
6        return n*factorial(n-1)
7
8    print('Recursive factorial with input 4:', factorial(4))
```
⤷   Recursive factorial with input 4: 24

We can trace through the stack push and pop sequence in code and create a recursive call "trace diagram" as shown in the following figure. The first call to the function checks if the input, 4, is equal to 1 on line 4. Since it is not, the code jumps to line 6 and multiplies the current input times a call to the function with input n - 1, (the value 3 in this case). Now in the stack, we push the activation record associated with 4 times the call to factorial with 3 as the input, and this is shown as *n*factorial(3)* in the trace diagram. We repeat the check if the current input, which is 3, is equal to 1, which is not, so we again execute line 6 where the current n is multiplied by a call to factorial with n - 1 or 2 as the input, and its activation record is pushed to the stack as *n*factorial(2)*. We then repeat the sequence for the input 2. Here we see that 2 is not equal to 1 so again we push its activation record to the stack, *n*factorial(1)*, this time with 2 as n times the call to factorial with input n - 1 or 1.

Now at this point in the sequence, the termination condition is met so we return 1 on line 5 and start unwinding the stack. To unwind, we perform the calculation called out in the last activation record pushed to the stack, *n*factorial(1)*, with *n* = 2 and factorial of 1 (which is 1), and we get the value 2. We then pop to the next layer's activation record which performs the returned value of

2 for the *factorial(2)* part times the input, 3, and we get the value 6. Finally, we perform the calculation called out in the 1st activation record pushed to the stack, *n*factorial(3)* where *factorial(3)* has propagated from the last popped activation record as 6, and that is multiplied by n or original input parameter of 4, which results in 24, and this is our answer; that is, the factorial of 4 is equal to 4 times 3 times 2 times 1 or 24.

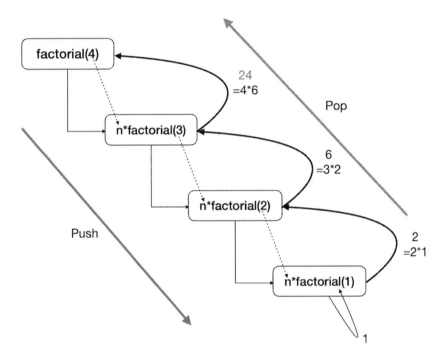

Now, say we had multiple recursive calls in a function? Let's look at how this works with another example. Previously, we discussed the Fibonacci sequence and how to generate the values in the sequence using Python loops. Here we will see how recursion can be used to find any one of the values in the sequence. The example code block follows and is run with an input parameter to find the value of the sequence at a specified index. Note that in this example, we use zero indexing, that is the first term in the sequence is indexed by 0, the 2nd value indexed by 1, and so on. In other words, for this example, if we want the 5th term in the sequence, we call the function with the input, 4.

Index	0	1	2	3	4	5	6	7	8	9	10
Fibonacci	0	1	1	2	3	5	8	13	21	34	55

```
1    #Return the nth number in a fibonacci sequence
2    #where n=0 represents the starting index of 0
3    #i.e. input 4 produces the 5th term, or "3"
4    #0,1,1,2,3,5,8,13,21,34,55,89,144
5
6    def fibonacci(n):
7        if(n<=1):
8            return n
9        return fibonacci(n-2) + fibonacci(n-1)
10
11   print('The 4th value in a recursive fibonacci:', fibonacci(4))
```

⤶ The 4th value in a recursive fibonacci: 3

In our recursive function, the base case with termination condition is shown in lines 7-8, which checks if the input parameter is less than or equal to 1, and if that condition is met then the stack is unwound by returning the input parameter, n, for the current function call.

If the termination condition is not met then the code makes two calls to the recursive function, one with input value, n - 2, and the other with, n - 1, then sums their returned values. This is shown in line 9.

The two recursive calls launch two branches in the following sequence trace diagram which represents all the activation records that are pushed to the stack. The process repeats as described for each branch; that is, the termination condition is checked, and if not met, the recursive calls are made again.

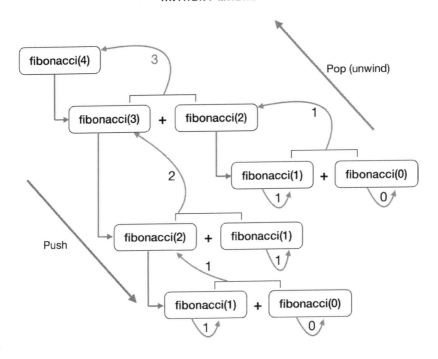

Now if the input value to the recursive function call is 1 or 0 then the termination condition is met, the input parameter is returned, and the stack unwinding occurs. You can see in the diagram, and by examining the code on line 8 that the *fibonacci* function returns 1 for each input parameter of 1 and returns 0 for each input parameter of 0, then for each layer in the sequence, the two *fibonacci* function return values are added and returned to the previous layer until the final sum is computed.

BINARY SEARCH

As we discussed when we introduced recursion, one of the more popular applications in data analytics is to implement search and sort algorithms. Many of these search and sort routines lend themselves well to recursion due their repetitive "divide and conquer" approach to the algorithm. The example that we show here is for binary search. This is a popular algorithm, and one which is studied extensively in computer science courses, so you may already be familiar with it. Binary search is an efficient algorithm that is used to find a position of a target value in a collection, and in Python, the collection would typically be a List or an array. And this search can be performed efficiently using recursive calls.

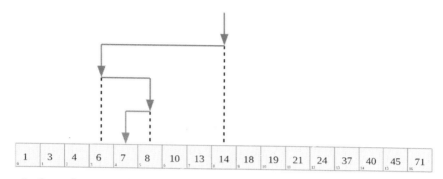

Attribution for image: Wikipedia Creative Commons
https://creativecommons.org/licenses/by/2.5 *by AlwaysAngry - Own work*

We first assume that the collection is sorted. The algorithm splits the array in half and compares a target value to the value in the middle of the collection. Then we can make some comparisons and decide which direction that we want to move for our next evaluation. Specifically, if the target is less than the middle value, then it must exist on the left half of the collection that would be towards the beginning or lower indices in the array. Conversely, if the target is greater than that middle value, it must be on the right side or towards the end of the array. We then can recursively split the half of the array into successive halves. Each time we split it in half, we are making a recursive call, and we do this continually until the target is found. This lends itself to complexity reductions from a standard multi-loop search algorithm. Specifically, the complexity efficiency for the worst-case and the average search would be on the order of the log of the number of elements in the array. Now we will walk through some code implementing binary search using recursion. We first show the algorithm implemented with pseudocode, which is an easier-to-read textual summary of the algorithm, then with a Python implementation in the following code blocks.

```
1    #Binary search pseudocode
2
3    def bin_search(input, target):
4        if middle element is equal to target:
5            return middle index
6        if middle element is greater than target:
7            bin_search left half of input
8        if middle element is less than target
9            bin_search right half of input
```

```
1    #Binary search using Recursion
2
3    def bin_search(input, left, right, target):
4
5        if right >= left:
6            mid = int((left + right)/2)
7
8            # Base / termination case
9            # If target is at the mid, return
10           if input[mid] == target:
11               return mid
12
13           #Recursive calls
14           # Target is smaller than mid so search the elements in left half
15           elif input[mid] > target:
16               return bin_search(input, left, mid-1, target)
17
18           # Target is larger than mid so search the elements in right half
19           else:
20               return bin_search(input, mid+1, right, target)
21       else:
22           # Target is not in input
23           return -1
24
25   #index (0, 1, 2, 3, 4, 5, 6, 7, 8, 9, 10, 11, 12, 13, 14, 15, 16)
26   my_list = [1, 3, 4, 6, 7, 8, 10, 13, 14, 18, 19, 21, 24, 37, 40, 45, 71]
27   print('The value 7 is located at index: ', bin_search(my_list, 0, len(my_list)-
     1, 7))
28   print('The value 10 is located at index: ', bin_search(my_list, 0, len(my_list)-
     1, 10))
29   print('The value 45 is located at index: ', bin_search(my_list, 0, len(my_list)-
     1, 45)
```

```
The value 7 is located at index: 4
The value 10 is located at index: 6
The value 45 is located at index: 15
```

We see in our function definition on line 3 that the input parameters include the input array and two pointers, one we call *left* and one *right*, and a target that we are searching for. The two pointers will represent the two ends of our "search window," which is the range of elements that we are searching through to find our desired target. At the start, our search window will be the entire array, so *left* and *right* will be the indices of the first and last element in the array, but over time we will make this window smaller and smaller as we search for our element. In the initial conditional statement on line 5, the two pointers, which are simply indices into the array, are checked to see if they have touched each other, because when this happens the array can no longer be split into smaller halves. We can view this as the "outer" base case, which if True will start the unwind process on any pushed activation records via line 23. If the right pointer index is greater than or equal to the left pointer index then we calculate a mid-position pointer index on line 6, which is equal to the left plus right divided by two. We also must cast the result to an integer because we are not able to index into an array with a fractional value which could be generated depending on the values of left and right.

Then we check the "inner" base case and check to see if the target is at that mid-position. If the condition statement evaluates True, then we found our target and we can start unwinding the stack and popping our activation records. If the condition evaluates false, recursive calls are made from the *else* clauses in the base case conditional statements. On line 15, we check if the value at that mid-position is greater than the target, and if true, the target is smaller than that mid-position value and therefore must be in the left-hand side of the search window, so we want to search those elements. This is executed with the recursive call on line 16, where we call our binary search function again with our window ranging from *left* to *mid* - 1, which represents the range of elements in the left half of the search window.

In the other else case, on line 19, the target is larger than the value at the mid pointer, so we will want to search the right-hand side of the array. In that case, we will make another recursive call of binary search with a new window ranging from *mid* + 1 to *right*, which represents the range of elements in the right half of the search window.

This process of evaluating the input with adjusted left and right pointers is repeated with the recursive calls until the target is found.

MEMOIZATION

Now, there exists is a technique in recursion called "memoization" where we take advantage of the fact that sometimes several function calls are repeated. We see this in the example for the Fibonacci sequence in the following code block.

```
1    #Fibonacci with Recursion and Memoization
2
3    import time
4
5    memoi = {}
6    def fib_memoi(n):
7        if n in memoi:
8            return memoi[n]
9        if n<=1:
10           memoi[n]=1
11           return 1
12       memoi[n] = fib_memoi(n-1) + fib_memoi(n-2) #add value to memoi[key]
13       print(memoi)
14       return memoi[n]
15
16   t0_memoi = time.time()
17   fib_memoization = fib_memoi(10)
18   t1_memoi = time.time()
19
20
21   def fib_recur(n):
22       if(n<=1):
23           return n
24       return fib_recur(n-2) + fib_recur(n-1)
25
26   t0_recur = time.time()
27   fib_recursive = fib_recur(10)
28   t1_recur = time.time()
29
30   print('Total time recursive: ', round(t1_recur-t0_recur, 10))
31   print('Total time memoization: ', round(t1_memoi-t0_memoi, 10))
```

> Total time recursive: 0.01168251
> Total time memoization: 0.0051362514

Memorization utilizes what is called a memory lookup, or sometimes called lookup tables to store previously calculated values which are the results of a recursive call. In our implementation, we can then add the result of the recursive call as a value to a Python Dictionary with a specific key. Then the next recursive call that we want to make, we can check to see if that key is already in the Dictionary and if it is we can retrieve it from there, and in that case will result in efficiency improvements which ultimately speed up our algorithm execution. A diagram of the sequence trace for the Fibonacci function is shown. With the trace diagram, we can easily count how many function calls are made for the different trace paths. Any call made more than one time is stored in the dictionary, and this can then be retrieved without the need to store a full activation record each time. For example, the highlighted sections in the middle and right side of the trace diagram shown could be removed since these would have been stored in a lookup table via the lower left side of the trace.

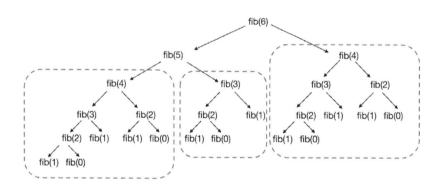

Where the total number of each distinct call to fib(n) is shown in the following table. The point here is that all but 1 of the total number of calls could be stored in a lookup table (or Dictionary).

Function call	Total number of calls
fib(4)	2
fib(3)	3
fib(2)	5
fib(1)	8
fib(0)	5

3.2:
FILE INPUT-OUTPUT

Next, we will discuss Python file input and output, or "File I/O". Most computer languages support File I/O and the ability for their applications to communicate with each other by reading from and writing to data files, and we will look at how we can do this with Python. File operations such as opening, closing, reading, writing, and appending are all common and used frequently in most computer applications. The following table summarizes common modes found in most File I/O libraries.

Mode	Description
r	Open a file for reading (default)
w	Open a file for writing. Creates a new file if it does not exist or truncates the file if it does exist.
x	Open a file for exclusive creation. If the file already exists the operation fails.
a	Open a file for appending at the end without truncating it. Creates a new file if it doesn't exist.
t	Open a file in text mode (default).
b	Open a file in binary mode.
+	Open a file for updating (both reading and writing).

The first functions that programmers need to be familiar with to work with a file are the "open" and "close" operations. Opening a file is intuitive but necessary to do before we perform any reading or writing to the file, that is you need to open the file before you can read from it or write to it.

The common modes we will use with the "open" command and include the following:

'r' : to open a file for reading

'w' : to open a file for writing. If the file already exists it will be overwritten, otherwise a new file will be created.

'+' : to open a file for both reading and writing.

Closing is a bit more confusing, mostly because many programmers sometimes make the mistake of forgetting to explicitly close a file after they are done using it, and even though it may not cause an error in the code execution, it may result in the computer crashing over time due to too many files being opened at one time, and this can also result in security vulnerabilities.

Two of the most common file types that are used in machine learning applications include the CSV and JSON file types.

CSV stands for "Comma Separated Values" and is the generic format of a spreadsheet consisting of rows and columns. In machine learning, a dataset may be represented in CSV format where each row comprises a sample or "example" as it is called in machine learning, and each column comprises the features, or independent variables in the dataset . An example dataset stored as a CSV file is shown in the following table. Here, each column represents a "feature" or independent variable, and each row an "example". We will discuss these terms in much more detail later.

Year	Month	Interest Rate	Unemployment Rate	GDP	Stock Index Price
2018	12	2.73	5.8	22.2	1464
2018	11	2.7	5.75	20.6	1394
2018	10	2.63	5.68	21.7	1357
2018	9	2.4	5.65	19.7	1293
2018	8	2.37	5.63	22.1	1256
2018	7	2.77	5.62	19.5	1254
2018	6	2.53	5.72	18.7	1234
2018	5	2.23	5.83	22	1230
2018	4	2.67	5.78	21.6	1195
2018	3	2.6	5.73	19.4	1175
2018	2	2.43	5.7	21.9	1167
2018	1	2.2	5.6	21.8	1159
2017	12	2.5	6.08	21.5	1147

Alternatively, JSON refers to "JavaScript Object Notation" and is comprised of a hierarchy of "key - value" pairs. These file types are used generically as the preferred data transport mechanism in many web communication protocols, and are also commonly used with machine learning image classifiers to annotate objects that can be used to train object detection algorithms. An example dataset record stored as a JSON entry is shown in the following figure.

```
{
    firstName: "Jim",
    lastName: "Smith",
    gender: "male",
    age: 24,
    address: {
        streetAddress: "1268",
        city: "San Diego",
        state: "CA",
        postalCode: "92128"
    },
    phoneNumbers: [
        {
            type: "home",
            number: "7573627627"
        }
    ]
}
```

CSV FILE IO

Let's look at how we can read a CSV file by walking through the following example code block. First, we need to import the CSV library in line 4 to access the file read functions that we will use later in the code. We will be demonstrating file read operations using a dataset courtesy of open.canada.ca at https://open. canada.ca/data/en/dataset/98f1a129-f628-4ce4-b24d-6f16bf24dd64/resource/ e61e33a6-3522-43c7-b3ef-0128a05e87c7 To follow along with the example or try for yourself, please download the file from the site provided and upload it to you're the top-level of your Google drive (MyDrive).

Since we are working in the Google Colab environment, you will need to make sure that you have mounted your Google drive and point the environment to the top-level drive folder so that you can open and process the file. We show this in lines 6-11. Lines 7-8 will mount the Google drive to allow Colab to access the folder, and line 11 executes the Linux command *cd* which stands for "change directory" and points the environment to the Google drive folder that contains the CSV file.

```
1    #File Input/Output - CSV
2    #Reading from a file
3
4    import csv
5
6    #Mount google drive for access to data
7    from google.colab import drive
8    drive.mount('/content/drive/', force_remount=True)
9
10   #Point to the directory that contains the csv file
11   %cd '/content/drive/MyDrive/'
12
13   #Read the data file
14   try:
15       dataFile = open('MY2019-Fuel-Consumption-Ratings.csv', 'r' )
16       dataReader = csv.reader(dataFile, delimiter=';')
17
18       data = []
19       for row in dataReader:
20           data.append(row)
21       print(data[1:4])
22   except IOError:
23       print('File read failed!')
```

Mounted at /content/drive
[['2019,Acura,MDX SH-AWD,SUV: Small,3.5,6,AS
9,Z,12.2,9.0,10.8,26,252,4,3'],
['2019,Acura,MDX SH-AWD A-SPEC,SUV: Small,3.5,6,AS
9,Z,12.2,9.5,11.0,26,258,4,3'],
['2019,Acura,MDX Hybrid AWD,SUV: Small,3.0,6,AM
7,Z,9.1,9.0,9.0,31,210,5,3']]

Next, we need to open the file in read mode as shown in line 15. Here the variable *dataFile* is what is known as a file handle, or reference to the file which we will use as an input parameter when calling the CSV library functions. Note that we have encapsulated the file open and read operations within exception handling; that is, within the *try* clause, to catch potential Input-Output Errors, which could happen if the file being opened is in the wrong directory (folder) or does not exist. Now, let's look at the CSV library Applications Programming Interface (API). The link to the API is here: https://docs.python.org/3/library/csv.html. We will use the *reader* function as shown on line 16 to access the data in the file and store it in the data structure *dataReader*.

Now, as shown on line 18, we initialize a list to store the data and then loop over all rows in *dataReader*, appending each row to our *data* variable. Upon completion of the loop, the data from the file is now ready to be processed, and we show a simple print of a slice of the file on line 21. Finally, note the exception handler "except" clause that prints a message if an *IOError* exception is thrown.

Next let's use the file write function from the CSV library to write some data to a file. From the same link as the reader API, we can use the "writer" function which allows us to write to a csv file, one row at a time. We show an example in the following code block. Note that we have commented out the import and mounting code from the code block as it is assumed that this code is run after running the previous code block, where the environment has already been set up and the library imported.

```
1   #File Input/Output - CSV
2   #Writing to a File
3
4   #import csv
5
6   #Mount google drive for access to data
7   #from google.colab import drive
8   #drive.mount('/content/drive/', force_remount=True)
9
10  #Write a datafile
11  try:
12      outDataFile = open('OutputFuelConsumptionRatings.csv', mode='w')
13      dataWriter = csv.writer(outDataFile, delimiter=',')
14      for i in range(len(data)):
15          dataWriter.writerow(data[i])
16
17      outDataFile.close()
18
19  except IOError:
20      print('File write failed!')
```

As with the file read operation, we use exception handling on lines 11 and 19 if the file IO operation fails. We open the file on line 12 in write mode, and set up a reference to the writer file handle on line 13. Then for each entry in the data list we created in the file read example shown above, we write a row to the file in the loop in lines 14-15. Finally, we close the file. After executing this code, you should be able to see the new file from the file manager panel on the left side of your Colab notebook, it'll be located in the same folder as you placed the original CSV file.

JSON FILE IO

Next, we will look at how to read a JSON file. As described earlier, the JSON format is based on key-value pairs, like the Python Dictionary data structure. Now viewing a JSON file is not as easy as simply reading a CSV with a spreadsheet application. However, many open-source readers exist, for example, the viewer at https://jsonformatter.org/json-viewer is one example (*Copyright © JSON Formatter 2020 3.5*).

Fortunately, for our code implementations there is a Python API to read and write JSON files. And because JSON is similar in structure to Python Dictionaries, we can directly convert a Dictionary into a JSON data structure.

A link to the JSON API is shown here: https://docs.python.org/3/library/json.html which provides example encoding and decoding functions that can be used in our Python scripts. Below, we show an example file that we will read via the JSON API. Alternatively, you can find one yourself or create one using the view link provided. To execute the JSON File IO code shown you should upload an example JSON file to your Google drive as was described previously.

```
example_json.json  ×

 1 {
 2     "firstName": "Jim",
 3     "lastName": "Smith",
 4     "gender": "male",
 5     "age": 24,
 6     "address": {
 7         "streetAddress": "1268",
 8         "city": "San Diego",
 9         "state": "CA",
10         "postalCode": "92128"
11     },
12     "phoneNumbers": [
13         { "type": "home", "number": "7573627627" }
14     ]
15 }
```

The example shown in the following code block will import the JSON library, mount the Google drive, and point the environment to the current working directory (folder). As with the CSV reader function, we encapsulate the code with the *IOError* exception handler, then open the file as shown in line 14 and assign a reference file handle *f*. Line 15 shows loading the file into the data structure *dataJSON*, which will be in a standard Python Dictionary format. We can then access the individual values by providing the keys as shown in lines 19-21.

```
1    #File Input/Output - JSON
2
3    import json
4
5    #Mount google drive for access to data
6    from google.colab import drive
7    drive.mount('/content/drive/', force_remount=True)
8
9    #Point to the directory that contains the json file
10   %cd '/content/drive/MyDrive/'
11
12   #Open and read JSON file from folder
13   try:
14       with open('example_json.json') as f:
15           dataJSON = json.load(f)
16   except IOError:
17       print('Read file failed!')
18
19   print('Example JSON first name: ', dataJSON['firstName'])
20   print('Example JSON last name: ', dataJSON['lastName'])
21   print('Example JSON city: ', dataJSON['address']['city'])
```

```
Example JSON first name: Jim
Example JSON last name: Smith
Example JSON city: San Diego
```

3.3:
OBJECT-ORIENTED
PROGRAMMING

Python is an object-oriented language, meaning it supports the concept of a "class" that can be activated to create objects which are self-contained entities residing in the computer's memory.

Now why do we care whether a language supports object-oriented concepts? Suppose we want to create student records in a school, or account records in a bank, or neuron nodes in a neural network? Each of these examples might need multiple copies of a base template but may also need some amount of customization. For example, all students have a name, ID, gender, and age so having a common template would be desired with the ability to customize each of the listed fields. In this case the student record would be most appropriately implemented using an object-oriented programming language. Therefore, we'll cover generic object-oriented programming, or OOP, concepts here, then we'll narrow the discussion down to those concepts most applicable in machine learning.

Let's first look at a few of the definitions summarized in the following table.

Class	User-defined prototype or blueprint that is used when creating a distinct unit or 'object' in a computer application. The characteristics of the class are incorporated when creating an object.
Object	The distinct physical memory that is allocated for variables and functions when a computer program "instantiates" an object from a Class.

Inheritance	Allows one class to take on the characteristics of another class
Encapsulation	Protects data in an object by restricting access to methods and variables
Abstraction	Hides implementation details from a user of a class

A "Class" is a blueprint the programmer writes to define the structure and behavior of objects in a program.

An "Object" is a unique instance created from a class during program execution.

"Inheritance" allows the creation of new classes based on existing ones, inheriting their characteristics, and allowing for further specialization. For example, as depicted in the following figure, you could have a generic Bicycle class, having characteristics such as wheels, frame, and seat, and then create new child classes such as Mountain Bike or Road Bike that would add more specific information such as rugged or smoother tires.

Bicycle

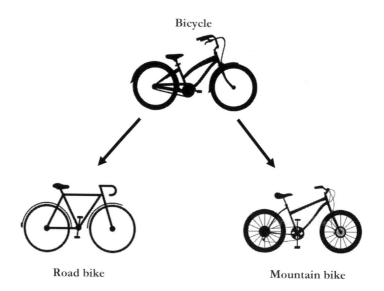

Road bike   Mountain bike

"Encapsulation" restricts access to certain class variables and data through accessor functions, ensuring data privacy and controlled access. This could be useful in, for instance, a bank record object, where we would want to keep personal information hidden and secure.

"Abstraction" hides implementation details, providing a clear interface while concealing inner workings.

Let's look at the graphical example shown in the following diagram to gain a conceptual understanding of OOP.

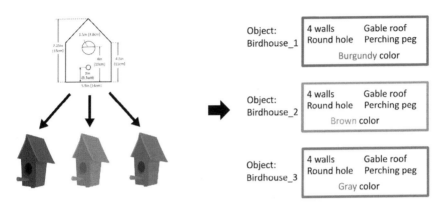

We previously stated that a *Class* is a blueprints of what eventually becomes one or more *objects* which are the separate physical entities created by instantiating the blueprint into each individual instance. In our example diagram we see that the blueprint is a common template for a birdhouse, and each of the instances have several common features, but each birdhouse instance also has a distinguishing characteristic, in this case its color. We create these instances by "constructing" or building the actual birdhouses based on the blueprint, then we personalize each of them by painting them a unique color. Now to translate this concept into what happens in a computer, our blueprint (*Class*) is instantiated into objects as distinct instances residing in their own segment of memory by a process called "construction". Each of the instances have several of the same features but they each also have a unique feature - the color in this example. These features would be stored as variables in each of the instance memory segment.

Now let's consider a more specific example. Here, we create a *Student* class with several features as shown in the following diagram and described below.

```
                        Student

Attribute variables:        Instance variables:
   stdCount                    Name
                               ID
Accessor methods:              Grades
   getTotalStudentCount        GPA
   getName
   getID                    Modifier methods:
   getGrades                   setGrades
   getGPA                      calcGPA
```

"Attribute variables" are features that are shared among all instances of the class. In this example, *stdCount*, the number of students, is the only attribute variable, and it will be the same value across all Student objects.

"Instance variables" are features that are unique to the object and are created when instantiating the object. *Name, ID, Grades,* and *GPA* are the instance variables here since each *Student* should have their own unique value for these features. These variables are not typically accessible from code residing outside the instantiated object.

"Accessor methods" are functions that support encapsulation, which allow read access and calculations to be performed with or on the instance variables. Accessor methods usually return something, for example calculated result, to the calling function.

"Modifier methods" are functions that also support encapsulation and allow write access to the instance variables in addition to performing calculations on those variables.

Now that we have a *Student* class designed with the features described previously, we can use this template to help build our student database application by creating three *Student* objects in computer memory as shown below.

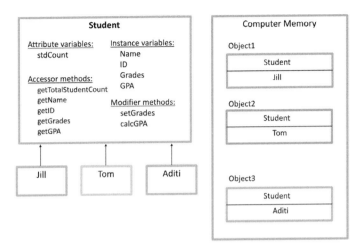

The first step we'd need to perform is to construct the objects and populate the feature list defined in the class for each of the students in our school, in this case the Name, ID, and Grades. A diagram is shown below. Most OOP languages allow programmers to instantiate the objects with a set of parameters that can be input during the construction of the objects. Alternatively, the objects may be constructed with default values assigned to the instance variables, then the parameters could be set after construction using modifier methods.

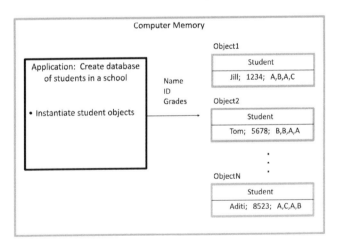

Next, we can set new grades that each student has received, for example by calling the *setGrades* modifier method. A diagram is shown below. We can also perform calculations, such as the current GPA for an individual student by calling the *calcGPA* modifier method

In this case each individual GPA is stored in the object's instance variable *GPA*.

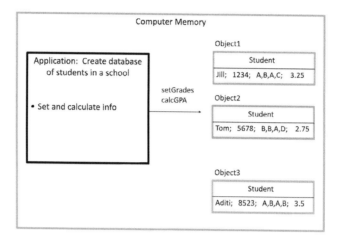

After setting or calculating values that are stored in the object's instance variables, we can then read the individual student information using the accessor methods. This is an example of encapsulation. A diagram of this is shown below.

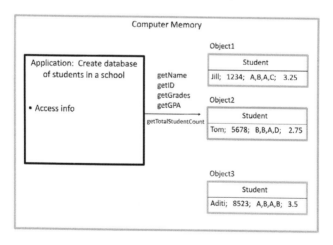

Ideally, we do not want to access the contents of the individual instance variables such as *Name, ID, Grades,* and *GPA* directly as they are parameters which are private to the objects, but we can use the accessor methods shown to read them. In

this case, the programmer may have built-in security protocols as part of the code that executes when the accessor method is called. For example, the *getGPA* method may require a passcode to access a student's *GPA* instance variable. We can also access the attribute variable *stdCount* using the accessor method *getTotalStudent-Count* which will be a count of all the student objects that have been constructed.

Let's now look at how we would implement this example in the following code block.

```
1    #Base Classes and methods
2
3    class Student:                          #class declaration
4        stdCount = 0                        #class attribute - common to all objs
5
6        def __init__(self, name, id):       #constructor
7            self.name = name                #instance vars: name, id, gpa
8            self.id = id
9            self.stdGPA = 0.0
10           Student.stdCount += 1           #inc total student count
11
12       def getName(self):                  #accessor (getter): name
13           return self.name
14
15       def getID(self):                    #accessor (getter): ID
16           return self.id
17
18       def getTotalStudentCount(self):     #accessor: total student count
19           return self.stdCount
20
21       def getGrades(self):                #accessor: grades list
22           return self.grades
23
24       def getGPA(self):                   #accessor: student GPA
25           self.calcGPA()
26           return self.stdGPA
27
28       def setGrades(self, stdGrades):     #modifier (setter): student grades
29           self.grades = stdGrades
30
31       def calcGPA(self):                  #modifier: calculate GPA
32           self.gradesSum = 0
33           for i in self.grades:
34               self.gradesSum = self.gradesSum + i
35           self.stdGPA = self.gradesSum/len(self.grades)
```

We declare our class using the *Class* keyword as shown on line 3 and name it something descriptive with the convention to capitalize the first letter of the word. Next, we define our "constructor" on line 6 which is defined with the keyword *init* preceded by two underscores and followed by two underscores. The constructor is called when we instantiate an object from this class in our main program. Here we see that the constructor takes in three parameters. *Self* is used to identify a reference to the class we're currently in, or as a reference to the instance of this class. You will see this reference to *self* as an input parameter in each of the function headers in this class. The other parameters, *name* and *id* are input when the main code instantiates the object, and the constructor then sets the instance variables *self.name* and *self.id* to the input parameters, then initializes the instance variable *self.stdGPA* and the attribute variable *Student.stdCount*. Note that *Student.stdCount* is not defined as *self* since it belongs to the *Student* class and not an individual instance (object).

The accessor methods are defined on lines 12, 15, 18, 21, and 24, where each function returns one of the instance variables. In these methods, a programmer could implement access control code, such as the entry of a password or PIN, to allow the instance variable to be returned. Also note that in the *getGPA* method, a call to the *calcGPA* method is made so that the most up to date calculation is performed.

Finally, the modifier methods are defined on lines 28 and 31, and usually perform some sort of calculation resulting in an update to the instance variables, but typically do not return anything.

The main program is shown in the following code block and instantiates the objects by calling the class constructor on lines 2 and 3, assigning a reference to the objects, in this case *student1* and *student2*.

Now to access the methods inside the class, we simply identify the object reference and the method we want separated with a period. In this example we are printing out the *name* and *id* for each of the student objects we constructed along with the total number of students.

```
1    #Create objects
2    student1 = Student('Jane', 12345)
3    student2 = Student('Tim', 98765)
4
5    #Accessing methods
6    print('Student1:', student1.getName(), ' ', student1.getID())
7    print('Student2:', student2.getName(), ' ', student2.getID())
8    print('Total number of students:', Student.getTotalStudentCount(self=Student))
```

⤷   Student1: Jane 12345
      Student2: Tim 98765
      Total number of students: 2

INHERITANCE

Previously, we discussed creating classes and instantiating or constructing objects from those classes. We covered how a "class" is used as a blueprint to create the base object, and then discussed ways for programmers to customize the base object with more specific characteristics. We showed how this can be applied to a student record where the base class, which defined generic characteristics, was made more specific during construction. And finally, we looked at a Python code example, implementing a class. Next let's look at how inheritance works. We show a graphical representation of general inheritance in the following diagram.

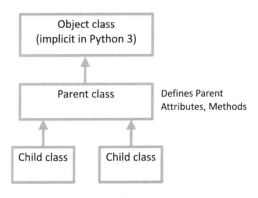

The base class in most OOP language hierarchies is called the "Object" class. All class hierarchies are derived from this base class. Here we define a "Parent"

class that connects to the base Object class, and two child classes that connect to the parent class.

In our computer memory model, the objects are instantiated for each of the individual "child" instances as shown in the following diagram.

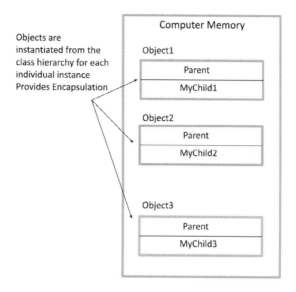

Now, each of these objects inherit the characteristics or features from the parent class and a base set of features in the child class, but each will have some distinguishing characteristics, for example, their name, age, gender, etc.

Next, we'll see how we can incorporate inheritance in this example.

We originally constructed our students using the base *Student* class, but say we want to categorize each of them as either high-school or junior-high-school students. Now, why would we want to do this? Well, say we have parameters that only fit one of the categories, for example SAT or ACT test scores. These parameters would only apply to High School students, and not Jr. High School students, so we wouldn't need those instance variables to be part of our base Student class since it would just waste memory to store those parameters for a large portion of the total student population. What we can do is create classes for each of these categories. For example, we create a class called *HighSchoolStudent* and another called *JrHighSchoolStudent*, and configure them as child classes with the Student class as their common parent. In this case, the classes *HighSchoolStudent* and *JrHighSchoolStudent*, are able to reuse the common characteristics of the base *Student* class, and are then able to define additional characteristics specific to their categories. We show a graphical representation of the inheritance hierarchy in the following diagram.

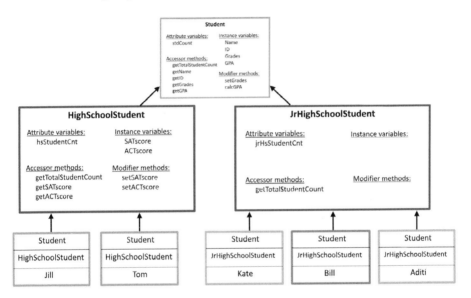

Let's see how we can implement as shown in the following code blocks. We have already presented the base *Student* class, but if you need a refresher, please review the previous units in the chapter to walk through the code. What we have here are the two child classes that define the categories for high schoolers and jr. high schoolers. The class declarations are shown in the code listing. The *Class* keyword is followed by the class name and the parent class in parentheses. This establishes the parent - child relationship in the hierarchy.

We show the *HighSchoolStudent* class in the following code block. The child class constructor on lines 4 – 8 first calls the constructor of the parent *Student* class with the name and ID of the student. Recall the *name* and *id* already exist as parameters in the *Student* class so we don't need to recreate those variables in this class since they will be populated from the fields in the parent class. We also initialize the high school student counter attribute variable *hsStdCount* and SAT and ACT score instances variables. The accessor methods on lines 10 - 17 simply return the instance or attribute variables, and the modifier methods on lines 19 - 23 set the instance variables with the parameters that are passed in.

```
1    class HighSchoolStudent(Student):          #child class inherits Student
2        hsStdCount = 0                          #class attribute
3
4        def __init__(self, name, id):          #constructor
5            Student.__init__(self, name, id)    #call parent constructor
6            HighSchoolStudent.hsStdCount += 1   #student counter
7            self.satScore = 0
8            self.actScore = 0
9
10       def getTotalStudentCount(self):         #accessor student count
11           return self.hsStdCount
12
13       def getSATscore(self):
14           return self.satScore
15
16       def getACTscore(self):
17           return self.actScore
18
19       def setSATscore(self, score):
20           self.satScore = score
21
22       def setACTscore(self, score):
23           self.actScore = score
```

The *JrHighSchoolStudent* class is shown in the following code block. The constructor, as with the *HighSchoolStudent* class, calls the constructor of the parent *Student* class with the *name* and *id* of the student. The *JrHighSchoolStudent* constructor also initializes the attribute variable which keeps count of the total number of Jr high school students by incrementing itself every time a new student is constructed. In this class we only have one accessor which is reading the student count. If we had more information that was only relevant to a Jr. High school student, then we would add the instance variables and appropriate accessor and modifier methods in this class.

```
1    class JrHighSchoolStudent(Student):          #child class inherits Student
2        jrHsStdCount = 0
3
4        def __init__(self, name, id):
5            Student.__init__(self, name, id)
6            JrHighSchoolStudent.jrHsStdCount += 1   #student counter
7
8        def getTotalStudentCount(self):           #accessor student count
9            return self.jrHsStdCount
```

Next, we show the main code used to construct the objects in the following code block. As with the base Student class example, we construct our child objects, either *HighSchoolStudent* or *JrHighSchoolStudent* via assigning a reference variable and calling the class constructor. We then can call the modifier methods to set the class instance variables for each student. Note that we are able to use the *setGrades* function even though it is not defined in either class; this is because this function has been defined in the *Student* class and has been inherited by both child classes

```
1    #Create objects (2 high school, 3 jr. high students)
2    #Invoke Modifier methods
3
4    student1 = HighSchoolStudent('Jill', 84752)
5    student1.setGrades([3.0, 4.0, 4.5, 2.0])
6    student1.setSATscore(1200)
7    student1.setACTscore(32)
8    student2 = HighSchoolStudent('Tom', 83729)
9    student2.setGrades([3.2, 4.0, 2.7, 3.0])
10   student3 = JrHighSchoolStudent('Kate', 63738)
11   student3.setGrades([3.2, 3.4, 3.7, 3.0])
12   student4 = JrHighSchoolStudent('Bill', 61129)
13   student4.setGrades([1.7, 2.0, 2.7, 3.0])
14   student5 = JrHighSchoolStudent('Aditi', 69410)
15   student5.setGrades([2.3, 3.2, 2.7, 2.9])
```

At this point our student objects are initialized and stored in separate segments of memory in our computer. We can then read the instance or attribute variables using the class accessor methods. Note that in some cases we are calling the accessor methods from the parent class, and in other cases we are calling the methods from the child class. We can also access the attribute variables, in this case the total count of students using the method *getTotalStudentCount*. However, note the syntax we need to use in the parameter list. In this case we need to identify the class type. We show the outputs from each of the print statements which call the accessor methods from both the high school and jr. high school students. Also note that we were able to directly access the instance variables defined *student1* as well as the *stdCount* variable from the *Student* class. We will address this concept next.

```
1   #Invoke Accessor methods
2
3   print('Student1:', student1.getName(), ' ', student1.getID(),\
4       ' ', student1.getGrades(), ' ', student1.getGPA(),\
5       ' ', student1.getSATscore(), ' ', student1.getACTscore())
6   print('Student2:', student2.getName(), ' ', student2.getID(),\
7       ' ', student2.getGrades(), ' ', student2.getGPA(),\
8       ' ', student2.getSATscore(), ' ', student2.getACTscore())
9   print('Student3:', student3.getName(), ' ', student3.getID(),
10      ' ', student3.getGrades(), ' ', student3.getGPA())
11  print('Student4:', student4.getName(), ' ', student4.getID(),
12      ' ', student4.getGrades(), ' ', student4.getGPA())
13  print('Student5:', student5.getName(), ' ', student5.getID(),
14      ' ', student5.getGrades(), ' ', student5.getGPA())
15  print('Total number of students:', \
16      Student.getTotalStudentCount(self=Student))
17  print('Number of high school students: ', \
18      HighSchoolStudent.getTotalStudentCount(self=HighSchoolStudent))
19  print('Number of junior high school students: ', \
20      JrHighSchoolStudent.getTotalStudentCount(self=JrHighSchoolStudent))
21
22  #Test direct access to public instance vars
23  print('Student1 name (direct var access):', student1.name)
24  print('Student count (direct var access):', Student.stdCount)
```

```
Student1: Jill 84752 [3.0, 4.0, 4.5, 2.0] 3.375 1200 32
Student2: Tom 83729 [3.2, 4.0, 2.7, 3.0] 3.225 0 0
Student3: Kate 63738 [3.2, 3.4, 3.7, 3.0] 3.325
Student4: Bill 61129 [1.7, 2.0, 2.7, 3.0] 2.35
Student5: Aditi 69410 [2.3, 3.2, 2.7, 2.9] 2.775
Total number of students: 5
Number of high school students: 2
Number of junior high school students: 3
Student1 name (direct var access): Jill
Student count (direct var access): 5
```

One final note about inheritance. The models we presented here are not limited to a single inheritance layer. We could continue to add "children" to the classes as shown here with a *HighSchoolAthlete* child class inheriting from the *HighSchoolStudent* class, which in turn is a child of the *Student* class as shown in the following inheritance hierarchy diagram.

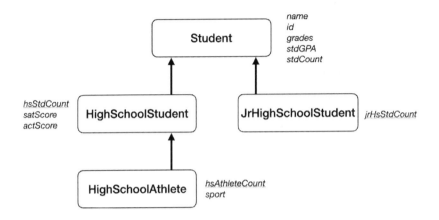

ENCAPSULATION

Previously, we mentioned "encapsulation" several times as the mechanism which restricts access to a variable existing in an object created from one class to outside entities. This important concept is relied upon by many institutions, including banks for client account information, schools for student records, online payment systems, and almost any login system.

We generally use encapsulation to prevent sensitive user information from being accessible to software entities outside of the constructed objects, and we do this by declaring our instance variables that store user sensitive information as "private".

In Python we can identify a variable as private by adding a double underscore prefix to the variable name. This would serve the purpose of keeping the variable local to only the object which it belongs to, and as a result, would then require an accessor method to read it.

Recall previously, we introduced the concept of the accessor method as a way to read the instance variables defined in our classes, but we also showed that we could access them directly from the main "runner" code, similar to how we could call the class methods. For example, previously, we accessed the name of *student1* in the print statements using simply *student1.name*. We could have blocked this access using encapsulation, by declaring our variables private (with the double underscore prefix), and by doing this would no longer be able to access the variable directly. We see an example of how to do this in the following code block. For example, here we have our Student class defined but we've added several private instance variables (*__encName, __id, __stdGPA, __grades*) which we know are private since they include the double underscore prefix.

```
1    class Student:                          #class declaration
2       stdCount = 0                         #class attribute - common to all objs
3
4       def __init__(self, name, id):        #constructor
5          self.name = name                  #instance vars: name (not private)
6          self.__encName = name             #private instance var
7          self.__id = id
8          self.__stdGPA = 0.0
9          self.__grades = []
10         Student.stdCount += 1             #inc total student count
11
12      def getName(self):                   #accessor (getter): name
13         return self.name
14
15      def getEncName(self):                #accessor (getter): encName
16         return self.__encName
17
18      def getID(self):                     #accessor (getter): ID
19         return self.__id
20
21      def getTotalStudentCount(self):      #accessor: total student count
22         return self.stdCount
23
24      def getGrades(self):                 #accessor: grades list
25         return self.__grades
26
27      def getGPA(self):                    #accessor: student gpa
28         self.calcGPA()
29         return self.__stdGPA
30
31      def setGrades(self, stdGrades):      #modifier (setter): student grades
32         self.__grades = stdGrades
33
34      def calcGPA(self):                   #modifier: calculate GPA
35         if(len(self.__grades) == 0):
36            return 0
37         self.__gradesSum = 0
38         for i in self.__grades:
39            self.__gradesSum = self.__gradesSum + i
40            self.__stdGPA = self.__gradesSum/len(self.__grades)
41
```

Next, we create our objects in the following code block. Note on lines 6 – 7 we attempt to access the student names directly (without the use of an accessor method). This is valid since *name* is not declared private in the *Student* class of the above code block. We also attempt to access Student1's *id* on line 8, but here we must use the accessor method *getID* since *id* is private. Finally, we attempt to access the Student1's GPA directly via its private instance variable __*encName*. When we run this code, we see the following output. The error, *AttributeError* is thrown because we are trying to access *student1.__stdGPA* directly.

```
1    #Create objects
2    student1 = Student('Jane', 12345)
3    student2 = Student('Tim', 98765)
4
5    #Direct access
6    print('Student1:', student1.name)
7    print('Student2:', student2.name)
8    print('Student1 ID:', student1.getID())
9
10   #Try to read instance variables
11   print('Student1 GPA (ATTEMPTED direct private var access):', student1.__stdGPA)
```

```
Student1: Jane
Student2: Tim
Student1 ID: 12345
--------------------------------------------------------------------
AttributeError                        Traceback (most recent call last)
<ipython-input-10-5a988101409a> in <cell line: 67>()
     65 print('Student2:', student2.name)
     66 print('Student1 ID:', student1.getID())
---> 67 print('Student1 GPA (ATTEMPTED direct private var access):', student1.__stdGPA)
     68
     69 print('\n\n')

AttributeError: 'Student' object has no attribute '__stdGPA'
```

3.4:
ADVANCED FUNCTIONS

Previously, we discussed the basics of Python, mostly applied to data structures in the collections libraries. Next, we'll discuss several advanced functions supported in the standard Python library that are useful for data processing and in machine learning applications. Specifically, we'll discuss the *map, zip, filter* and *reduce* functions which are useful for processing the basic collections data structures we've studied. Then we'll discuss the Python *lambda* function to see how it can be used to make our code more efficient. While it is not required that you use these advanced functions in your implementations, you should be able to recognize and interpret them if they are encountered in reference code.

ADVANCED FUNCTIONS - *MAP*
The first function we'll look at is the Python *map* function. The API link is shown here.

map API: https://docs.python.org/3/library/functions.html#map.

The *map* function works with an iterator; that is, a data structure that has a collection of items which we can traverse through, for example with a *for* loop. An example usage of the *map* function is shown in the following code block.

```
1    # Python map() example
2
3    myList1 = [1, 2, 3, 4, 5]
4
5    # Multiply each member of list by scalar
6    def scalarMult(input, k):
7        return input*k
8
9
10   # Traditional approach ---------
11   sclrMult1 = []
12   for x in myList1:
13       sclrMult1.append(scalarMult(x, 3))
14   print('Traditional Approach: ', sclrMult1)
15
16   # Map approach -----------------
17   mult = [3] * len(myList1) #list of multipliers of length myList1
18   sclrMult2 = map(scalarMult, myList1, mult)
19   print('Map Approach: ', list(sclrMult2)) # Convert object to list
```

⟶ Traditional Approach: [3, 6, 9, 12, 15]
   Map Approach: [3, 6, 9, 12, 15]

The example shows how you could implement an operation that multiplies each element in a list (which could also be interpreted as a multidimensional vector) by a scalar value (3 in the example). The list we will work on is shown on line 3, and the function that implements the scalar multiply operation is shown on lines 6-7. Here the function simply inputs a number and the multiplier, then returns the product of the two inputs. A traditional implementation, shown in lines 11-13, iterates through the list, then calls the *scalarMult* function for each item in the list, appending the product returned by the function to a result list shown on line 13. Note this requires calling the *scalarMult* function for each item in the list.

Now, a more condensed version using the *map* function on shown on line 18. We start by initializing a list that holds the values of the scalar multipliers which is "broadcast" to the length of *myList1* in line 17. In other words, after line 17 is executed, the list *mult* will store [3, 3, 3, 3, 3]. The syntax of the *map* function on line 18 includes passing the function reference to *scalarMult*, the list we want to modify, and the broadcast multiplier list. The *map* function will then call *scalarMult*, passing to it every item in the *myList* data structure and corresponding item in *mult*. The *map* return data structure will be an object, so we need to cast it to a list, as shown on line 19, so that we can print it out. Note that both implementations yield the same results, but that the map function does not require our code to include a loop.

ADVANCED FUNCTIONS - *ZIP*

The next function we will describe is the Python *zip* function. The API link is here.

zip API: https://docs.python.org/3/library/functions.html#zip

The *zip* function, like the *map* function, works with a list of iterables. It creates an iterator that collects the items from each of the iterable data structures that are passed into it and allows us to access each of the iterables together one element at a time. The *zip* function is very convenient, for example, if we want to perform operations between 2 collections such as lists. An example usage of the *zip* function is shown in the following code block.

```
1    #Python zip() example
2
3    myList2 = [1, 3, 8, 4, 9]
4    myList3 = [2, 2, 7, 5, 8]
5
6    # Traditional approach
7    # Add two lists
8    addList1 = []
9    for x in range(0,len(myList2)):
10       addList1.append(myList2[x] + myList3[x])
11   print('Traditional Approach: ', addList1)
12
13   # Zip approach
14   # Add two lists - iterate at the same time
15   addList2 = []
16   for x, y in zip(myList2, myList3):
17       addList2.append(x + y)
18   print('Zip approach: ', addList2)
```

```
Traditional Approach: [3, 5, 15, 9, 17]
Zip approach: [3, 5, 15, 9, 17]
```

We first show how you might implement an operation that performs an element-by-element addition of the values of two lists. The lists that are added together are shown in lines 3-4, and the code that implements the element-by-element addition using a traditional for-loop is shown in lines 9-10 which appends the sum to a resultant list in line 11.

A more condensed approach using the *zip* function is shown in line 16. We start by initializing an empty list on line 15, then iterate over the two lists using variables x and y in the 'for-each', with the two lists being "zipped" together so that each iterator accesses the corresponding list items, one item at a time.

We show the printed outputs for both implementations and see that they yield the same results. Note that the traditional implementation requires that both lists are of the same length, otherwise the for-loop will generate an exception when the iterator attempts to access an out of bounds item in one of the lists. Conversely, the *zip* function will iterate until the length of the shortest list has been met, then will terminate the loop – so the lists in the *zip* function may be different lengths, and the function will not throw an exception.

ADVANCED FUNCTIONS – *FILTER*

Next we'll look at the Python *filter* function. The API link is here.

Filter API: https://docs.python.org/3/library/functions.html#filter

The *filter* function provides a way to test each item in a sequence as true by invoking a function on the item and appending the returned value from the function into one of our iterator data structures. An example usage of the *filter* function is shown in the following code block.

```
1    #Python filter() example
2
3    myList4 = [1, 2, 3, 4, 5, 6, 7, 8, 9, 10]
4
5    def odd(x):
6        return x % 2 != 0
7
8    # Traditional approach
9    # Find odd numbers
10   myOdds1 = []
11   for x in myList4:
12       if odd(x):
13           myOdds1.append(x)
14   print('Traditional Approach: ', myOdds1)
15
16   # Filter approach
17   # Find odd numbers
18   myOdds2 = filter(odd, myList4)
19   print('Filter Approach: ', list(myOdds2))
```

Traditional Approach: [1, 3, 5, 7, 9]
Filter Approach: [1, 3, 5, 7, 9]

We first show a traditional Python implementation, and in this case our code assembles all the values in a list that are odd. The traditional code iterates through a list using a for-loop on line 11-13, and calls a function which returns a Boolean, reflecting whether the input number is odd, and if it is odd then the code appends the value to a new list.

A more condensed approach is shown using the *filter* function on line 18. In this case, a reference to the *odd* function is passed to the *filter* along with the input list. We can see the printed output and see that the two implementations output the same values.

ADVANCED FUNCTIONS - *REDUCE*

Next, we will describe the Python *reduce* function. The API link is here.

Reduce API: https://docs.python.org/2/library/functions.html#reduce

The function implements a condensed way to work on two items at a time in an iterable data structure. An example is shown in the following code block.

```
1    #Python reduce() example
2
3    from functools import reduce
4
5    def addFunc(a, b):
6        return a + b
7
8    # Traditional approach
9    # Add numbers in a list 2 at a time
10   myList5 = [0, 1, 2, 3, 4, 5]
11   sum = 0
12   for i in range(0, len(myList5)-1, 2):
13       sum = sum + addFunc(myList5[i], myList5[i+1])
14   print('Traditional Approach: ', sum)
15
16   # Reduce approach
17   # Add numbers in a list 2 at a time
18   sum2 = reduce(addFunc, myList5)
19   print('Reduce Approach: ', sum2)
```

> Traditional Approach: 15
> Reduce Approach: 15

We first show a traditional Python implementation on lines 10-13. The code iterates through a list using a for-loop, passing two adjacent items from the list to the *addFunc* function which returns the sum of the two items, and then subsequently accumulated in the loop into the variable *sum*.

A more condensed approach is shown using the *reduce* function on line 18. In this case, a reference to the *addFunc* function, is passed to the *reduce* function along with the input list. Because we only pass in a single list, the reduce function executes *addFunc* and implements the accumulation function automatically since it iterates through the list, first calling *addFunc* on the first two elements, and then passing the returned value into another call of *addFunc* along with the next item in the list. This is repeated until the function has executed on all the elements in the iterable. We can see the printed output and see that the two implementations output the same values.

ADVANCED FUNCTIONS - *LAMBDA*

Finally, we will look at a common approach to provide abstraction to our code. A *lambda* is what is called an anonymous function and is used with other functions to make code more concise and convenient. A *lambda* is typically used when the operation needed is something small - usually a single line or two of code, and we often use it with the *map, filter*, and *reduce* functions we discussed previously. A *lambda* syntax includes using the keyword 'lambda' followed by any number of arguments (including 0), then a colon, and the operation. An example is shown in the following code block.

```
1    #Python lambda example
2
3    # Traditional approach
4    # Find numbers in a list that are less than 40
5    myList6 = [11, 16, 5, 65, 2, 74, 55, 18, 20, 13, 15, 83]
6    outList = []
7    for x in myList6:
8        if(x < 40):
9            outList.append(x)
10   print('Traditional Approach:', outList)
11
12   # Lambda approach
13   # Find numbers in a list that are less than 40
14   outList = (filter(lambda x: x < 40, myList6))
15   print('Lambda Approach:', list(outList))
```

Traditional Approach: [11, 16, 5, 2, 18, 20, 13, 15]
Lambda Approach: [11, 16, 5, 2, 18, 20, 13, 15]

Here, we first show a traditional Python implementation. In this case the code checks if a value in a list is less than 40 and if it is, the value is added to an output list. The traditional code iterates through a list using the for-loop on line 7, then checks the value in the list, and appends it to the output list if it is less than 40.

The *lambda* approach is shown on line 14 using a filter function with the operation implemented using a reference to the lambda and passing the input list to a Python filter. In this case, a reference to the lambda function *lambda x: x<40, myList6*, is passed to the Python *filter* function along with the input list. We can see the printed output list and note the two implementations output the same values.

CHAPTER 4:

INTRODUCTION TO PYTHON DATA ANALYTICS AND MACHINE LEARNING LIBRARIES

In this chapter we will introduce the most common Python libraries used in the pre-processing and visualization stages of data analytics. The topics described in this Module include the Python Numpy, Pandas, and Maplotlib libraries.

LEARNING OBJECTIVES

By the end of this chapter, you will be able to do the following:

- Create and use a Numpy ndarray in a Python script
- Incorporate Numpy functions into Python scripts to determine and modify the dimension, size, and shape of an ndarray
- Implement processing function on Numpy arrays
- Create a Pandas series and dataframe in a Python script using built-in data structures and Numpy arrays
- Incorporate Pandas functions into Python scripts to calculate data statistics
- Implement processing function on Pandas series and dataframes
- Format and display graphs of data from Python built-in, Numpy, and Pandas data structures
- Create multiple plots displaying multiple graph types

4.1:

NUMPY LIBRARY

NumPy is a Python library that provides an efficient and robust way of creating and processing multidimensional arrays in your code. While you could do this with traditional Python lists, there are many built-in linear algebra functions, and efficient optimizations, such as the ability to process multidimensional arrays using what is called "vectorizing" that is not available if implementing with normal Python lists. NumPy uses the Python *array* data structure, and as we know from the Python Data Structures chapter, this requires that the data be homogeneous, meaning that every member of the array has the same type. To use NumPy in our code, we need to import the library, and the industry standard way to do this is: *import numpy as np*, then from that point on in our code, we can reference *np* to access the library functions.

Let's look at some examples in the following code block.

```
1   import numpy as np
2
3   #1-D array
4   arr_1D = np.array([1, 2, 3, 4])
5   print('1D array:', arr_1D)
6
7   #2-D array
8   arr_2D = np.array([[1, 2, 3, 4], [5, 6, 7, 8], [9, 10, 11, 12]])
9   print('\n2D array:\n', arr_2D)
```

```
1D array: [1 2 3 4]

2D array:
 [[ 1 2 3 4]
 [ 5 6 7 8]
 [ 9 10 11 12]]
```

To create simple 1D and 2D arrays, we use the declarations on lines 4 and 8. Line 4 constructs an array with one axis, which is also known as a vector, and this can be done by passing a Python list to the method *np.array()* then assigning it to a variable. On line 8, we create a two-dimensional array using the same method, except here we pass a 2D list to the *np.array()* method and this creates an array with two axes, which is known as a matrix.

When working with multidimensional arrays, especially when implementing machine learning algorithms, it is extremely important to know the shape of the data structure you are working with. In NumPy, the shape refers to the length of each axis or dimension in the array (NumPy refers to each of the dimensions as axes). Therefore, *np.shape* returns a Tuple containing the length of each axis. Now the axis in every NumPy array has an intrinsic order that can be referenced in other methods using zero-based indexing. The following image shows examples of 1D, 2D and 3D NumPy arrays along with each of their axes and shapes. For example, a 1D array has only one axis (axis 0), and the shape is shown as the length of axis 0. Since *np.shape* returns a Python Tuple, and recall that creating a Tuple with one item requires adding a comma after it, we see the shape displayed in the example image as (4,) where the comma followed by a blank indicates no additional axes exist. Similarly, a 2D array would have a shape equal to the number of rows by the number of columns, and a 3D shape would be in order of the rows, columns, depth.

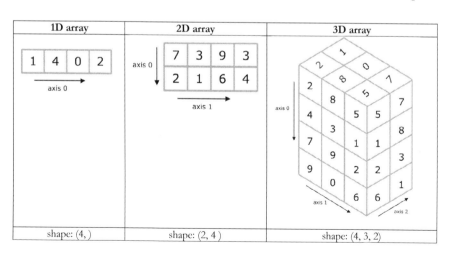

1D array	2D array	3D array
shape: (4,)	shape: (2, 4)	shape: (4, 3, 2)

SHAPING NUMPY ARRAYS

An example is shown in the following code block to illustrate the NumPy shapes for different array dimension formats. In the first example on line 5, a standard Python list is passed to the NumPy *array* method to create a one-dimensional array with shape (4,) since only axis 0 exists. The example on line 8 produces a shape (4, 1) since the Python list is explicitly set up as a two-dimensional array with 4 rows and 1 column, where each row contains an array of length 1. And finally, in the example on line 11, the NumPy array is again explicitly set up as a two-dimensional array (note the double square brackets), this time with a single row and 4 columns.

```
1    # Shapes example
2
3    import numpy as np
4
5    x = np.array([1, 2, 3, 4])
6    print('1:', x.shape)
7
8    y = np.array([[1], [2], [3], [4]])
9    print('2:', y.shape)
10
11   z = np.array([[1, 2, 3, 4]])
12   print('3:', z.shape)
```

```
1: (4,)
2: (4, 1)
3: (1, 4)
(4,)
```

Initializing a NumPy array as shown in the previous example is fine for small datasets, but we may want to use a different method as the data we work with gets larger. Oftentimes, it is a good idea to create a uniform array of zeros or ones to use as building blocks for other arrays, or to initialize an array to a range of values. To do this, we can use the *np.zeros()*, *np.ones()*, or *np.arange()* methods. The *zeros* and *ones* methods input a Tuple of the array shape and create a NumPy array of that shape filled zeros or ones, while the *arange* method inputs optional start, stop, and step parameters, behaving in the same way as the Python built-in *range* function but returning a NumPy array instead. An example is shown in the following code block. Lines 3 and 4 show how to create a one-dimensional NumPy array of zeros and ones respectively. Note that NumPy supports simply passing in the number of zeros (without the comma) for a one-dimensional array, but to be consistent with our Tuple definition for a single value, we show it with previous notation. Lines 5 and 6 show how to create two-dimensional arrays of zeros and ones. And finally line 7 creates an array with eight items from 0 through 7.

```
1   import numpy as np
2
3   print(np.zeros((3,)))
4   print('\n',np.ones((3,)))
5   print('\n',np.zeros((2,2)))
6   print('\n',np.ones((4,3)))
7   print('\n',np.arange(8))
8   print('\n',np.arange(8).shape)
```

```
[0. 0. 0.]

[1. 1. 1.]

[[0. 0.]
 [0. 0.]]

[[1. 1. 1.]
 [1. 1. 1.]
 [1. 1. 1.]
 [1. 1. 1.]]

[0 1 2 3 4 5 6 7]
arange shape: (8,)
```

Each NumPy array that we create is what is called an *ndarray* object, which stands for N-dimensional array, and each object has attributes that store information about it. In OOP terms, this type of information is stored in object instance variables. There are several important attributes that will help throughout your coding and debugging process to ensure that you are working with the arrays that you are envisioning. A few of the most common attributes include *size*, *shape*, and *ndim*. The *size* attribute refers to the total number of elements the array contains. *Shape* reflects the dimensions of the array as was previously discussed. And the *ndim* attribute contains the number of dimensions, or axes, the array contains.

The following example code block shows how to reference each of these important attributes.

```
1   import numpy as np
2
3   #2-D array size, shape, and dimension
4
5   arr = np.array([[1, 2, 3, 4], [5, 6, 7, 8], [9, 10, 11, 12]])
6   print(arr.size, ' ', arr.shape, ' ', arr.ndim)
```

⤷ 12 (3, 4) 2

One common operation we may need to perform is rearranging the shape of our array. This is common for neural networks, where the input may be a matrix consisting of several features and several examples (data samples are known as "examples" in machine learning), and due to the operations required such as the dot product, we may need to rearrange the items in the array. Two common *ndarray* methods are *reshape* and *transpose*. An example is shown in the following code block. We create an array of 10 items in line 3, which will have shape (10,). When we call reshape on line 6, the items in the input array will be rearranged with the dimension of the shape tuple passed in. The transpose function will swap the rows with the columns, and can be done in NumPy with the *transpose* method or by appending a .*T* at the end of the array we wish to transpose, as shown in lines 9 and 12 respectively.

```
1    import numpy as np
2
3    a = np.arange(10)
4    print('\n',a)
5
6    b = a.reshape((2, 5))
7    print('\n',b)
8
9    c = b.transpose()
10   print('\n',c)
11
12   d = c.T
13   print('\n',d)
```

⊡→ [0 1 2 3 4 5 6 7 8 9]

[[0 1 2 3 4]
 [5 6 7 8 9]]

[[0 5]
 [1 6]
 [2 7]
 [3 8]
 [4 9]]

[[0 1 2 3 4]
 [5 6 7 8 9]]

Another useful function to modify the shape of an *ndarray* is the *squeeze* method. *Squeeze* is used to remove any axes that have length 1. This is useful, for example, if your data structure has three axes but only two of them are used and subsequent processing requires a 2D array. An example of this is shown in the following code block. We see in the output that the original 3D shape is (1, 2, 3), but since the first axis is 1, is it effectively unused and if we needed to perform an operation, say with the 2D array, we can transform the 3D shape to 2D as shown.

```
1   # Squeeze example
2
3   import numpy as np
4
5   #2D array in 3D format
6   my_3Darray = np.array([[[1, 2, 3], [4, 5, 6]]])
7   print('Original 3D array shape:', my_3Darray.shape)
8
9   #2D array
10  my_2Darray = np.arange(6).reshape(2,3)
11  print('2D array shape:', my_2Darray.shape)
12
13  my_squeezed_3Darray = np.squeeze(my_3Darray)
14  print('Squeezed 3D array:', my_squeezed_3Darray.shape)
```

⊡→ Original 3D array shape: (1, 2, 3)
2D array shape: (2, 3)
Squeezed 3D array: (2, 3)

SLICING NUMPY ARRAYS

To reference specific items in your NumPy array, we can use slicing as with Python lists. To do this, we access specific indices or ranges of values we want to pull from the array. An example is shown in the following code listing. In lines 4 and 5 we access all rows of the array and column 0 up to but not including column 1, which results in printing the first column. For the slice in line 8, we access rows 1 up to but not including row 2 and all columns, which results in printing the 2nd row. Now, note that the output generated from line 8 is a single row but has 2 dimensions as shown with the double brackets; that is, [[4 5 6]]. If we wanted to remove the unused dimension here, we could squeeze this result as shown in line 9, or simply access the single row as shown in line 10.

```
1   import numpy as np
2
3   a = np.array([[1, 2, 3], [4, 5, 6]])
4   print(a[0:2, 0:1])
5   print(a[:, 0:1]) # same as the above line
6
7   a = np.array([[1, 2, 3], [4, 5, 6], [7, 8, 9]])
8   print('\n 2D output:', a[1:2, :])
9   print('Squeezed output:', np.squeeze(a[1:2, :]))
10  print(a[1, :])
```

```
[[1]
 [4]]
[[1]
 [4]]

2D output [[4 5 6]]
Squeezed output [4 5 6]
[4 5 6]
```

NUMPY BASIC OPERATIONS

"Element-wise" operations are defined when basic operators are performed between two arrays of the same size. You can think of this as the same way that we add two matrices together; that is, we take the elements that are in the same position in each array, perform the operation, and then store the result in that position in the result array. An example is shown in the following code block. Several basic operations are performed for the two arrays of shape $(2, 4)$. Note that in each of the examples, the result is generated by taking the items from both arrays at the same index, performing the operation, then placing the result at the same index.

```
1   # Basic Operations
2
3   import numpy as np
4
5   a = np.arange(8)
6   a = a.reshape((2,4))
7   b = np.ones((2,4))
8
9   print(a)
10  print('\n a * (3 + b):\n', a * (3 + b))
11  print('\n a + (3 + b):\n', a + (3 + b))
12  print('\n b * (3 + a):\n', b * (3 + a))
13  print('\n a * (3 + (2+b)):\n', a * (3 + (2+b)))
14  print('\n a**2\n', a**2)
```

```
[[0 1 2 3]
 [4 5 6 7]]

a * (3 + b):
[[ 0. 4. 8. 12.]
 [16. 20. 24. 28.]]

a + (3 + b):
[[ 4. 5. 6. 7.]
 [ 8. 9. 10. 11.]]

b * (3 + a):
[[ 3. 4. 5. 6.]
 [ 7. 8. 9. 10.]]

a * (3 + (2+b)):
[[ 0. 6. 12. 18.]
 [24. 30. 36. 42.]]

a**2
[[ 0 1 4 9]
 [16 25 36 49]]
```

NUMPY MATRIX MULTIPLICATION

There are two methods of multiplying vectors or matrices that are applicable to machine learning algorithm implementations: the "element-wise" product (also known as the Hadamard product), and the "dot" product. We will cover each of these methods in the chapter on Linear Algebra, but will describe the NumPy operators and provide some examples here. The element-wise or Hadamard product is simply the product of each of the elements in the same row and column index in the two vectors or matrices. This therefore requires that the vector or matrices have the same shapes, and produces a vector or matrix with the same shape as well.

The dot product is a bit more complicated. When calculating a dot product on two matrices, the sum of the products of the elements in the ith row of the first matrix and the jth column of the second matrix are computed, and the result is placed in the resultant matrix at the position (i, j). Note that this requires some restrictions on the shapes of the matrices when computing the dot product, so some rearranging may be necessary. If this does not make sense to you, don't worry, we will cover this in detail in the Linear Algebra chapter. However, for completeness, an example of how these operations are performed in NumPy is shown in the following code block.

The matrices are created on lines 5-6, each with shape $(3, 3)$. NumPy supports two ways to compute element-wise (Hadamard) products as shown in lines 9-10, one with the *multiply* method, and the other with the "*" operator. Both produce the same result as shown in the output. For the dot product, NumPy supports three different methods, the "@" operator, the *dot* method, and the *matmul* method. Each of these have subtle differences that can be explored in the NumPy documentation, but for our purposes in implementing machine learning algorithms, where the multiply operations rarely exceed dimensions greater than 2, these methods produce the same results as shown in the output.

```
1   #Matrix multiply functions
2
3   import numpy as np
4
5   X1 = np.arange(9.0).reshape((3, 3))
6   X2 = -1*np.array([[0,1,2],[3,4,5],[6,7,8]])
7
8   #Element-wise (Hadamard) product
9   hadamard_1= np.multiply(X1, X2)
10  hadamard_2 = X1*X2
11
12  #Dot product
13  dot_1 = X1@X2
14  dot_2 = np.dot(X1, X2)
15  dot_3 = np.matmul(X1,X2)
16
17  print('X1:\n', X1)
18  print('\nX2:\n', X2)
19  print('\nhadamard_1:\n', hadamard_1)
20  print('\nhadamard_2:\n', hadamard_2)
21  print('\ndot_1:\n', dot_1)
22  print('\ndot_2:\n', dot_2)
23  print('\ndot_3:\n', dot_3)
```

off

X1:
[[0. 1. 2.]
 [3. 4. 5.]
 [6. 7. 8.]]

X2:
[[0 -1 -2]
 [-3 -4 -5]
 [-6 -7 -8]]

hadamard_1:
[[0. -1. -4.]
 [-9. -16. -25.]
 [-36. -49. -64.]]

hadamard_2:
[[0. -1. -4.]
 [-9. -16. -25.]
 [-36. -49. -64.]]

dot_1:
[[-15. -18. -21.]
 [-42. -54. -66.]
 [-69. -90. -111.]]

dot_2:
[[-15. -18. -21.]
 [-42. -54. -66.]
 [-69. -90. -111.]]

dot_3:
[[-15. -18. -21.]
 [-42. -54. -66.]
 [-69. -90. -111.]]

NUMPY FILE INPUT-OUTPUT

NumPy also supports File Input-output and has a custom file type with the extension .*npy* that stores the data in an *ndarray* object. The methods used to save and load your array are .*save* and .*load*. The .save method inputs a filename and an array, and saves that array under the filename with extension .*npy*. Alternatively, the .*load* method inputs a filename and returns an array containing the data from the .*npy* file. An example is shown in the following code block.

```
1   import numpy as np
2
3   a = np.array([[1, 5], [2, 6]])
4   np.save('first_example', a)
5
6   b = np.load('first_example.npy')
7   print('Loaded from first_example:\n', b)
8   np.savetxt('second_example.csv', b)
9
10  c = np.loadtxt('second_example.csv')
11  print('\nLoaded from csv saved file:\n', c)
```

⌐→ Loaded from first_example:
     [[1 5]
     [2 6]]

     Loaded from csv saved file:
     [[1. 5.]
     [2. 6.]]

A simple array is created on line 3 with shape (2, 2) and saved on line 4. You do not have to name the file with the *.npy* extension as NumPy will automatically append the extension to the end of your filename. The *.npy* file will be saved to your drive in your current working directory. Note that the saved filetype is not text (it is binary) so will not be readable with a standard text editor. On line 6, we assign the array returned by the *.load* method with the first example *.npy* file passed into it. Because we saved an NumPy array to this filename previously, we can see in the output that b is the same as our original a matrix.

Another method that we can use to store and load NumPy arrays is *savetext* and *.loadtext*. When we do this, we can save the arrays in a text format, so they can be read in a standard text editor or used by other applications that require text input. When we call *savetext*, as shown in line 8, we pass in a filename and an array. Note that we must specify the filename extension with this method, as you could save it as a *csv*, *txt*, or other file type. Also, note that numeric values stored will be converted to floating point format, even if read in as integers. When we use the method *.loadtext*, we pass in the same filename we saved b as previously, and store that array in c, we can see when we print it out it is the same array as b.

NUMPY DOCUMENTATION

We covered the basics of the NumPy library that we will build upon in future machine learning algorithm implementations, but by no means is this a comprehensive review. You will undoubtedly find yourself frequently visiting the API documentation at the link here: https://numpy.org/doc/ to check method format options and functionality, or even to browse for new methods that you may find useful in your implementations.

Alternatively, the NumPy library has a built-in help method, *help*, that you can call directly in your notebook as shown in the following code block. Here we call *help* and pass the method we are interested in, the *arange* method in this case, and we see a portion of the returned output.

```
1  import numpy as np
2
3  help(np.arange)
```

Help on built-in function arange in module numpy:

arange(...)
    arange([start,] stop[, step,], dtype=None, *, like=None)

    Return evenly spaced values within a given interval.

    Values are generated within the half-open interval ``[start, stop)``
    (in other words, the interval including `start` but excluding `stop`).
    For integer arguments the function is equivalent to the Python built-in
    `range` function, but returns an ndarray rather than a list.

    When using a non-integer step, such as 0.1, it is often better to use
    `numpy.linspace`. See the warnings section below for more information.

    Parameters
    ----
    start : integer or real, optional
        Start of interval. The interval includes this value. The default
        start value is 0.
    stop : integer or real
        End of interval. The interval does not include this value, except
        in some cases where `step` is not an integer and floating point
        round-off affects the length of `out`.
    step : integer or real, optional
        Spacing between values. For any output `out`, this is the distance
        between two adjacent values, ``out[i+1] - out[i]``. The default
        step size is 1. If `step` is specified as a position argument,
        `start` must also be given.
    dtype : dtype
        The type of the output array. If `dtype` is not given, infer the data
        type from the other input arguments.
    like : array_like
        Reference object to allow the creation of arrays which are not
        NumPy arrays. If an array-like passed in as ``like`` supports
        the ``__array_function__`` protocol, the result will be defined
        by it. In this case, it ensures the creation of an array object
        compatible with that passed in via this argument.

        .. versionadded:: 1.20.0

    Returns
    ----
    arange : ndarray
        Array of evenly spaced values.

4.2:

PANDAS LIBRARY

Next, we will describe the basics of the Python Pandas library. Like NumPy, Pandas is an extensive collection of methods useful in processing datasets, and one which most data scientists and machine learning engineers are familiar with.

Before we get into the details, we will comment a bit on datasets. A dataset typically has two items, the attributes, which from hereon will be referred to as "features" and/or independent variables because this is the standard convention used in Data Science and Machine Learning, and the examples. Features are unique characteristics that each example shares, and the examples are groupings of the feature data points that are shared by one item in the dataset. "Tabular" datasets are a specific type of dataset, in that they can be sorted and displayed as a series of rows and columns, like a spreadsheet. In this format, the features are shown along the columns and the examples along the rows. The illustration shown here is a portion of the dataset called "World Happiness Report 2019". The dataset can be accessed from the following link: https://worldhappiness.report/ed/2019/

Overall rank	Country or region	Score	GDP per capita	Social support	Healthy life expectancy	Freedom to make life choices	Generosity	Perceptions of corruption
1	Finland	7.769	1.34	1.587	0.986	0.596	0.153	0.393
2	Denmark	7.6	1.383	1.573	0.996	0.592	0.252	0.41
3	Norway	7.554	1.488	1.582	1.028	0.603	0.271	0.341
4	Iceland	7.494	1.38	1.624	1.026	0.591	0.354	0.118
5	Netherlands	7.488	1.396	1.522	0.999	0.557	0.322	0.298
6	Switzerland	7.48	1.452	1.526	1.052	0.572	0.263	0.343
7	Sweden	7.343	1.387	1.487	1.009	0.574	0.267	0.373
8	New Zealand	7.307	1.303	1.557	1.026	0.585	0.33	0.38
9	Canada	7.278	1.365	1.505	1.039	0.584	0.285	0.308
10	Austria	7.246	1.376	1.475	1.016	0.532	0.244	0.226
11	Australia	7.228	1.372	1.548	1.036	0.557	0.332	0.29
12	Costa Rica	7.167	1.034	1.441	0.963	0.558	0.144	0.093
13	Israel	7.139	1.276	1.455	1.029	0.371	0.261	0.082

Reference citation: Helliwell, J., Layard, R., & Sachs, J. (2019).
World Happiness Report 2019, New York: Sustainable Development Solutions Network.

As can be seen, each column represents a different feature of the dataset; for example, Country or region, Score, GDP per capita, and Social support are all features in this dataset. You can also observe that each example occupies one row. The first row represents Finland's data for each feature, the second row is Denmark's and so on.

There are other types of datasets, besides tabular, that exist such as "document-based" datasets. Common databases are typically stored as document-based datasets, and these are ones which are based on each example being like a Python object such that each feature may have several data points associated with it. While document-based datasets are important to understand and work with, we will focus on tabular datasets here.

Now that we have defined what tabular data is, we can describe the importance of the Pandas library. Pandas provides methods to manipulate and store tabular data in Python. And it is built upon NumPy, so we can use the same array manipulation methods that you learned previously.

To fully understand Pandas, we first need to understand the two data structures that are integral to its inner workings; that is, the *Series* and the *DataFrame*. A figure of each is shown below.

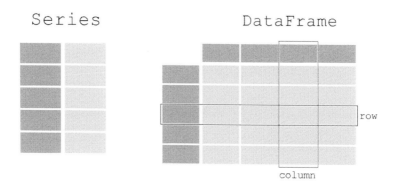

Reference citation: Images from
https://pandas.pydata.org/docs/getting_started/intro_tutorials/01_table_oriented.html

Pandas *Series* are one-dimensional columns of homogeneous data, where homogeneous data means that each piece of data is of the same type. Alternatively, *DataFrames* are two-dimensional stores for data where each column of the data is its own *Series*. This means that each *Series* represents one feature of the dataset over all examples, while the complete *DataFrame* includes all features (in the columns) and all examples (in the rows). To use Pandas in our code, we need to import the library, and the industry standard way to do this is: *import pandas as pd,* then from that point on in our code, we can reference *pd* to access the library functions.

PANDAS SERIES

We define a Pandas series as a one-dimensional labeled array. This is like a Python Dictionary where each item (the value) of the data structure has its own label (the key) associated with it. The following code block shows an example on how to create a Pandas series.

```
1   # Pandas Series creation
2
3   import pandas as pd
4   import numpy as np
5
6   pan_series1 = pd.Series(np.arange(3), index=['a', 'b', 'c'])
7
8   print('Series 1:\n', pan_series1)
```

```
Series 1:
 a 0
 b 1
 c 2
dtype: int64
```

The constructor on line 6 takes in two parameters: the data to be stored and the indices associated with them. However, there are several ways that data can be presented to the constructor, and each situation changes how the data should be passed in. For example, on line 6 *pan_series1* is a NumPy array with the values 0, 1, and 2 created by the *arange* method. Because NumPy arrays do not have a specific label index associated with the item, we can pass in a list of objects that can serve as the indices. The output shows the data is 0, 1, and 2 with a, b, and c respectively as the indices. We can also see that each item is stored as an integer, seen by the output *dtype: int64*.

We can convert a standard Python dictionary to a Pandas *Series* as shown in the following code block.

```
1   # Pandas Series creation
2
3   import pandas as pd
4   import numpy as np
5
6   dict2 = {'ayy': 3, 'bee': 4, 'see': 5}
7   pan_series2 = pd.Series(dict2)
8
9   print('Series 2\n', pan_series2)
```
```
Series 2
ayy 3
bee 4
see 5
dtype: int64
```

On line 6, we define a standard Python Dictionary. If we pass this dictionary into the Pandas *Series* constructor, we see that its output shows the dictionary keys for each pair as the data index and the dictionary values as the data.

We can also pass in the data to the Pandas *Series* constructor as a NumPy *array* without any indication of what we want the index to be as shown in the following code block. In this case the labels will simply be the indices of the array.

```
1   # Pandas Series creation
2
3   import pandas as pd
4   import numpy as np
5
6   pan_series3 = pd.Series(np.array([10, 11, 12]))
8
9   print('Series 3\n', pan_series3)
```
```
Series 3
0 10
1 11
2 12
dtype: int64
```

From the output, we can see that Pandas automatically sets the indices from zero up to the size of the data. There are many other possible ways to create Pandas series, however these examples should give you an idea of what is possible.

CONVERTING PANDAS SERIES TO NUMPY ARRAYS

If you want to extract a NumPy *array* from your Pandas *Series*, you can use the *to_numpy* method. This method will only store the data fields, ignoring the index fields. Examples are provided in the following code block.

```
1   import pandas as pd
2   import numpy as np
3
4   s = pd.Series(
5       ["one", "two", "three", "four"],
6       ["a", "b", "c", "d"]
7   )
8   arr = s.to_numpy()
9
10  print('Pandas series access:', s['a'])
11  print('\nPandas series slicing:\n', s[:2])
12  print('\nPandas series datatype:', s.dtype)
13  print('NumPy converted array:', arr)
14  print('NumPy array shape:', arr.shape)
```

```
Pandas series access: one

Pandas series slicing:
a one
b two
dtype: object

Pandas series datatype: object
NumPy converted array: ['one' 'two' 'three' 'four']
NumPy array shape: (4,)
```

The Pandas *Series* is defined on lines 4-8 using the standard value and index method described previously. Line 8 converts the series to a NumPy *array*. The remaining lines print various sliced accesses to the Pandas *Series* as well as the extracted NumPy *array*.

COMBINING PANDAS SERIES OBJECTS

Performing operations on Pandas *Series* can be done using traditional operators and most of the NumPy *array* methods. Part of the power of Pandas is that the data can be processed based on their index labels rather than their position. For example, in the following code block, we can see that s is a *Series* containing the data 1, 2, and 3 indexed with a, b, and c, and t is a *Series* containing the data 4, 5, and 6 indexed by b, c, and d. Note that the only indices these two *Series* share are b and c, so when we add them together on line 12, we can see b and c are the only indices that contain an output value. The values associated with a and d are turned into "Not-a-Number" (NaN) values. Also note that the data type (*dtype* in the output) has been changed to *float64*. Although we have not converted our data to a NumPy *array*, we can still pass it in to the NumPy math exponential function *exp* on line 13 which computes *e* to the power of every element. Both operations performed with NumPy functions return a Pandas *Series* which can be used in subsequent processing.

```
1    import pandas as pd
2    import numpy as np
3
4    s = pd.Series(
5        [1, 2, 3],
6        ["a", "b", "c"]
7    )
8    t = pd.Series(
9        [4, 5, 6],
10       ["b", "c", "d"]
11   )
12   print('Adding series:\n', s + t)
13   print('\nExponential:\n',np.exp(s))
```

```
Adding series:
a NaN
b 6.0
c 8.0
d NaN
dtype: float64

Exponentiation:
a 2.718282
b 7.389056
c 20.085537
dtype: float64
```

CREATING PANDAS DATAFRAMES

As described previously, Pandas *DataFrames* are 2-dimensional groupings of data where each column is a *Series* representing a feature in a dataset. Because of this grouping each column in a Pandas *DataFrame* is therefore comprised of the same data type, and because each *Series* in a *DataFrame* has a name (label), attached to it, we can reference the whole column by its feature name.

To create a Pandas *DataFrame*, we call its constructor, and as with *Series*, there exist several different options to pass in data. In addition, there are index and column parameters that can be used to label or filter the data, depending on the application. Several examples are shown in the following code block.

To start, we create a 2-dimensional NumPy *array* on line 4. Then, in the *DataFrame* constructor, we specify the feature labels with the "column" argument set equal to a list of the feature names, aaa and bbb. When we print the *DataFrame*, we can see that the NumPy *array* is the main body or data section in the *DataFrame*, and that the rows are indexed vertically starting at 0. We see that the columns are labeled with the feature names that were passed into the constructor as the Python list, aaa and bbb. Therefore, the Pandas *Series* attached to the feature label aaa contains the data 1 and 3, and the feature aaa contains the data 2 and 4.

```
1   import pandas as pd
2   import numpy as np
3
4   arr = np.array([[1, 2], [3, 4]])
5
6   a = pd.DataFrame(arr, columns=['aaa', 'bbb'])
7   b = pd.DataFrame({'one': arr[0][:], 'two': arr[1][:]})
8   c = pd.DataFrame(a, columns=['aaa'])
9
10  print('Original NumPy array:\n',arr)
11  print('\nNumPy convert to Pandas df - a :\n', a)
12  print('\nNumPy convert to Pandas df - b :\n', b)
13  print('\nAccess Pandas df - c :\n', c)
```

⤷ Original NumPy array:
   [[1 2]
   [3 4]]

   NumPy convert to Pandas df - *a* :
     aaa bbb
   0 1 2
   1 3 4

   NumPy convert to Pandas df - *b* :
     one two
   0 1 3
   1 2 4

   Access Pandas df - *c* :
     aaa
   0 1
   1 3

Alternatively, on line 7 we construct a *DataFrame* with a Python Dictionary of 1-dimensional NumPy *arrays*. Each key in the dictionary represents the name of the column, and each value of the dictionary represents the data contained in the series associated with that column. We can see that the column associated with the word "one" is the first row of the array named *arr*, which is the numbers 1, 2. The column associated with the word "two" is the second row of the array named *arr*. We can see this reflected in the output when we print *b*.

The last example shown in line 8 creates a *DataFrame* from another *DataFrame*. Here, we set *c* equal to *a*, but we extract out only column *aaa*. In the resulting output, we can see that the only *Series* that is used to construct *c* is the series from *a* associated with label *aaa* which we specified in the columns list.

PANDAS FILE INPUT-OUTPUT

Datasets are primarily stored in files or databases, so Pandas comes with several functions to import and export files to and from your programs. The link here https://pandas.pydata.org/pandas-docs/stable/user_guide/io.html provides a list of all the file types supported by Pandas for input-output. You will see many distinct file types listed for your application but the most common datasets that you will encounter are stored as comma-separated values (.csv), Excel files, Javascript Object Notation (.json), or Structured Query Language (SQL) databases.

A couple useful methods include *.head* and *.tail*, which allow you to preview the first five or last five examples in your *DataFrame*. In the example code block below, we read the happiness data CSV file referenced in the introduction, and then print its head. The output shows us a preview of the first five examples in the file.

```
1   import pandas as pd
2
3   df = pd.read_csv('happiness_data.csv')
4   print(df.head())
```

Overall rank	Country or region	Score	GDP per capita	Social support \
0	1	Finland 7.769	1.340	1.587
1	2	Denmark 7.600	1.383	1.573
2	3	Norway 7.554	1.488	1.582
3	4	Iceland 7.494	1.380	1.624
4	5	Netherlands 7.488	1.396	1.522

	Healthy life expectancy	Freedom to make life choices	Generosity \
0	0.986	0.596	0.153
1	0.996	0.592	0.252
2	1.028	0.603	0.271
3	1.026	0.591	0.354
4	0.999	0.557	0.322

	Perceptions of corruption
0	0.393
1	0.410
2	0.341
3	0.118
4	0.298

PANDAS DATAFRAMES

There are a variety of ways to access Pandas *DataFrames*. The most common is through accessing the *DataFrame* individual features (columns) or examples (rows). To access a column, we use square brackets and specify the name associated with the column to return a *Series*, and to access a row we can use the Pandas *.loc* method. An example is shown in the following code block.

```
1   import pandas as pd
2   import numpy as np
3
4   df = pd.DataFrame({
5       "one": pd.Series(np.arange(5) + 2),
6       "two": pd.Series(np.arange(5) * 10),
7       "three": pd.Series(np.ones(5, dtype=int) * 3)
8   })
9
10  print('Original DataFrame:\n',df)
11  print('\nSingle attribute (column), "one"\n', df["one"]
```

Original DataFrame:
```
   one two three
0   2    0    3
1   3   10    3
2   4   20    3
3   5   30    3
4   6   40    3
```

Single attribute (column), "one"
```
0   2
1   3
2   4
3   5
4   6
Name: one, dtype: int64
```

On lines 4-8, we create *df*, a Pandas *DataFrame* using the NumPy *arange* and *ones* methods. We see that it has 3 columns, labeled with the strings "one", "two", and "three".

To access a single column as shown in line 11, we index the column name within square brackets, and we can see that this is a *Series* with all indices associated with it, along with an extra "Name" label that identifies it with the name "one".

To delete a column as shown in the following code block, we can use the *pop* method. Here we simply specify the column name that we want to remove. Note that by referencing *df* with the *pop* method, the function is performed "in-place" which means it will update *df* directly. If we wanted to preserve the original *DataFrame*, then we should assign another variable to the output of *df.pop()*, such as, *df_modified = df.pop("two")*.

```
1   df.pop("two")
2   print('\nRemove feature, "two":\n',df)
```

Remove attribute, "two":
```
   one three
0   2    3
1   3    3
2   4    3
3   5    3
4   6    3
```

We can use the Pandas *assign* method to create columns out of other columns as shown in the following code block. This method returns a separate *DataFrame*, without modifying the original one we are referencing. We can see that we are assigning a new feature named "four", which should be equal to the feature "one" plus feature "three". When we print out the new *DataFrame*, we can see that it has removed the "two" column (from the previous example), and added a new column labeled "four", which is the sum of columns "one" and "three".

```
1   df = df.assign(four=df["one"] + df["three"])
2   print('\nModify\n',df)
3   print('\n Single example (row)\n', df.loc[1]
```

```
Modify
    one three four
0   2   3    5
1   3   3    6
2   4   3    7
3   5   3    8
4   6   3    9


Single example (row)
one      3
three    3
four     6
Name:  1, dtype: int64
```

Finally, if you would like to extract an individual example (row) as a *Series*, we use the *.loc* method as shown in line 3 of the above code block with the index provided within square brackets. The output shows the second row of the *DataFrame* (since we use zero-based indexing), and in its output, we see that the column names are the indices.

Most data types that you can load into Pandas can also be stored as files through Pandas after editing the *DataFrame*. Further, it is quite common to read a dataset into a Pandas *DataFrame*, then convert it to NumPy *array* for processing though both libraries can be used to clean and store datasets in a process known as Exploratory Data Analysis (EDA).

OTHER COMMON PANDAS FUNCTIONS

There are a multitude of Pandas functions available for use when processing a dataset. The open source API documentation is shown in the link https://pandas. pydata.org/docs/. Here we provide a few examples of common functions in the following code block.

```
1   import pandas as pd
2   import numpy as np
3
4   df = pd.DataFrame({
5       "one": pd.Series(np.arange(5) + 2),
6       "two": pd.Series(np.arange(5) * 10),
7       "three": pd.Series(np.ones(5, dtype=int) * 3)
8   })
9
10  print('Original DataFrame:\n',df)
11  print('\nFeature labels:\n',df.columns.array)
12  print('\nExample indices:\n', df.index.array)
13  print('\nDataFrame shape:\n', df.shape)
```

```
Original DataFrame:
    one two three
0    2   0    3
1    3  10    3
2    4  20    3
3    5  30    3
4    6  40    3

Attribute labels:
<PandasArray>
['one', 'two', 'three']
Length: 3, dtype: object

Example indices:
<PandasArray>
[0, 1, 2, 3, 4]
Length: 5, dtype: int64

DataFrame shape:
(5, 3)
```

As in the previous example, we create a *DataFrame* in lines 4-8. To get a list of all the feature (column) labels in order, we can access it through *.columns.array*, and to get a list of all the index labels, use *.index.array* as shown in lines 11 and 12 respectively. This applies to both *Series* and *DataFrames*. The methods are useful when needing to iterate through every column or row of the *DataFrame*. To get the shape of the DataFrame, use the *.shape* method as shown in line 13. This method is consistent with the *shape* method in NumPy.

Finally, there are a variety of ways to gather insights into your data. The following code block shows several examples. As shown in line 10, *.sum()* returns the sum of each of the features (columns). In line 11, *.mean* provides an average of the columns. And *.max* and *.min* return the maximum and minimum value of each column (*.max* is shown in line 12).

```
1    import pandas as pd
2    import numpy as np
3
4    df = pd.DataFrame({
5        "one": pd.Series(np.arange(5) + 2),
6        "two": pd.Series(np.arange(5) * 10),
7        "three": pd.Series(np.ones(5, dtype=int) * 3)
8    })
9    print('Original DataFrame:\n',df)
10   print('\nFeature sums:\n', df.sum())
11   print('\n Feature means:\n', df.mean())
12   print('\n Feature max values:\n', df.max())
13   print('\nDataFrame description:\n',df.describe())
```

Original DataFrame:
```
   one two three
0   2   0   3
1   3  10   3
2   4  20   3
3   5  30   3
4   6  40   3
```

Attribute sums:
```
one      20
two     100
three    15
dtype: int64
```

Attribute means:
```
one      4.0
two     20.0
three    3.0
dtype: float64
```

Attribute max values:
```
one      6
two     40
three    3
dtype: int64
```

DataFrame description:

	one	two	three
count	5.000000	5.000000	5.0
mean	4.000000	20.000000	3.0
std.	1.581139	15.811388	0.0
min	2.000000	0.000000	3.0
25%	3.000000	10.000000	3.0
50%	4.000000	20.000000	3.0
75%	5.000000	30.000000	3.0
max	6.000000	40.000000	3.0

Pandas also provides a useful summary of the *DataFrame* without the need to call each of the methods described above with the *.describe* method as shown in line 13 in the above code block. This will provide a list of statistics about each feature (column) that will give you an overview of your data. The statistics include the number of examples in the *DataFrame*, and for each feature, its mean, standard deviation, min, max and percentiles which can be used to determine interquartile ranges (IQR) that are useful to identify dataset outliers (IQR will be covered in the statistic chapter).

PANDAS DOCUMENTATION

Like NumPy, we covered the basics of the Pandas library, but this is not a comprehensive review. You will find yourself frequently visiting the API documentation at the link here: https://pandas.pydata.org/docs/reference/index.html to check method format options and functionality, or even to browse for new methods that you may find useful in your implementations.

And like the NumPy library, Pandas also has a built-in help method, *help*, that you can call directly in your notebook for inline descriptions of the available methods.

4.3:
MAPLOTLIB

The final Python library that we will cover is the common data visualization package that is used extensively in Machine Learning and Data Science applications called Matplotlib. A generic example figure of how we can visualize data with Matplotlib follows.

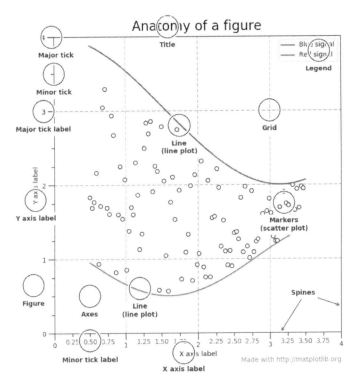

Almost everything in the diagram shown can be edited and changed through various settings and parameters in Matplotlib figures. This library can work with both Python built-in data structures; for example Lists, and NumPy arrays as inputs for all the functions, so we will be able to easily integrate it with our NumPy and Pandas based code.

Like NumPy and Pandas, Matplotlib supports extensive functionality that could consume an entire book, and many tutorials are available, so we will limit our focus to the functions needed specific to visualizing data in support of the Machine Learning and Data Science applications that we will implement, mainly using the module called *pyplot*. The *pyplot* module will allow us to make simple graphs in 2 and 3 dimensions to help visualize our data.

Every plot that we make is made up of two main objects, a figure object, and an axes object. The figure object contains all the plot elements such as the size, colors, border details, subplot definitions, and other layout particulars. The axes object represents one plot or subplot in a figure and includes the plot type (scatter, bar, pie, etc.), labels and titles, and legends or other annotations included on the plot. To use Matplotlib in our code, we need to import the library, and the industry standard way to do this is: ***import** matplotlib.pyplot **as** plt,* then from that point on in our code, we can reference *plt* to access the library functions.

PYPLOT

As mentioned previously, we will be using the *pyplot* interface to create our graphs. Each *pyplot* function is used to set up the visualizations on the graph, and then the method *show* is called to display it. The following example code block shows how we can create basic scatter and line plots.

In the following scatter plot example, we must provide the X and Y coordinates for our plot, and in this example, we pass a Python List of X-coordinates and Y-coordinates, in that order, to the scatter function on line 5. Many other optional configuration parameters may also be passed to the function to set the type of marker, colors, and so on, but they all have default parameters so are not required. We can set the axis *label* for the x and y axes, and plot *title* as shown in lines 6-8, then display the plot by calling the *show* function on line 9.

```
1   # Scatter plot
2
3   import matplotlib.pyplot as plt
4
5   plt.scatter([1, 2, 3, 4], [1, 2, 3, 4])
6   plt.ylabel('y label')
7   plt.xlabel('x label')
8   plt.title('Plot title')
9   plt.show()
```

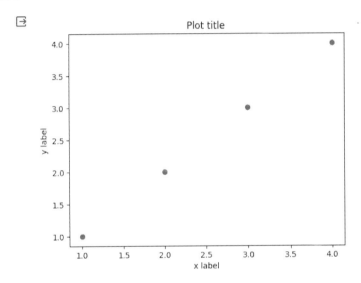

In the following line plot example, we similarly need to provide the x and y coordinates, then call the *plot* function, but this time we pass NumPy *arrays* and pass them to the function on line 8. The *plot* method will automatically assume the points are connected and draw a line through them. As with the scatter function, there are many optional parameters that can be passed to the plot function to display point markers, change colors, and more. You should experiment with the APIs to get a feel for the different plot options available.

```
1    # Line plot
2
3    import matplotlib.pyplot as plt
4    import numpy as np
5
6    x = np.array([1, 3, 5, 7])
7    y = np.array([2, 4, 6, 8])
8    plt.plot(x, y)
9    plt.title('Plot title')
10   plt.ylabel('even points')
11   plt.xlabel('odd points')
12   plt.show()
```

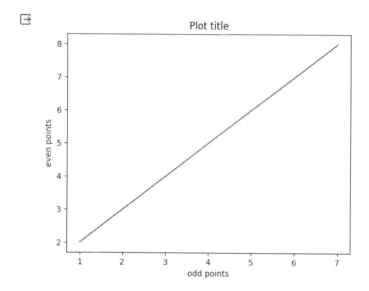

FIGURE SIZING AND SUB-PLOTS

Changing the size of your plots, can be done with the *figure* method by setting the *figsize* variable to the ratio you want to show along the horizontal and vertical directions, which is scaled in inches. This is shown in the following example code block on line 6. Here we set the figure size to be 9 inches wide and 3 inches tall. Note that depending on your code development environment console output, the actual size may vary, but the ratio of width to height should be maintained.

To include more than one graph in your plots, the *subplot* method can be used. The subplot API includes three parameters: the number of rows to divide the figure into, the number of columns to divide the figure into, and the index of the specific *subplot* you want to modify. With this subplot formatting, any methods you call underneath will only apply to that *subplot* until you designate another afterwards. For example, at line 10 we show *subplot(1, 3, 1)* which designates 1 row, 3 subplots, and we index the first subplot to place a scatterplot in that position (line 11). Then in line 13, we reference the second subplot and place a bar plot in that position. And finally in line 16, we reference the third subplot and place a stemplot in that spot.

```
1    # Figure sizing and Subplots
2
3    import matplotlib.pyplot as plt
4    import numpy as np
5
6    plt.figure(figsize=(9, 3))
7    x = np.array([1, 2, 3, 4])
8    y = np.array([2, 4, 6, 8])
9
10   plt.subplot(1, 3, 1)
11   plt.scatter(x, y)
12
13   plt.subplot(1, 3, 2)
14   plt.bar(x, y)
15
16   plt.subplot(1, 3, 3)
17   plt.stem(x, y)
18
19   plt.show()
```

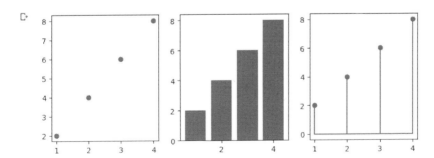

PLOT TYPES

The following table lists many of the plot types available in Matplotlib. The top 5 listed plots show the most common that you will likely use, but you should check out the Matplotlib gallery at the link shown to get more details on each of the available plot types so that you can decide which ones are most useful for your application. https://matplotlib.org/3.1.0/gallery/index.html.

plt.plot()	# lines & markers
plt.scatter()	# scatter plot
plt.hist()	# histogram
plt.bar()	# bar chart
plt.stem()	# stem plot
plt.barh()	# horizontal bar chart
plt.boxplot()	# box and whisker plot
plt.hist2d()	# 2d histogram
plt.pie()	# pie chart
plt.polar()	# polar graph
plt.stackplot()	# stacked area plot
plt.step()	# step plot
plt.quiver()	# plot of arrows

Next, we show examples using Matplotlib with NumPy and Pandas. This should provide a basic working knowledge from which you can create visualizations for your datasets and application results, but as with the NumPy and Pandas libraries, you should use the open-source documentation to customize Matplotlib for your own applications.

The following code blocks shows an example which creates a Pandas *DataFrame* comprised of 2 *Series* formed with the NumPy *arange* function on lines 7-10.

We then set the figure size to be 4 units wide and 8 units tall on line 12. Next, we define and set up two subplots. In our first *subplot* on lines 14-15, we pass the actual *Series* returned by the columns associated with attributes *one* and *two* from the *DataFrame* as the X and Y parameters, along with a string that designates the format of the graph, which we will discuss next. Note that in passing in the *Series* associated with the names *one* and *two*, we are passing in lists as objects that contain the actual data as the X and Y parameters. We see the results of this in the output figure. The column associated with the string "one" is plotted on the horizontal x-axis, and the column that we associate with the string "two" is on the vertical.

In our next subplot on line 17-18, we show how the *data* input parameter can be used. This is used for labeled data, so if you want to work with an entire *DataFrame*, you may want to use this method. What we do here is pass in the label for X and Y (*one* and *two* respectively), then declare a different format string and pass in our *DataFrame* as the variable data. The labels we pass in are those corresponding to the columns we want to plot, so we end up with the exact same graph just with different formatting. Either of these methods will work fine for plotting the data, but if you are using a *DataFrame*, you may find that the second set of parameters is easier to use.

```
1    # Pandas DataFrame plots
2
3    import matplotlib.pyplot as plt
4    import pandas as pd
5    import numpy as np
6
7    df = pd.DataFrame({
8        "one": pd.Series(np.arange(5) + 2),
9        "two": pd.Series(np.arange(5) * 10),
10   })
11
12   plt.figure(figsize=(4, 8))
13
14   plt.subplot(2, 1, 1)
15   plt.plot(df["one"], df["two"], "o--m")
16
17   plt.subplot(2, 1, 2)
18   plt.plot("one", "two", "D:k", data=df)
19
20   plt.show()
```

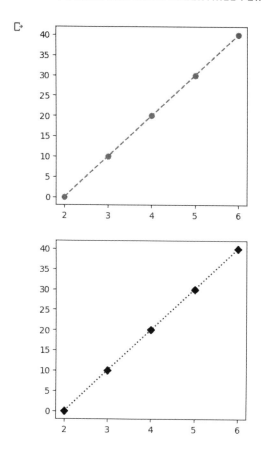

FORMAT STRINGS

The format string specifies 3 attributes to the plot: the type of marker, the line style, and the color of the line. This is done by having a character or group of characters that represent each style and then having them ordered in a string which is parsed by *pyplot* and translated to your graph as was shown as the last parameter in the previous code listing on line 15. Your format parameters must be specified in the following order: marker first, then the line, and finally the color. An example of some of the marker types, line types, and colors is shown in the following table. These are not the only attributes available, however, so refer to the open-source documentation for a full list that best suits your needs.

Marker		Line		Color	
.	point	-	solid line	b	blue
o	Circle	--	dashed line	k	black
D	diamond	-.	dash-dot	r	red
*	star	:	dotted line	m	magenta

For markers, a period (".") means that data will be represented by a point, lowercase "o" represents a circle, capital "D" a diamond, and an asterisk presents a star. Next, some of the line parameters options include the dash to create a solid line, two dashes for a dashed line, a dash followed by a period for a dash-dot alternating line, and a colon to create a dotted line. Again, check out the reference documentation for more options. Finally, you can change the color by adding a character at the end of the format attribute string. For example, use "b" for blue, "g" for green, "r" for red, and others as defined in the documentation.

There are many more formatting options that you can experiment with. An example is shown in the following code block. The most common options that are shown here allow you to set the *title* (line 20), *labels* (lines 21-22), limits (*lim*) on your x and y ranges (lines 23-24), tick marks (*xticks, yticks*) visibility (lines 25-26), and adding a *legend* to multiple datasets that are plotted on the same graph (line 27).

Finally, you can *annotate* your plot with symbols, arrows, and descriptive text anywhere on the graphs to make them more readable. An example is shown on lines 29-34 which places an arrow and text highlighting the intersection point between to two plots.

```
1   # More Matplotlib format examples
2
3   import matplotlib.pyplot as plt
4   import pandas as pd
5   import numpy as np
6
7   df1 = pd.DataFrame({
8       "one": pd.Series(np.arange(5) + 2),
9       "two": pd.Series(np.arange(5) * 10),
10  })
11
12  df2 = pd.DataFrame({
13      "three": pd.Series(np.arange(10)),
14      "four": pd.Series(np.arange(10, 1, -2) * 4),
15  })
16
17  plt.plot(df1["one"], df1["two"], "o--m", label="DataFrame_1")
18  plt.plot(df2["three"], df2["four"], "D-k", label="DataFrame_2")
19
20  plt.title("Example Graph")
21  plt.xlabel("Numbers")
22  plt.ylabel("Bigger Numbers")
23  plt.xlim(0, 7)
24  plt.ylim(0, 50)
25  plt.xticks(np.arange(0, 7))
26  plt.yticks(np.arange(0, 6) * 10)
27  plt.legend(loc=1)
28
29  plt.annotate(
30      "Intersection",
31      xy=(3.35, 12),
32      xytext=(3.0, 30),
33      arrowprops=dict(facecolor="blue", shrink=0.1)
34  )
35  plt.show()
```

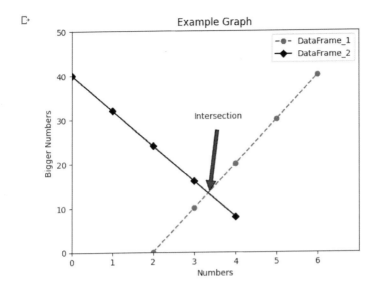

MATPLOTLIB DOCUMENTATION

As with NumPy and Pandas, we covered the basics of the Matplotlib library that we will build upon in our machine learning implementations, but this is not a comprehensive review. You will find yourself frequently visiting the API documentation at the link here: https://matplotlib.org/stable/ to check method format options and functionality, or even to browse for new methods that you may find useful in your implementations.

And like the NumPy and Pandas libraries, Matplotlib also has a built-in help method, *help*, that you can call directly in your notebook for inline descriptions of the available methods.

SECTION 2:

MATHEMATICS PRIMER FOR MACHINE LEARNING

In the previous section we focused on the Python language, then introduced the three most common libraries used in data analytics pre-processing and machine learning.

This section will focus on the mathematics needed to develop machine learning algorithms, namely statistics, linear algebra, and calculus.

This section forms the fundamental mathematics that we will need to understand most of the concepts behind the traditional machine-learning algorithms such as regression, classification, feature reduction, recommender systems, and in neural network applications in deep learning.

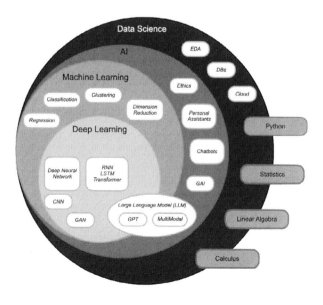

CHAPTER 5:
Statistics Introduction for Machine Learning

This chapter focuses on Statistics and its application to machine learning.

LEARNING OBJECTIVES

By the end of this chapter, you will be able to do the following:

- Identify a variable as either categorical or quantitative
- Calculate marginal and joint relative frequency from a contingency table
- Identify a dotplot, stemplot, boxplot, and histogram
- Describe the shape, center, and variability of a distribution
- Calculate the mean, median, mode, variance and standard deviation in a distribution
- Identify the shape of a normal, left skew, and right skew distribution
- Calculate the InterQuartile Range (IQR) and outliers in a distribution

5.1:
DISPLAYING AND INTERPRETING DATA - PART 1

STATISTICAL TARGETS

We will first discuss what a statistical target is and how we will work with it. We need to learn as much information about the target as possible so that we are better informed on how to analyze the data we collect, which may or may not precisely predict the target, and may or may not be influenced by some bias as shown in the following figure.

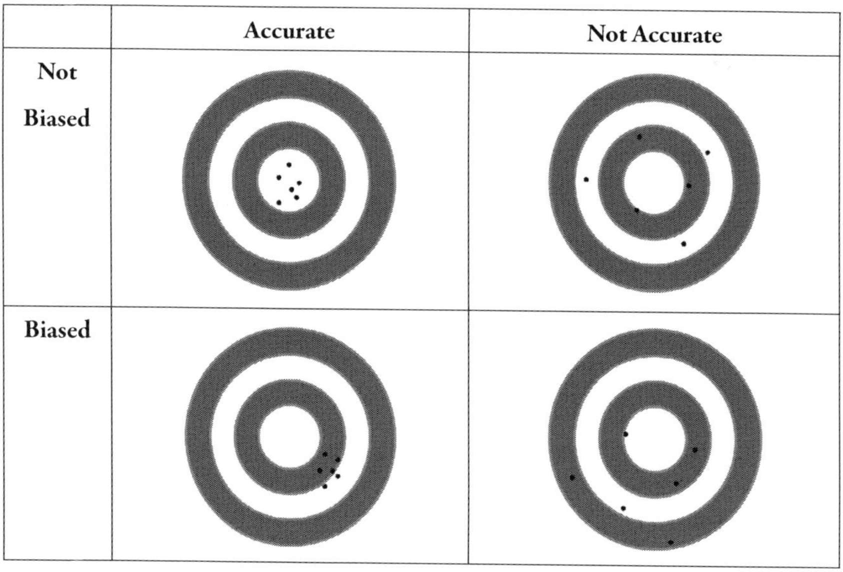

	Accurate	Not Accurate
Not Biased		
Biased		

The first thing we need to do is identify the individuals which are commonly comprised of elements and variables in the dataset. Once we know the type of variables we have, we can figure out how to best interpret and display the data. We typically do this by creating a graphical representation from which we can identify some of its key properties, and that allows us to describe the data in "Statistics" language. We call this SOCV or SOCS, which we will define soon, but before we do that let's take a step back and ask, what exactly is statistics?

Statistics is the science of collecting, analyzing, and making conclusions from data. As mentioned, our data is made up of individuals or elements which comprise the object that is described in our dataset. Some examples of individuals include, but are not limited to, people, households, countries, animals, trees, and schools to name a few.

We also have variables in the dataset. Now, the variables can be categorical; that is, they define a category or group and usually have a text-based descriptor, such as name, color, or gender. This is also known as a qualitative variable. Alternatively, the variable can be quantitative; that is, is a number which represents a measurable quantity and may be represented as an integer, floating point, or binary value such as height, blood pressure level, or MPG. Quantitative variables as also called "numerical variables".

Let's look at some examples of categorical and quantitative variables. Remember that the qualitative variables define categories or groups, while the quantitative variables can be represented with numeric quantities.

Categorical Variables	Quantitative Variables
Gender	Weight
Dog Breed	Income
Employment Status	GDP
Religion	Cholesterol level
Ethnicity	MPG
Vehicle Model	Circumference

In statistics, we need to first understand this general classification of our data before we can do any analysis on it. Let's look at an example. Here we have a table with five elements in the dataset, each with an ID and 4 additional features, 3 of which are quantitative; that is height, weight, and cholesterol, and one categorical; that is, smoking status.

ID	Height (cm)	Weight (kg)	Smoking Status	Cholesterol (mg/dL)
55678	175	68	Yes	170
55694	168	70	No	181
55729	172	55	Yes	178
55875	177	65	Yes	150
54012	159	50	No	145

Based on this data, we can ask the following question. Does smoking influence cholesterol? Can you tell by examining this data visually whether smoking influences an individual's cholesterol level? This example illustrates the type of questions that statisticians and data scientists strive to solve; that is, to provide a conclusion based on analyzing a collection of data.

To form a response to the question, we need to examine the data more closely. And there are many ways we can do that. For instance, here we show several examples of how one might display the data for a response to a survey question on a preferred communication method.

Preferred Communication Method	Frequency	Relative Frequency
Cell Phone	2	2/10 = 20%
Social Media	1	1/10 = 10%
In Person	3	3/10 = 30%
Text message	4	4/10 = 40%

The first type is the frequency table, which shows the total number of individuals who selected each category. The second type is the relative frequency table, which shows the proportion of the individual who selected each category.

The following code block shows how we can capture this data in a Matplotlib visualization in a bar graph and a pie chart.

```
1    #Graph generation for preferred communication
2
3    import matplotlib.pyplot as plt
4    import numpy as np
5
6    plt.figure(figsize=(12, 3))
7    x = np.array(['Cell phone', 'Social Media', 'In-person', 'Text Message'])
8    y = np.array([20, 10, 30, 40])
9    colors = ['blue', 'orange', 'green', 'red']
10
11   plt.subplot(1, 2, 1)
12   plt.bar(x, y, color=colors)
13   plt.title('Preferred Communication Method')
14
15   plt.subplot(1, 2, 2)
16   plt.pie(y, labels=x, colors=colors)
17   plt.title('Preferred Communication Method')
18
19   plt.show()
```

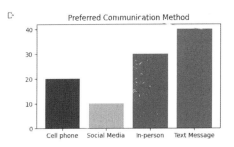

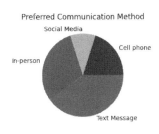

Now, are there such thing as bad displays of data? Yes! The link shows several examples of visualizations that distort the data and may be misleading. https://www.businessinsider.com/the-27-worst-charts-of-all-time-2013-6 It is important that if we provide a visual interpretation, we do so objectively with minimal distortions.

When we create a display graph, we want to do a couple of things. First, we need to identify the individual or elements in the dataset, and second, we want to include the context when describing the displayed data. An example is shown in the following code block. Here a graph is generated which shows for a sample of 2000 streaming video subscribers who took a survey on favorite movie genres, the results showed that "romance" and "action" were most preferred, followed closely behind by "comedy" and "sci-fi". As shown, the least preferred genre was "drama".

```
1    #Graph generation from video streaming survey
2
3    import matplotlib.pyplot as plt
4    import numpy as np
5
6    x = np.array(['Comedy', 'Action', 'Romance', 'Drama', 'Sci-Fi'])
7    y = np.array([400, 500, 600, 100, 400])
8    colors = ['blue', 'orange', 'green', 'red', 'cyan']
9
10   plt.bar(x, y, color=colors)
11   plt.title('Favorite Movie Genre')
12
13   plt.show()
```

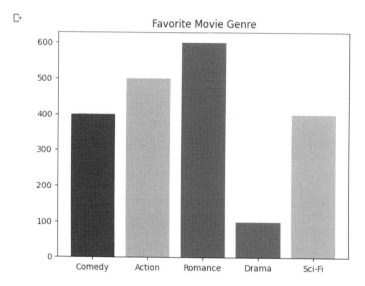

RELATIVE FREQUENCIES

The methods we have learned are appropriate for displaying data for a single categorical variable. However, often we are interested in seeing if there is a relationship between two categorical variables. We define a "two-way table" or "contingency table" as one which summarizes data on the relationships between two categorical variables for some group of individuals or elements. The following shows examples that display different representations of the same data.

		Annual Income			
		<60K	60K-120K	>120K	Total
Degree Type	Associates	24	17	7	48
	Bachelors	24	40	27	91
	Masters	10	20	15	45
	Doctorate	0	3	19	22
Total		58	80	68	206

➡

		Annual Income			
		<60K	60K-120K	>120K	Total
Degree Type	Associates	.116	.083	.034	.23
	Bachelors	.116	.194	.131	.44
	Masters	.049	.097	.073	.22
	Doctorate	0	.015	.092	.11
Total		.28	.39	.33	1

The term relative frequency is used in Statistics to refer to converting frequency data into a percentage. We can define what is called "marginal relative frequency", which is computed as the row or column total divided by the overall total and allows us to answer questions shown in the example table, such as what percent of respondents have an income less than 60,000. We can also define the "joint relative frequency" in which each cell is converted to a ratio of the cell total divided by the overall total, and this allows us to answer questions more directly by looking at the cell itself. For example, we can determine what percent of respondents that have a Doctorate degree and make over $120,000?

Let's look at an example of how we can interpret a contingency table of passengers on the famous luxury cruise ship, the Titanic.

		Class of Travel of Travel			
		First	Second	Third	Total
Survival Status	Survived	197	94	151	442
	Died	122	167	476	765
Total		319	261	627	1207

Titanic struck an iceberg in 1912 while traveling across the Atlantic and sank, and many people perished. Passengers in those days were split into classes depending on their socio-economic status. The table shows frequency data; that is, how many died and how many survived for each of the three classes of passengers. We will consider several example questions that can be found through interpretation of this relative frequency table.

1. Why might it be useful to change the data from frequencies to relative frequencies?

So that we can compare the values more accurately. You cannot compare the death frequencies for each class since there were not an equal number of First, Second, and Third class passengers.

2. What percent of Titanic passengers were First class?

   319/1207 = 26% (this is a marginal relative frequency)

3. What percent of Titanic passengers died?

   765/1207 = 63% (this is a marginal relative frequency)

4. What percent of Titanic passengers were First class passengers who died?

   122/1207 = 10% (this is a joint relative frequency)

5. What percentage of First-class passengers died on the Titanic?

   122/319 = 38% (this is a conditional relative frequency) - we will use these a lot when analyzing probabilities

COMPARATIVE BAR CHARTS

Next, we show couple other examples of data visualization using bar charts and the associated code used to produce them. Consider the following data which shows people's political affiliation, and whether they currently own or are planning to buy an Electric Vehicle (EV).

Political Party	Own or plan to buy an Electric Vehicle		
	No - Never	Maybe	Yes - Definitely
Republican	72	25	3
Democrat	16	30	54
Independent	36	42	22

The following code blocks produce both side-by-side and stacked bar charts using the Python libraries (NumPy and Matplotlib) we have covered in previously.

In the first code block, we provide the data to be graphed in lines 6-9 then create an array of indices into the Python List (shown on line 6) using the NumPy *arange* method on line 12. We then create a bar chart using the Matplotlib *bar* method, setting the x coordinates of the bars (offset by 0.2), the height of the bars which are defined by the values in the Lists on lines 7-9, the width of the bars (set to 0.2), and placing labels on the x-axis corresponding to the List variable names on lines 7-9.

```
1    # Side-by-side bar chart
2
3    import numpy as np
4    import matplotlib.pyplot as plt
5
6    X = ['Republican','Democrat', 'Independent']
7    Never = [72, 16, 36]
8    Maybe = [25, 30, 42]
9    Yes = [3, 54, 22]
10
11
12   X_axis = np.arange(len(X))
13
14   plt.bar(X_axis - 0.2, Never, 0.2, label = 'Never')
15   plt.bar(X_axis + 0.0, Maybe, 0.2, label = 'Maybe')
16   plt.bar(X_axis + 0.2, Yes, 0.2, label = 'Yes')
17
18   plt.xticks(X_axis, X)
19   plt.xlabel("Political Affiliation")
20   plt.ylabel("Number of Members")
21   plt.title("Political Party vs. EV ownership")
22   plt.legend(title="EV ownership")
23   plt.show()
```

The second code block creates a Python List of the x-axis labels on line 6 then a Python Dictionary of the EV use categories (keys) and corresponding number of members in each political party (values) on lines 8-12. A loop is used on line 17 to iterate through the Dictionary keys and values, creating a stacked bar via updating the y-coordinate of the *bottom* of each bar by the number of members in each of the political affiliation at each loop iteration.

```python
1    # Stacked bar chart
2
3    import numpy as np
4    import matplotlib.pyplot as plt
5
6    X = ['Republican','Democrat', 'Independent']
7
8    EV_use = {
9        'Never' : np.array([72, 16, 36]),
10       'Maybe' : np.array([25, 30, 42]),
11       'Yes' : np.array([3, 54, 22])
12   }
13
14   X_axis = np.arange(len(X))
15   bottom=np.zeros(3)
16
17   for use, members in EV_use.items():
18       plt.bar(X_axis, members, 0.2, label = use, bottom=bottom)
19       bottom += members
20
21   plt.xticks(X_axis, X)
22   plt.xlabel("Political Affiliation")
23   plt.ylabel("Number of Members")
24   plt.title("Political Party vs. EV use")
25   plt.legend(title="EV use", bbox_to_anchor=(1.05, 1))
26   plt.show()
```

The charts show the relationships between people's political party and those who own or plan to purchase an Electric Vehicle. The left chart shows the graph in a side-by-side bar chart, where each EV ownership bar is placed along the horizontal axis. The chart on the right shows the same data in a segmented bar chart where each of the EV ownership bars are placed vertically on top of each other. These charts allow us to visually identify possible associations or relationships between two variables.

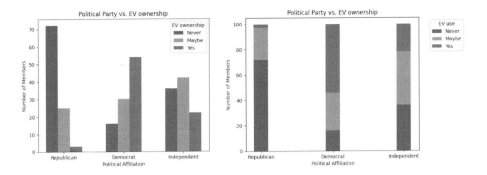

Do you think there is an association in the displayed data? It appears that people who are members of the Democratic party are more likely to own or purchase an Electric Vehicle, and conversely members of the Republican party are more unlikely. Can you infer other associations not explicitly called out with this data? Perhaps an Electric Vehicle maker may not want to spend as much money on infrastructure, such as charging stations, in Republican dominated ("red") states. Or perhaps a marketing campaign to spur interest in EV's in red states may be warranted due to an untapped market. A data scientist working for an EV company could attempt to find interpretations like this to provide advantages to the business case. However, even though we say there is an association here, we do not imply causation, where causation is defined as the condition when one variable influences the other (causing the other). We will discuss causation and the related "correlation" later in this chapter.

Finally, we will consider a few more ways to visualize our data. You can find online documentation for each of the graph types shown and we will look at how to display them with software tools later, but we will provide an introduction or review of each of the most common visualizations used by statisticians.

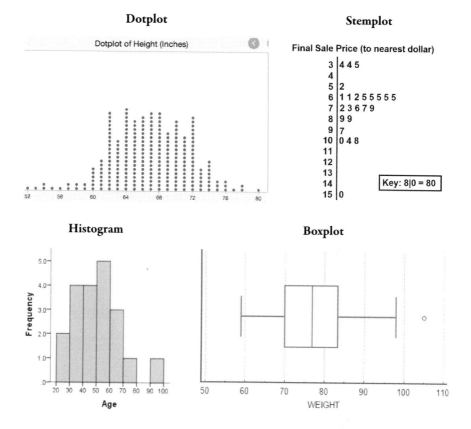

Dotplot

Stemplot

Histogram

Boxplot

In a Dotplot, each individual data value is represented by a dot, placed above its appropriate position on a number line. The Dotplot displays the frequency of a variable as a vertical collection of dots, so the greater the number of dots in a stack, the higher the frequency of that variable.

In a Stemplot, each individual data value is separated into two parts, a "stem" and a "leaf", separated by a vertical line. We typically use a Stemplot when we have a small to medium number of quantitative variables to analyze. The stem consists of the largest value digits and is positioned to the left of the vertical line, while the leaf consists of the lower value digits which are placed on the right of the vertical line. The stems are ordered from lowest to highest in the vertical column, and the leaves are arranged from lowest to highest to the right of the appropriate stem. As an example, the first line in the example Stemplot represents the final sale prices of $34, $34, and $35. In other words, we take the 3 from the left of the line as the most significant digit and combine it with the other digits to the right of the line to form the data values. The Stemplot is not a common type of plot used today but was a fast way to sketch data distributions by hand before computers did that work for us.

Histograms are better for displaying large sets of quantitative data. For example, you would not want to plot 1,000 pieces of a data on a Dotplot. Histograms group data into equal intervals and plot the data as bars. The heights of the bars represent the frequencies or relative frequencies of values in each interval. We will use histograms frequently with machine learning algorithm visualizations so you should become comfortable with recognizing and working with them.

Finally, another popular visualization for statisticians and data scientists is the Boxplot. We will describe and use the Boxplot in detail when we start analyzing data as it contains many statistical measures that we will use with our machine learning algorithm implementations.

5.2:
Displaying and Interpreting Data - Part 2

Next, we will revisit the acronym we mentioned previously, "SOCV". We introduced this as the way we describe our data in Statistics language. When describing distributions of a quantitative variable you can use a graph to look for an overall pattern and for clear departures from that pattern, both of which are important. Overall patterns can be described by focusing on "Shape" (the "S" in SOCV), "Center" (the "C" in SOCV) and "Variability" (the "V" in SOCV). Departures from this pattern can be seen in the form of "Outliers" (the "O" in SOCV) which are observations that fall outside the overall pattern. Note that we need to always be sure to include context when asked to describe a distribution. This means using the variable name, not just the units the variable is measured in.

SHAPE (SOCV)

First, we will describe the "Shape" characteristic of SOCV. When we evaluate a dotplot, stemplot, or histogram, we want to look for the major peaks, that is whether it has a single peak, 2 peaks (also called bimodal), more than 2 peaks (or multimodal), or uniform (which is basically a flat distribution). We also want to look to see if our data is clustered or if there are any obvious gaps in the distribution. And finally, we would also like to know if the shape has symmetry or if it is skewed. The following figure shows examples of left and right skewed distributions.

Left Skewed   **Right Skewed**

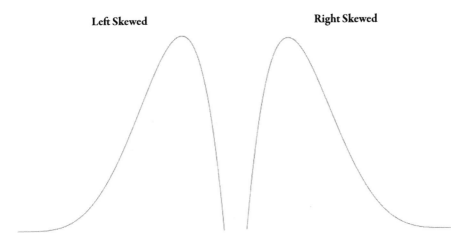

Now it may seem counterintuitive that the skewed left figure has the peak to the right. But the peak or mound is where most of the data is, and the "skew" describes where the outlier or odd data is. The actual definition of the verb 'skew' is "to distort especially from a true value or symmetrical form." So, the skew is referring to what is odd or different, and therefore something with a low outlier will be skewed to the left.

Next, we provide a few distribution examples in the following figures. The first example shows the roll of a die which represents a uniform distribution that is roughly symmetric and has no clear peaks.

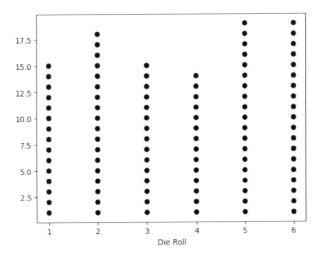

The next example shows a bimodal distribution. This distribution represents the duration of the eruptions (in minutes) of the famous geyser, Old Faithful, and has two distinct clusters with peaks at around 1.9 mins and 4.6 minutes.

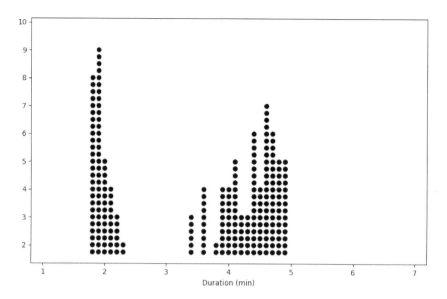

The final example shows a distribution of quiz scores with a skewed left shape and some gaps in the data. The distribution is skewed to the left with a single peak at 20 pts. There are two small gaps at 12 and 16.

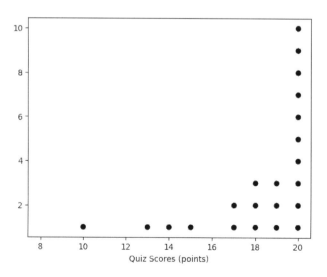

CENTER (SOCV)

Next, we will discuss the "center" in SOCV. We usually describe the center in terms of the "mean" and the "median". *Mean* and *Median* are both common measures of center, but there is a time and a place for when each should be used.

The *mean* is the average of all the individual data values. To find the mean, we sum together all the values (observations) and divide them by the total number of observations. The *mean* is easy to find, but it is also sensitive to outlier values, and thus is also known as a non-resistant statistical measure; in other words, the mean is not resistant to outlier values.

The *median* is the midpoint of a distribution, such that half of the observations are smaller, and half are larger. Again, this is an easy and probably familiar calculation to you in that we just need to find the middle value in the dataset. The only actual calculation for the median is if there exists an even number of values, and in that case the *median* is simply the average (or *mean*) of the two middle values.

Whether we should be describing our distribution center using the *mean* or the *median* depends on the shape of the distribution and whether any outliers exist. So, if we were asked to describe a distribution center, which should we use? If the *mean* is approximately equal to the *median*, then we have a symmetric distribution, and we could use either. However, if we have a skewed distribution, then the *mean* will be impacted by the outlier values, and in that case, we should use the *median*. The following figure shows examples of the mean and median for Normal, Left skewed and Right skewed distributions.

Normal Distribution

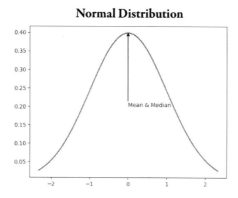

Left Skew   **Right Skew**

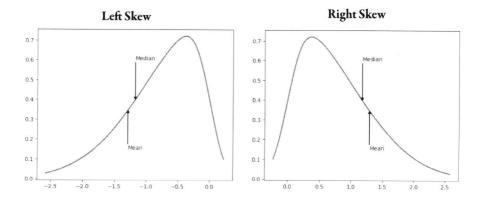

VARIABILITY (SOCV)

Next, we will discuss the "variability" in SOCV. We usually describe the variability in our data in terms of the parameters: Range, Standard Deviation, and Interquartile Range.

The *range* is defined as the maximum value minus the minimum value, and we note that range is a single number. For example, we do NOT say that the *range* is "between 2 and 5", instead we would say the *range* is 3. The range is another parameter that is easy to compute. However, the *range* is not a resistant statistical measure and can be misleading depending on the shape of the distribution as we can see in the example image which shows the same *range* for two very different distributions. Here we see that the *range* is approximately equal to 20 for both distributions.

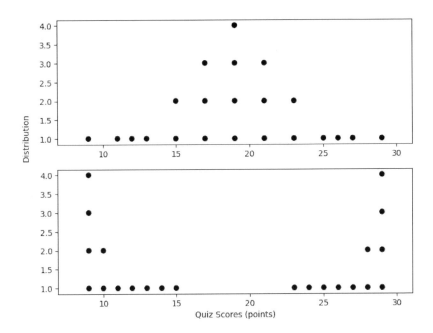

'The *standard deviation*, measures the typical distances of the values in a distribution from the mean. Now the *standard deviation* is very useful when working with certain types of distributions that we will work with later in this chapter. For example, in the above figure we saw that the range was the same for both distributions, but the variation of the values is different from the *mean*. While the *standard deviation* is a powerful measure, it is somewhat complicated to compute. We will discuss the standard deviation in more detail next.

Finally, we can describe our variability using what is called the *interquartile range*, or IQR, which is the distance between the first and third "quartiles" of a distribution. The quartiles are simply the values that divide the data into quarters as if the values were placed on a number line. In this case quartile 1 would be the lowest 25% of the values, quartile 2 would be the next 25% of the values up to the median, 3rd quartile would be the second highest 25% of the values above the median, and quartile 4 would be the highest 25% of the values. Then, our *interquartile range* defines the distance between the 1st and 3rd quartile, and this is our first statistically resistant measure because we can ignore any outliers that would exist in the 1st or 4th quartiles; that is, the outer quartiles where the outliers would fall. We will discuss the detailed IQR calculations next.

DESCRIBING VARIABILITY - STANDARD DEVIATION

First, we will discuss the *standard deviation* in more detail since this will be one of the more important measures in describing variability in our distributions and is used repeatedly in Data Science and Machine Learning. At a high level, the *standard deviation* provides a distance measure of the values in a distribution to the mean of the distribution. The standard deviation is most valuable when used with symmetric distributions, such as the well-known "normal" or "Gaussian" distribution shown below.

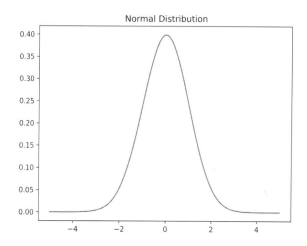

The formula for the standard deviation takes on the following two forms:

Population Standard deviation   **Sample Standard deviation**

$$s_x = \sqrt{\frac{\Sigma_i(x_i - \bar{x})^2}{n}}$$ and $$s_x = \sqrt{\frac{\Sigma_i(x_i - \bar{x})^2}{n - 1}}$$

Now you will rarely need to do this calculation by hand, but it is important to know the process so that you can understand its use in machine learning algorithms, as well as understand the difference between the two equation forms in your Python implementations. Both formulas take the square root of the sum of the square differences between each sample in the dataset and its *mean*. This summation effectively computes the sum of all the distances from each sample to the *mean*, where the square is taken so that each distance is a positive value. The summation result is then divided by n or n - 1, where n is the number of samples in the dataset. We refer to the first equation (divide by n) as the "population" *standard deviation* and this second (divide by n - 1) as the "sample" or "Bessel-corrected" *standard deviation*.

So why do we need this correction? First, we need to clarify a couple terms used in statistics. We call the entire group that you want to analyze and make conclusions about a "population", and a subset of the population is referred to as a "sample". The *standard deviation* provided in the first equation is just an estimate of the population *standard deviation*; in other words, it is an estimate of the average distance of all the values in the population to the *mean* of the population. Now we usually do not know the entire population *mean*, and as a result are not able to calculate the deviations from it. So, instead we typically use the *mean* of a sample population. However, because the sample *mean* can be thought of as the exact balancing point of the data that we have, and not necessarily of the entire population, the data will almost always be closer to the sample *mean*, than to the population *mean*. Thus, if we use the sample *mean* in the first formula, the sum of the squared deviations from the *mean* will underestimate the sum of the squared deviations from the actual population *mean*. To correct for this, we divide by a slightly smaller number when finding the average; that is, n - 1, instead of n, and this is known as the Bessel correction. So, in other words, if we have access to the entire population, we should use the first formula (population *standard deviation*), and if we only have a sample of the population, then we use the second (sample *standard deviation*).

Now, why do we care about any of this? Since we are going to be using this statistical measure in many of our machine learning algorithm implementations, we should not only use the correct formula for our dataset, we also need to know which form the common libraries, specifically NumPy and Pandas, use to calculate it, and it turns out the default NumPy function implements the *population standard deviation* (the divide by n case), while Pandas implements the Bessel-corrected or *sample standard deviation* (the divide by n – 1 case). The following code block shows each of the calculations shown in the above equations along with the NumPy and Pandas library implementations. The output confirms that the default NumPy *std* function produces the *population standard deviation* while Pandas produces the Bessel-corrected *sample standard deviation*. Note that if the *sample standard deviation* is required, then NumPy can be configured to calculate it using the "Delta Degrees of Freedom" input parameter *ddof=1* which sets the divisor to n - 1, and thus calculates the *sample standard deviation* as shown in the console output.

```
1   #Standard deviation in Numpy and Pandas
2   import numpy as np
3   import pandas as pd
4
5   X = np.array([1, 2, 3, 4, 5, 6, 7, 8, 9, 10])
6
7   df = pd.DataFrame({'X': X})
8
9   #Hand calculations
10  mean = np.mean(X)
11  sx = np.sqrt(np.sum((X-mean)**2)/len(X))
12  sx_bessel = np.sqrt(np.sum((X-mean)**2)/(len(X)-1))
13
14  #Library calculations
15  sx_numpy = np.std(X)
16  sx_pandas = df.std()
17
18  print('Hand calc population std:', np.round(sx, 5))
19  print('Hand calc sample std (with Bessel correction):', np.round(sx_bessel, 5))
20  print('NumPy std:', np.round(X.std(), 5 ))
21  print('NumPy std (with ddof=1):', np.round(X.std(ddof=1), 5 ))
22  print('Pandas std:', np.round(df.std(), 5))
```

```
Hand calc population std: 2.87228
Hand calc sample std (with Bessel correction): 3.02765
NumPy std: 2.87228
NumPy std (with ddof=1): 3.02765
Pandas std: X    3.02765
dtype: float64
```

ANTHONY MAURO

To complete the discussion on standard deviation, we will note that *variance* is simply the *standard deviation* squared, sx². We typically use the *standard deviation* in our statistical analysis, with *variance* being used in a broader sense to reflect the degree to which each data point differs from the mean, and *standard deviation* being used as a measure of dispersion (or spread) of values around their mean.

DESCRIBING VARIABILITY - INTERQUARTILE RANGE (IQR)

Next we will discuss the interquartile range, or *IQR*, details. As was described previously, the interquartile range is the distance between the first (Q1) and third (Q3) quartiles of a distribution.

The formula and steps in calculating the interquartile range include the following. We first need to partition the dataset into quartiles by dividing it into 4 groups having roughly the same number of values. We can do this by arranging the data values from smallest to largest then finding the overall *median* of the dataset. Next, recall the *IQR* is defined as the range of the middle half of the distribution, so we need to find the *median* of quartile 3 (or Q3) and the *median* of quartile 1 (or Q1). In other words, our 1st quartile (Q1) is defined by the *median* of the data values that are to the left of the overall dataset *median*, and our 3rd quartile (Q3) is the *median* of the data values that are to the right of the overall *median*. And therefore, the *IQR* is the range of the middle half of the distribution or simply the media of Q3 minus the median of Q1.

The following figure shows where the quartiles fall in a Normal distribution with 0 mean and standard deviation of 1. In this case Q1 and Q3 fall at around −0.67 and +0.67 respectively.

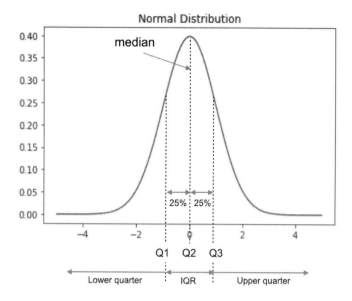

Now we'll through an example to calculate the *IQR* on a simple dataset. The dataset represents, for 20 households, the number of years a homeowner has lived in their house.

data = np.array([14, 7, 6, 5, 12, 38, 8, 7, 10, 10, 10, 11, 4, 5, 22, 7, 5, 10, 35, 7])

First we create a dotplot of the data to visualize the distribution.

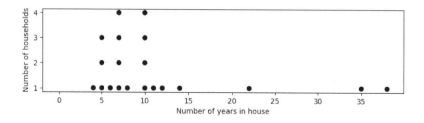

Then we list out all the data values in order and find the overall *median* (the middle value in the ordered list). Next, to find Q1, we find the *median* of the data to the left of the overall *median* and we see it is the average of the values 6 and 7, or 6.5. Then to find Q3, we find the *median* of the data to the right of the overall *median*, and that turns out to be 11.5. Finally, our IQR is therefore Q3 - Q1 or 11.5 - 6.5 = 5.

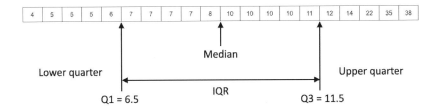

The following Python function computes the *IQR* from an input dataset. NumPy offers a function shown on lines 8-9 called *percentile* which can be used to compute Q1 and Q3. Note there are several methods parameters that can be specified in the API to estimate the quartiles, here we use parameter *midpoint*.

```
1    #Calculate the Q1, Q3, and IQR
2
3    def IQR_calculator(dataIn):
4        #dataIn = list of data
5        #return IQR, Q1, Q3
6
7        #Calculate first and third quartiles (Q1, Q3) using numpy percentile function
8        Q1 = np.percentile(dataIn, 25, method = 'midpoint')
9        Q3 = np.percentile(dataIn, 75, method = 'midpoint')
10
11       # Calculate the Interquartile range
12       IQR = Q3 - Q1
13       return IQR, Q1, Q3
```

Now we previously mentioned that the *IQR* is a resistant statistical measure since it ignores the smallest and largest 25% of the data, which is where the outliers would be located. In other words, the *IQR* is resistant to being skewed by outlier values in our dataset.

Further, outliers can be identified using the *IQR*. We define the following rule: an observation (or value in our dataset) is defined as an outlier if it falls further than 1.5 IQR's above the third quartile (Q3), which we call "high outliers" or 1.5 IQR's below the first quartile (Q1), "low outliers". We show an example dataset with the *IQR* parameters defined, along with the calculations used to identify the outliers in the following figure.

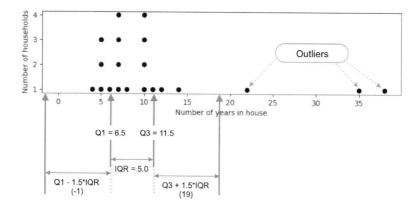

The following code block shows how we can calculate the outlier thresholds and find the outliers in a dataset.

```
1    #Calculate the IQR outlier thresholds
2    def IQR_outlier_thresholds(IQR, Q1, Q3):
3        #IQR = interquartile range
4        #Q1, Q3 = Quartile 1, 3
5        #return tuple of low and high outlier thresholds
6
7        highOutlierThresh = Q3 + 1.5*IQR
8        lowOutlierThresh = Q1 - 1.5*IQR
9        return lowOutlierThresh, highOutlierThresh
10
11   #Find the outliers
12   def IQR_find_outliers(dataIn, lowT, highT):
13       #dataIn = list of data
14       #highT = high outlier threshold
15       #lowT = low outlier threshold
16       #return list of low outliers, list of high outliers
17
18       outlierLow = []
19       outlierHigh = []
20       for i in dataIn:
21       if i < lowT:
22           outlierLow.append(i)
23       if i > highT:
24           outlierHigh.append(i)
25       return outlierLow, outlierHigh
```

And to complete our example, we show the final calling sequence to find the quartiles, *IQR*, outlier thresholds and finally any outliers that exist in our dataset.

```
1   #IQR example
2
3   import numpy as np;
4   import matplotlib.pyplot as plt
5
6   data = np.array([14, 7, 6, 5, 12, 38, 8, 7, 10, 10, 10, 11, 4, 5, 22, 7, 5, 10, 35, 7])
7
8   IQR, Q1, Q3 = IQR_calculator(data)
9   lowT, highT = IQR_outlier_thresholds(IQR, Q1, Q3)
10  outlierLow, outlierHigh = IQR_find_outliers(data, lowT, highT)
11
12  print('IQR, Q1, Q3:', IQR, Q1, Q3)
13  print('IQR thresholds:', lowT, highT)
14  print('Low Outliers:', outlierLow)
15  print('High Outliers:', outlierHigh)
```

```
IQR, Q1, Q3: 5.0 6.5 11.5
IQR thresholds: -1.0 19.0
Low Outliers: []
High Outliers: [38, 22, 35]
```

Now why is it important to identify outliers in our dataset? In data science we want to have as accurate information as possible, and an outlier in a dataset may indicate incorrectly entered data or even a misstatement. Additionally, determining outliers is an important consideration when choosing a machine learning algorithm. For example, the unsupervised "clustering" algorithm called K-means may be negatively affected if outliers exist so a preprocessing step to identify and possibly remove them may be warranted to improve performance. With that in mind, we can utilize the *IQR* method to help us determine what constitutes an outlier in our dataset.

Alternatively, the outlier may be accurate but may provide an interesting occurrence that is noteworthy. But the most important reason to identify outliers in our data is so that we can note the possible impact they may have on our summary statistics, such as with the *mean, range,* or *standard deviation.*

VISUALIZING DATA STATISTICS WITH BOXPLOTS

Now we introduced the visualization graph called the "boxplot" previously, but here we will discuss it in more detail. A boxplot is another useful way of displaying quantitative data. The boxplot helps visualize a distribution by focusing on 5 important values in the distribution, also known as "Five-Number Summary". Those 5 values include the (1) Minimum, (2) Q1, (3) Median, (4) Q3, and (5) Maximum. We see an example of each of these properties in the following figure.

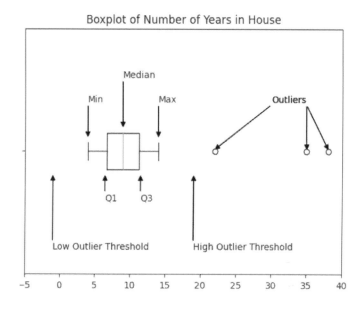

The left side of the box represents the first quartile (Q1), and the right side, the third quartile (Q3). Then the width of the box represents the *IQR*. The vertical line inside the box is the median.

The horizontal lines protruding from the box extend to the minimum and the maximum values of the dataset, excluding any outliers, and are commonly called "whiskers". The ends of the whiskers are marked by two shorter vertical lines. Values higher than Q3 + 1.5 • IQR, or lower than Q1 - 1.5 • IQR are considered outliers and are plotted to the right of the high outlier threshold or to the left of the low outlier threshold.

The steps in creating a box plot include the following: First we find and identify the five-number summary, that is the *Minimum*, *Q1*, *Median*, *Q3* and *Maximum*. Next, we identify any outliers using our *IQR* outlier rule. Then, we draw and label the horizontal axis, making sure to accurately scale the axis. Then we draw a box that spans between Q1 and Q3, and mark the *median* with a vertical line. And finally, we draw lines that extend from each edge of the box to the *maximum* and *minimum* values, and mark any outliers. The following code block shows how the above figure boxplot was generated, along with the outlier annotations.

```
1   #Boxplot and IQR example
2
3   import numpy as np;
4   import matplotlib.pyplot as plt
5
6   data = np.array([14, 7, 6, 5, 12, 38, 8, 7, 10, 10, 10, 11, 4, 5, 22, 7, 5, 10, 35, 7])
7
8   IQR, Q1, Q3 = IQR_calculator(data)
9   lowT, highT = IQR_outlier_thresholds(IQR, Q1, Q3)
10  outlierLow, outlierHigh = IQR_find_outliers(data, lowT, highT)
11
12  plt.boxplot(data, vert=0)
13  plt.title('Boxplot of Number of Years in House')
14  plt.xlim(-5,40)
15
16  for i in outlierHigh:
17      plt.annotate(
18          "Outliers",
19          xytext=(30.0, 1.2),
20          xy=(i, 1.01),
21          arrowprops=dict(facecolor="black", width=0.1, headwidth=5, headlength=5)
22  )
```

INTERPRETING TRANSFORMED DATA

A common task that a data scientist performs is called Exploratory Data Analysis (EDA), which means they analyze a dataset prior to applying a machine learning model to summarize the main statistical characteristics, and this is usually done using visual methods and SOCV. We have looked at some of the techniques involved in visualizing data via different plot types and SOCV measures previously. We'll now look at some examples on the effects that transforming a dataset may have on the statistical characteristics.

Imagine you had a dotplot for a set of quiz scores as shown in the following figure. What effect does adding or subtracting a constant have on a distribution?

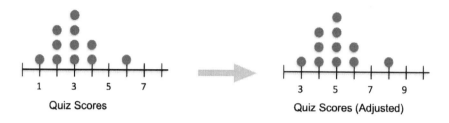

Your teacher feels like the scores are too low and adds 2 points to each student's score. What effect does this have on the data? When asked "what effect" an action has on the data, we are looking for any changes in the SOCV; that is, the *shape*, the *center* (or the *mean* in this case), *variability* (or the *standard deviation*) and *outliers* in the data.

We know the center will be affected since the *mean* or *median* will increase by 2 points. The *variability* will not be affected since the *IQR*, *range* and *standard deviation* will not change (try computing it for yourself if you are not sure). Finally, the *shape* will not be affected as can be seen in the dotplot itself because the entire distribution is just shifted two points to the right.

Now imagine you had a dotplot for a set of quiz scores, and your teacher wants to convert the scores into percentages. The test was out of 25 points, so she multiplies all the scores by 4. So, this time we're looking for the effect the action of multiplying the values in our population has on SOCV.

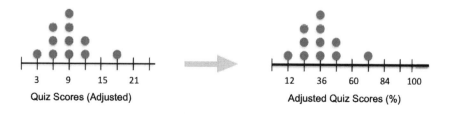

As with the previous example, we know the *center* will be affected, that is, the *mean* will be multiplied by 4. The *variability* will be affected in this case (and recall that the variability was not affected in the previous example when adding/subtracting to the values). The *IQR*, *range*, and *standard deviation* will be multiplied by 4. Finally, the *shape* will not be affected. Again, as with the previous example, the entire distribution moves along the axes, but the general *shape* remains the same.

Let's consider one more example. Suppose you have a set of data for mean temperatures in the El Portal village of Yosemite National Park, measured in degrees Celsius. The annual mean temperature is 16.35 °C, with a standard deviation of 6.38 °C. Here we want to answer what effect a combination of transforms (multiplying/dividing and addition/subtraction) has on a distribution?

We use the familiar conversion formula to translate the temperature given in Celsius to Fahrenheit, where:

$$°F = \frac{9}{5}°C + 32$$

The converted monthly temperatures are shown in the table.

Month	Min (°C)	Max (°C)	Mean (°C)	Min (°F)	Max (°F)	Mean (°F)
January	3	12	7.5	37	54	45.5
February	5	15	10	41	59	50
March	6	18	12	43	64	53.6
April	8	22	15	46	72	59
May	12	27	19.5	54	81	67.1
June	14	31	22.5	57	88	72.5
July	17	34	25.5	63	93	77.9
August	17	33	25	63	91	77
September	14	31	22.5	57	88	72.5
October	11	25	18	52	77	64.4
November	6	17	11.5	43	63	52.7
December	3	12	7.5	37	54	45.5

Reference citation: Data from
https://www.climatestotravel.com/climate/united-states/yosemite.
Copyright Climatestotravel.com.

We want to find the annual *mean* temperatures in degrees Fahrenheit and the *standard deviation*. As described previously, the *mean* is affected by addition/subtraction AND multiplication/division, and the *standard deviation* is ONLY affected by multiplication/division. We can now interpret the results. The original conversion to °F includes both a 9/5 scale (multiplication and division) and an offset (+ 32). Since both factors will affect the *mean* we will see it increase to:

$$\left(\frac{9}{5}\right) \cdot 16.35 + 32 = 61.43 \text{ °F}$$

The *standard deviation* will be affected by:

$$\left(\frac{9}{5}\right) \cdot 6.38 = 11.48 \text{ °F}$$

Note that we do not include the +32 scaling because addition does not affect the *variability*. In other words, the temperature readings typically vary from the mean by about 11.48 degrees Fahrenheit.

Z-SCORE

Next, we will discuss the Z-score. Z-scores provide us with a mechanism to evaluate and compare metrics from a 'normal' population, that is, where the population follows a normal distribution as shown in the following figure.

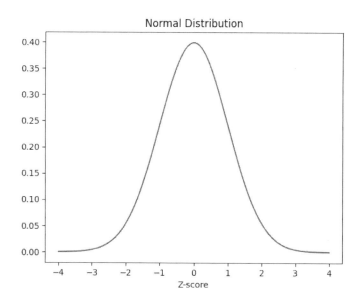

Now we won't get into the details about the different types of distributions that exist nor what a probability density function is as those topics are covered in most standard high school statistics courses. We will, however, discuss the normal distribution since it is the most important type of probability density function that has a shape as shown in the figure and allows us to model many real-world datasets, as well as evaluate several of the statistical metrics we have discussed so far. For the normal distribution shown, the mean is at the center or peak of the distribution and the standard deviation is a unit of measure from the mean.

The Z-score is also known as the "standard score" or "standardized score" and tells us how many standard deviations away from the mean a value falls, and in what direction. From an intuitive point of view then, an observation that has a large Z-score can be considered "unusual" or a possible outlier. A Z-score is also directional. A positive Z-score means the observation was higher than the mean, while a negative Z-score means the observation was less than the mean. Finally, the units of a Z-score are NOT the same as the units of the observed data. The units are in "standard deviations", in other words, a Z-score of '1' means 1 standard deviation from the mean.

The Z-score is defined as:

$$Z-Score = \frac{Value - Mean}{Standard\ Deviation}$$

Now what can we do with a Z-score? We can calculate the probability of a value occurring within our normal distribution, and we can also compare two scores from different normal distributions which we will show in several examples later. An example Z-score look-up table is shown in the following figure.

Standard Normal Probabilities

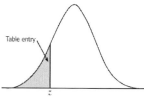

Table entry

Table entry for z is the area under the standard normal curve to the left of z.

z	.00	.01	.02	.03	.04	.05	.06	.07	.08	.09
−3.4	.0003	.0003	.0003	.0003	.0003	.0003	.0003	.0003	.0003	.0002
−3.3	.0005	.0005	.0005	.0004	.0004	.0004	.0004	.0004	.0004	.0003
−3.2	.0007	.0007	.0006	.0006	.0006	.0006	.0006	.0005	.0005	.0005
−3.1	.0010	.0009	.0009	.0009	.0008	.0008	.0008	.0008	.0007	.0007
−3.0	.0013	.0013	.0013	.0012	.0012	.0011	.0011	.0011	.0010	.0010
−2.9	.0019	.0018	.0018	.0017	.0016	.0016	.0015	.0015	.0014	.0014
−2.8	.0026	.0025	.0024	.0023	.0023	.0022	.0021	.0021	.0020	.0019
−2.7	.0035	.0034	.0033	.0032	.0031	.0030	.0029	.0028	.0027	.0026
−2.6	.0047	.0045	.0044	.0043	.0041	.0040	.0039	.0038	.0037	.0036
−2.5	.0062	.0060	.0059	.0057	.0055	.0054	.0052	.0051	.0049	.0048
−2.4	.0082	.0080	.0078	.0075	.0073	.0071	.0069	.0068	.0066	.0064
−2.3	.0107	.0104	.0102	.0099	.0096	.0094	.0091	.0089	.0087	.0084
−2.2	.0139	.0136	.0132	.0129	.0125	.0122	.0119	.0116	.0113	.0110
−2.1	.0179	.0174	.0170	.0166	.0162	.0158	.0154	.0150	.0146	.0143

Reference citation: Image from https://byjus.com/maths/z-score-table/.

We will illustrate the Z-score by way of an example. We are given the following age data for 25 respondents to a survey.

n	Mean	Standard Deviation	Min	Q1	Median	Q3	Max
25	35.44	8.77	12	31.5	38	41.5	48

Given the following statistical measures in the table shown answer the following questions:

1. Find and interpret the Z-score for Brooks, who is 18 years old

2. Find the age of Samantha, who had a standardized score of 1.66

For Question 1. the Z-score is the difference between Brooks' age and the mean, divided by the standard deviation, or: $(18 - 35.44)/8.77 = -1.99$. This means that Brooks' age falls 1.99 *standard deviations* below the *mean* age of 35.44 years.

For Question 2, we see that Samantha is 1.66 *standard deviations* from the *mean* age, so to solve for her age we need to solve the Z-score equation algebraically; that is, we need to take 1.66, which is the difference between Samantha's age and the *mean*, then divide that by the *standard deviation*. If we solve the algebra, we see that Samantha is approximately 50 years old.

Now we will summarize a few things about the normal distribution and Z-scores, then we'll walkthrough a few more examples. First, the normal distribution is described by a symmetric, single-peaked, bell-shaped density curve called a Normal curve. Any Normal distribution is completely specified by two numbers, its mean and standard deviation. Normal Distributions are commonly used in inference which means we can use this distribution to deduce properties in the data to do things like calculate critical values for confidence intervals, and test statistics for hypothesis tests. Next, regarding the basic function of Z-scores, they are a simple way to standardize data (for example, to get rid of the units), so that we can compare values from many different datasets. And if data is normally distributed, Z-scores can help us evaluate how likely it is that we will see a particular value in the dataset.

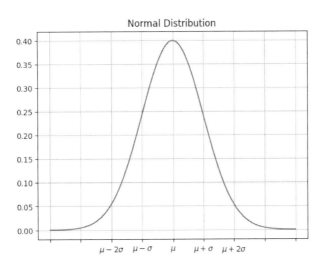

And if data is normally distributed, Z-scores can help us evaluate how likely it is that we will see a particular value in the dataset. The following figure shows what percentage of normally distributed data falls between +1, + 2, and + 3, standard deviations from the mean. We see in the figure that approximately 68% of the data will reside within + 1 standard deviation, and almost 100% between + 3 standard deviations.

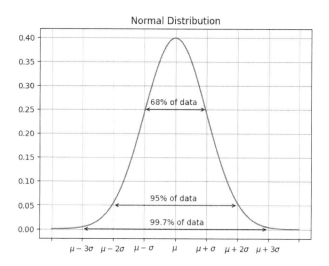

Z-TABLES

The following table shows look-up values for what is called a left-hand Z-table for negative Z-scores, and another left-hand table for positive Z-scores. Recall, the Z-scores to the right of the *mean* are positive and the Z-scores to the left of the *mean* are negative. Both tables, however, always represents the proportion of the total area under the normal curve which is left of the Z-score, regardless of whether it is positive or negative. The area value can be looked up in this table by combining the first two digits of the left-most column with the hundreds digit in the top row to get the desired Z-score, then locating the value at the intersection.

Negative z-scores   z   0

Positive z-scores   0   z

z	0.00	0.01	0.02	0.03	0.04	0.05	0.06	0.07	0.08	0.09
-3.4	0.0003	0.0003	0.0003	0.0003	0.0003	0.0003	0.0003	0.0003	0.0003	0.0002
-3.3	0.0005	0.0005	0.0005	0.0004	0.0004	0.0004	0.0004	0.0004	0.0004	0.0003
-3.2	0.0007	0.0007	0.0006	0.0006	0.0006	0.0006	0.0006	0.0005	0.0005	0.0005
-3.1	0.0010	0.0009	0.0009	0.0009	0.0008	0.0008	0.0008	0.0008	0.0007	0.0007
-3.0	0.0013	0.0013	0.0013	0.0012	0.0012	0.0011	0.0011	0.0011	0.0010	0.0010
-2.9	0.0019	0.0018	0.0018	0.0017	0.0016	0.0016	0.0015	0.0015	0.0014	0.0014
-2.8	0.0026	0.0025	0.0024	0.0023	0.0023	0.0022	0.0021	0.0021	0.0020	0.0019
-2.7	0.0035	0.0034	0.0033	0.0032	0.0031	0.0030	0.0029	0.0028	0.0027	0.0026
-2.6	0.0047	0.0045	0.0044	0.0043	0.0041	0.0040	0.0039	0.0038	0.0037	0.0036
-2.5	0.0062	0.0060	0.0059	0.0057	0.0055	0.0054	0.0052	0.0051	0.0049	0.0048
-2.4	0.0082	0.0080	0.0078	0.0075	0.0073	0.0071	0.0069	0.0068	0.0066	0.0064
-2.3	0.0107	0.0104	0.0102	0.0099	0.0096	0.0094	0.0091	0.0089	0.0087	0.0084
-2.2	0.0139	0.0136	0.0132	0.0129	0.0125	0.0122	0.0119	0.0116	0.0113	0.0110
-2.1	0.0179	0.0174	0.0170	0.0166	0.0162	0.0158	0.0154	0.0150	0.0146	0.0143
-2.0	0.0228	0.0222	0.0217	0.0212	0.0207	0.0202	0.0197	0.0192	0.0188	0.0183
-1.9	0.0287	0.0281	0.0274	0.0268	0.0262	0.0256	0.0250	0.0244	0.0239	0.0233
-1.8	0.0359	0.0351	0.0344	0.0336	0.0329	0.0322	0.0314	0.0307	0.0301	0.0294
-1.7	0.0446	0.0436	0.0427	0.0418	0.0409	0.0401	0.0392	0.0384	0.0375	0.0367
-1.6	0.0548	0.0537	0.0526	0.0516	0.0505	0.0495	0.0485	0.0475	0.0465	0.0455
-1.5	0.0668	0.0655	0.0643	0.0630	0.0618	0.0606	0.0594	0.0582	0.0571	0.0559
-1.4	0.0808	0.0793	0.0778	0.0764	0.0749	0.0735	0.0721	0.0708	0.0694	0.0681
-1.3	0.0968	0.0951	0.0934	0.0918	0.0901	0.0885	0.0869	0.0853	0.0838	0.0823
-1.2	0.1151	0.1131	0.1112	0.1093	0.1075	0.1056	0.1038	0.1020	0.1003	0.0985
-1.1	0.1357	0.1335	0.1314	0.1292	0.1271	0.1251	0.1230	0.1210	0.1190	0.1170
-1.0	0.1587	0.1562	0.1539	0.1515	0.1492	0.1469	0.1446	0.1423	0.1401	0.1379
-0.9	0.1841	0.1814	0.1788	0.1762	0.1736	0.1711	0.1685	0.1660	0.1635	0.1611
-0.8	0.2119	0.2090	0.2061	0.2033	0.2005	0.1977	0.1949	0.1922	0.1894	0.1867
-0.7	0.2420	0.2389	0.2358	0.2327	0.2296	0.2266	0.2236	0.2206	0.2177	0.2148
-0.6	0.2743	0.2709	0.2676	0.2643	0.2611	0.2578	0.2546	0.2514	0.2483	0.2451
-0.5	0.3085	0.3050	0.3015	0.2981	0.2946	0.2912	0.2877	0.2843	0.2810	0.2776
-0.4	0.3446	0.3409	0.3372	0.3336	0.3300	0.3264	0.3228	0.3192	0.3156	0.3121
-0.3	0.3821	0.3783	0.3745	0.3707	0.3669	0.3632	0.3594	0.3557	0.3520	0.3483
-0.2	0.4207	0.4168	0.4129	0.4090	0.4052	0.4013	0.3974	0.3936	0.3897	0.3859
-0.1	0.4602	0.4562	0.4522	0.4483	0.4443	0.4404	0.4364	0.4325	0.4286	0.4247
-0.0	0.5000	0.4960	0.4920	0.4880	0.4840	0.4801	0.4761	0.4721	0.4681	0.4641

z	0.00	0.01	0.02	0.03	0.04	0.05	0.06	0.07	0.08	0.09
0.0	0.5000	0.5040	0.5080	0.5120	0.5160	0.5199	0.5239	0.5279	0.5319	0.5359
0.1	0.5398	0.5438	0.5478	0.5517	0.5557	0.5596	0.5636	0.5675	0.5714	0.5753
0.2	0.5793	0.5832	0.5871	0.5910	0.5948	0.5987	0.6026	0.6064	0.6103	0.6141
0.3	0.6179	0.6217	0.6255	0.6293	0.6331	0.6368	0.6406	0.6443	0.6480	0.6517
0.4	0.6554	0.6591	0.6628	0.6664	0.6700	0.6736	0.6772	0.6808	0.6844	0.6879
0.5	0.6915	0.6950	0.6985	0.7019	0.7054	0.7088	0.7123	0.7157	0.7190	0.7224
0.6	0.7257	0.7291	0.7324	0.7357	0.7389	0.7422	0.7454	0.7486	0.7517	0.7549
0.7	0.7580	0.7611	0.7642	0.7673	0.7704	0.7734	0.7764	0.7794	0.7823	0.7852
0.8	0.7881	0.7910	0.7939	0.7967	0.7995	0.8023	0.8051	0.8078	0.8106	0.8133
0.9	0.8159	0.8186	0.8212	0.8238	0.8264	0.8289	0.8315	0.8340	0.8365	0.8389
1.0	0.8413	0.8438	0.8461	0.8485	0.8508	0.8531	0.8554	0.8577	0.8599	0.8621
1.1	0.8643	0.8665	0.8686	0.8708	0.8729	0.8749	0.8770	0.8790	0.8810	0.8830
1.2	0.8849	0.8869	0.8888	0.8907	0.8925	0.8944	0.8962	0.8980	0.8997	0.9015
1.3	0.9032	0.9049	0.9066	0.9082	0.9099	0.9115	0.9131	0.9147	0.9162	0.9177
1.4	0.9192	0.9207	0.9222	0.9236	0.9251	0.9265	0.9279	0.9292	0.9306	0.9319
1.5	0.9332	0.9345	0.9357	0.9370	0.9382	0.9394	0.9406	0.9418	0.9429	0.9441
1.6	0.9452	0.9463	0.9474	0.9484	0.9495	0.9505	0.9515	0.9525	0.9535	0.9545
1.7	0.9554	0.9564	0.9573	0.9582	0.9591	0.9599	0.9608	0.9616	0.9625	0.9633
1.8	0.9641	0.9649	0.9656	0.9664	0.9671	0.9678	0.9686	0.9693	0.9699	0.9706
1.9	0.9713	0.9719	0.9726	0.9732	0.9738	0.9744	0.9750	0.9756	0.9761	0.9767
2.0	0.9772	0.9778	0.9783	0.9788	0.9793	0.9798	0.9803	0.9808	0.9812	0.9817
2.1	0.9821	0.9826	0.9830	0.9834	0.9838	0.9842	0.9846	0.9850	0.9854	0.9857
2.2	0.9861	0.9864	0.9868	0.9871	0.9875	0.9878	0.9881	0.9884	0.9887	0.9890
2.3	0.9893	0.9896	0.9898	0.9901	0.9904	0.9906	0.9909	0.9911	0.9913	0.9916
2.4	0.9918	0.9920	0.9922	0.9925	0.9927	0.9929	0.9931	0.9932	0.9934	0.9936
2.5	0.9938	0.9940	0.9941	0.9943	0.9945	0.9946	0.9948	0.9949	0.9951	0.9952
2.6	0.9953	0.9955	0.9956	0.9957	0.9959	0.9960	0.9961	0.9962	0.9963	0.9964
2.7	0.9965	0.9966	0.9967	0.9968	0.9969	0.9970	0.9971	0.9972	0.9973	0.9974
2.8	0.9974	0.9975	0.9976	0.9977	0.9977	0.9978	0.9979	0.9979	0.9980	0.9981
2.9	0.9981	0.9982	0.9982	0.9983	0.9984	0.9984	0.9985	0.9985	0.9986	0.9986
3.0	0.9987	0.9987	0.9987	0.9988	0.9988	0.9989	0.9989	0.9989	0.9990	0.9990
3.1	0.9990	0.9991	0.9991	0.9991	0.9992	0.9992	0.9992	0.9992	0.9993	0.9993
3.2	0.9993	0.9993	0.9994	0.9994	0.9994	0.9994	0.9994	0.9995	0.9995	0.9995
3.3	0.9995	0.9995	0.9995	0.9996	0.9996	0.9996	0.9996	0.9996	0.9996	0.9997
3.4	0.9997	0.9997	0.9997	0.9997	0.9997	0.9997	0.9997	0.9997	0.9997	0.9998

Reference citation: Image from
https://ask.learncbse.in/t/use-the-standard-normal-table-to-find-the-z-score-that-correspondents-to-the-given-percentile/22162.

For example, we can easily confirm this area property by looking at the Z-scores 0.00 or -0.00. These Z-scores represent the number of standard deviations the value is located from the mean and since it is zero, we are positioned on top of the mean which would be located at the peak of the normal curve. In this case the proportion of the total area under the normal curve to the left of this Z-score would be half the total area (50%) since the normal curve is symmetric about its mean, and from the table we see the value at the intersection of 0.0 (row) and 0.00 (column) is 0.5000, or 50%.

Another way of looking at this is if you look up the score in the Z-table, you can tell what percentage of the population is above or below your score. For example, say we calculated a Z-score of -2.47, we can find the percentage of the population that is below the score by using a left-hand z-table and finding the value which intersects -2.4 (row) and .07 (column) which is 0.0068, or 0.68%. This means that 0.68% of the total population is below this Z-score. And if we wanted to know the percentage of the population above this score then we simply subtract that value from 100%, or for our example 99.32% of the population is above this z-score.

To illustrate the use of a Z-table, we'll go through an example.

The scores on the math section of the SAT exam for the 1.6 million students who took the test in a given year followed a Normal distribution with a mean of 508 and standard deviation of 110. What percent of students who took the SAT scored less than 350 on the math section?

Solution:

- Step 1: Calculate the Z-score: $(350 - 508)/110 = -1.44$. The means that a score of 350 falls 1.44 standard deviations below the mean.
- Step 2: Use the left-handed Z-score table, since we are looking for the area that is less than the Z-score, to find the area to the left of the value; that is, we find the intersection between -1.4 (row) and 0.04 (column) which yields the value 0.0749, or 7.49%

Thus, we can conclude that about 7.5% of students (or 1.6 million x 0.075 = 120,000 students) who took the SAT scored less than 350 on the math section.

Z-SCORE TRANSFORMATIONS

Finally, we will summarize how the transformations we discussed affect the Z-score by way of an example.

Assume we have the set of quiz scores shown in the following dotplot, and we want to generate the standardized scores (or Z-scores) for the dataset.

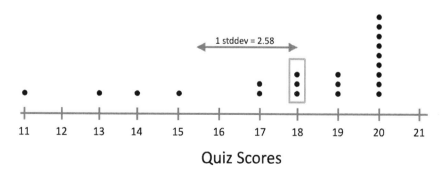

Quiz Scores

The following code listing shows how we can calculate the mean, standard deviation, and Z-scores, in Python with the NumPy library.

```
1    # Z-scores
2    import numpy as np
3    import matplotlib.pyplot as plt
4
5
6    def calc_zscores(data):
7        #data is the input data list
8        #return mean, standard deviation, and z-scores
9
10       mean = np.mean(data)
11       stddev = np.std(data)
12       zScores = (data - mean)/stddev
13       return(mean, stddev, zScores)
14
15
16   X = np.array([11, 13, 14, 15, 17, 17, 18, 18, 18, 19,
17                 19, 19, 20, 20, 20, 20, 20, 20, 20, 20, 20])
18   mean, std_dev, z_scores = calc_zscores(X)
19   print('Mean:', mean)
20   print('Standard Deviation:', np.round(std_dev, 2))
21   print('Z-scores:\n', np.round(z_scores, 2))
```

```
Mean: 18.0
Standard Deviation: 2.58
Z-scores:
[-2.71 -1.94 -1.55 -1.16 -0.39 -0.39 0. 0. 0. 0.39 0.39 0.39
 0.77 0.77 0.77 0.77 0.77 0.77 0.77 0.77 0.77]
```

Recall that transforming data into Z-scores involves subtracting a constant and dividing by a constant.

$$Z-Score = \frac{Value - Mean}{Standard\ Deviation}$$

We see that our dataset transforms to the following graph of standardized or Z-scores, and we can note the following conclusions.

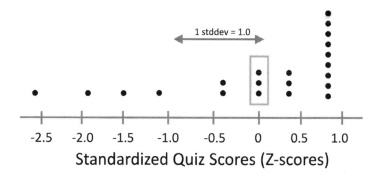

Standardized Quiz Scores (Z-scores)

First, the SHAPE of the distribution of Z-scores remains unchanged. Next, the mean of the distribution of Z-scores is always 0. This is because the transformation shifts the mean of the dataset distribution to 0 due to the subtraction that is done in the numerator of the Z-score equation of all the values by its mean. Note, the shifting of data is also known as "centering".

Finally, the standard deviation of the distribution of Z-scores is always 1. This is because we effectively compress all the values in the dataset by the standard deviation due to the division in the denominator of the Z-score equation such that any dataset value that was 1 standard deviation away from the mean (or 2.65 in the example) becomes 1 standard deviation, or 2.65 divided by 2.65 in this case.

CHAPTER 6:
Linear Algebra
Introduction
for Machine Learning

In this chapter, we'll introduce Linear Algebra and its applications to machine learning, including objects and their operations, special vectors and matrices, and applications of linear algebra.

LEARNING OBJECTIVES

By the end of this chapter, you will be able to do the following:

- Identify a format a scalar, vector, matrix, and tensor
- Perform vector addition, subtraction and multiplication
- Perform matrix addition and subtraction
- Perform matrix scalar multiplication, elementwise, and standard multiplication
- Create an n x n identity matrix
- Create the transpose of a matrix
- Calculate the determinant, cofactor, and adjugate of a matrix
- Calculate the inverse of a generic and diagonal matrix
- Calculate the L1 and L2 norm of a vector
- Calculate the covariance of a matrix
- Apply Eigenvalue decomposition to a dataset

6.1:
Introduction to Linear Algebra for Machine Learning

The use of Linear Algebra allows us to efficiently implement many machine learning algorithms, ranging from those characterized as "traditional", such as Regression and Classification, as well as more specialized algorithms such as Artificial Neural Networks, where a diagram of a Multi-layer Perceptron model (also known as a Deep Neural Network) is shown with an input dataset matrix and corresponding weight and bias matrices below.

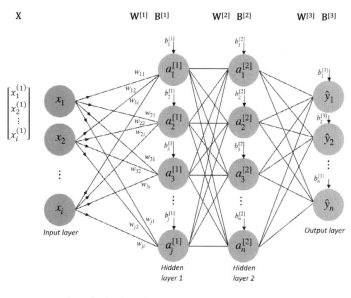

$$w_{xy} \rightarrow \begin{cases} x = destination\ node \\ y = source\ node \end{cases}$$

$$Z^{[1]} = W^{[1]} \cdot X + B^{[1]} = \begin{bmatrix} z_1^{[1](1)} \\ z_2^{[1](1)} \\ \vdots \\ z_j^{[1](1)} \end{bmatrix} = \begin{bmatrix} w_{11}^{[1]} & w_{12}^{[1]} & \cdots & w_{1i}^{[1]} \\ w_{21}^{[1]} & w_{22}^{[1]} & \cdots & w_{2i}^{[1]} \\ \vdots & \vdots & & \vdots \\ w_{j1}^{[1]} & w_{j2}^{[1]} & \cdots & w_{ji}^{[1]} \end{bmatrix} \cdot \begin{bmatrix} x_1^{(1)} \\ x_2^{(1)} \\ \vdots \\ x_j^{(1)} \end{bmatrix} + \begin{bmatrix} b_1^{[1]} \\ b_2^{[1]} \\ \vdots \\ b_j^{[1]} \end{bmatrix}$$

We will introduce the basic definitions and operations associated with scalars, vectors, matrices including tensors, and then we'll provide examples of their use in machine learning algorithms such as with Eigenvalue decomposition, which is used in feature reduction techniques, such as Principal Component analysis which maximizes the variances between independent variables along axes called principal components. Here, we will show several code examples to implement basic vector and matrix operations with both standard Python lists and using the NumPy library. After reviewing the code examples, you should see how much more efficient using the NumPy library will be based on its vectorized function implementations.

FUNDAMENTAL DATA OBJECTS

The fundamental objects that we'll use include the following:

- *Scalars* are what we are most familiar with in our normal exposure to number systems, consisting of magnitude and sign.
- *Vectors* contain both magnitude and direction and are comprised of an ordered group of scalars.
- *Matrices* include ordered groups of vectors.
- *Tensors* are a generalized collection of vectors or matrices.

An example representation of each of the data objects is shown in the following figure.

Scalar	Vector	Matrix	Tensor
1	$\begin{bmatrix} 1 \\ 2 \end{bmatrix}$	$\begin{bmatrix} 1 & 2 \\ 3 & 4 \end{bmatrix}$	$\begin{bmatrix} [1\ 2] & [3\ 4] \\ [5\ 6] & [7\ 8] \end{bmatrix}$

First, we'll discuss the *scalar*. As mentioned previously, scalars are what we are working with in our day-to-day use of numbers. The scalar is one of the basic building blocks of linear algebra, and it represents the magnitude of a feature in a dataset. We show a few examples in the following figure, such as volume, time, and temperature, and these represent their units of measure in terms of scalar values.

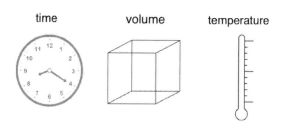

Next, a *vector* is comprised of an ordered group of scalars. In programming languages such as Python, we represent them in lists or arrays, where each element is a scalar and may represent, for example a feature, or independent variable, in a dataset. A vector contains both magnitude and direction and is usually represented in 2-D diagrams as an arrow with a length of the arrow proportional to the magnitude and the head of the arrow pointing in its direction. For example, the vector [10, 3] could be drawn on a 2-D coordinate system by placing the starting point (tail) at coordinate (0, 0), then placing the end point (head) by moving 10 units along the positive x-axis, and 3 units along the positive y-axis. The magnitude and direction could then be determined using right-triangle geometry and trigonometry.

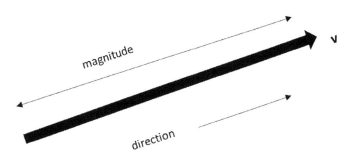

The size of a *vector* is equal to the number of scalars it contains, which could represent the number of dimensions in a coordinate system or the number of features in a dataset. Vectors are typically written using the notation shown in either horizontal or vertical form.

$$[x_1 \; x_2 \; x_3 \; \cdots \; x_i] \quad \begin{bmatrix} x_1 \\ x_2 \\ x_3 \\ \vdots \\ x_j \end{bmatrix}$$

A *matrix* is a group of vectors arranged in rows or columns, and is usually implemented as a collection of scalars arranged as individual elements in a 2-D data structure. The size of a matrix is equal to the number of elements it contains, and its shape is equal to the number of rows and columns it contains. In the example matrix shown below, the size would then be j • i and the shape would be (j, i). We note that the size and shape are sometimes used interchangeably, but we'll adhere to the definition stated here; that is, the size is the total number of elements, and the shape is the number of rows and columns which the matrix contains.

$$W^{[1]} = \begin{bmatrix} w_{11}^{[1]} & w_{12}^{[1]} & \cdots & w_{1i}^{[1]} \\ w_{21}^{[1]} & w_{22}^{[1]} & \cdots & w_{2i}^{[1]} \\ \vdots & \vdots & & \vdots \\ w_{j1}^{[1]} & w_{j2}^{[1]} & \cdots & w_{ji}^{[1]} \end{bmatrix}$$

Finally, a *tensor* is a generalization of the preceding objects with shapes ranging from zero for a scalar, to j for a vector where j is the number of elements, to (j, i), where j is the number of rows and i is the number of columns in a two-dimensional data structure, to (j, i, m) for a 3D tensor, where j is the number of rows, i is the number of columns and m is the depth of a three-dimensional cube. A tensor can continue to add dimensions, but we typically do not use more than 4 dimensions in most machine learning applications. A summary is shown in the following table.

Label	Scalar	Tensor-1D	Tensor-2D	Tensor-3D
Rank	0	1	2	3
Shape	[]	[j]	[j, i]	[j, i, m]
Example	7	$[x_1 \ x_2 \ \cdots \ x_i]$	$\begin{bmatrix} w_{11}^{[1]} & w_{12}^{[1]} & \cdots & w_{1i}^{[1]} \\ w_{21}^{[1]} & w_{22}^{[1]} & \cdots & w_{2i}^{[1]} \\ \vdots & \vdots & & \vdots \\ w_{j1}^{[1]} & w_{j2}^{[1]} & \cdots & w_{ji}^{[1]} \end{bmatrix}$	$\begin{bmatrix} \begin{bmatrix} w_{11}^{[m]} & w_{12}^{[m]} & \cdots & w_{1i}^{[m]} \\ w_{11}^{[2]} & w_{12}^{[2]} & \cdots & w_{1i}^{[2]} \\ \begin{bmatrix} w_{11}^{[1]} & w_{12}^{[1]} & \cdots & w_{1i}^{[1]} \\ w_{21}^{[1]} & w_{22}^{[1]} & \cdots & w_{2i}^{[1]} \\ \vdots & \vdots & & \vdots \\ w_{j1}^{[1]} & w_{j2}^{[1]} & \cdots & w_{ji}^{[1]} \end{bmatrix} \end{bmatrix} \end{bmatrix}$

VECTOR OPERATIONS

Next, we'll look at some common vector operations. In machine learning vector notation, the first element of a vector of size i has subscript 1 and the last element, subscript i, but when implementing with a Python data structure we use zero-based indexing, which requires the first element in the vector to be accessed with index 0, and the last element, with i − 1.

VECTOR OPERATIONS - ADDITION

Now one of the most basic vector operations is addition, where vectors of equal sizes are added together, one pair of elements at a time, where the pair added share the same index.

$$A = \begin{bmatrix} a_1 \\ a_2 \\ \vdots \\ a_j \end{bmatrix} \quad B = \begin{bmatrix} b_1 \\ b_2 \\ \vdots \\ b_j \end{bmatrix} \quad C = A + B = \begin{bmatrix} a_1 + b_1 \\ a_2 + b_2 \\ \vdots \\ a_j + b_j \end{bmatrix}$$

Here we show the element-by-element vector addition example, resulting in the vector C as the sum of A and B.

$$A = \begin{bmatrix} 1 \\ 2 \\ 3 \end{bmatrix} \quad B = \begin{bmatrix} 4 \\ 5 \\ 6 \end{bmatrix} \quad C = A + B = \begin{bmatrix} 5 \\ 7 \\ 9 \end{bmatrix}$$

The following code block and console output provides an example of vector addition with standard Python Lists and NumPy arrays.

```
1   #Vector Addition
2
3   import numpy as np
4
5   #Using Python Lists
6   A = [1, 2, 3]
7   B = [4, 5, 6]
8   C = []
9   for j in range(len(A)):
10      C.append(A[j] + B[j])
11
12  #Using NumPy
13  A_np = np.array([1, 2, 3])
14  B_np = np.array([4, 5, 6])
15  C_np = A_np + B_np
16
17  print('Python list:', C)
18  print('Numpy array:', C_np)
```

⤷ Python list: [5, 7, 9]
   Numpy array: [5 7 9]

VECTOR OPERATIONS - SCALAR MULTIPLICATION

Now a vector may be scaled by a value, through a process called scalar multiplication, where each element of the vector is multiplied by the scalar.

$$A = \begin{bmatrix} a_1 \\ a_2 \\ \vdots \\ a_j \end{bmatrix} \qquad c * A = \begin{bmatrix} c * a_1 \\ c * a_2 \\ \vdots \\ c * a_j \end{bmatrix}$$

The following example shows how we can perform scalar multiplication. If c is a scalar and A is a vector of size three, we can scale A by c, where the resultant matrix is the product of each element of the vector A and the scalar c.

$$A = \begin{bmatrix} 1 \\ 2 \\ 3 \end{bmatrix} \quad c = 7 \quad c * A = \begin{bmatrix} 7 * 1 \\ 7 * 2 \\ 7 * 3 \end{bmatrix} = \begin{bmatrix} 7 \\ 14 \\ 21 \end{bmatrix}$$

The following code block and console output provides an example of scalar multiplication with standard Python Lists and NumPy arrays.

1	#Scalar Multiplication
2	
3	import numpy as np
4	
5	#Using Python Lists
6	A = [1, 2, 3]
7	C = []
8	for j in range(len(A)):
9	C.append(7*A[j])
10	
11	#Using NumPy
12	A_np = np.array([1, 2, 3])
13	C_np = 7*A_np
14	
15	print('Python list:', C)
16	print('Numpy array:', C_np)

⤷ Python list: [7, 14, 21]
Numpy array: [7 14 21]

VECTOR OPERATIONS - DOT PRODUCT

One of the more important operations that we will implement with vectors is the "dot product". Geometrically, the dot product of two vectors is found by multiplying their Euclidean magnitude (or norm); that is, the square root of the sum of the squares of the elements, and the cosine of the angle between them. In other words, the geometric dot product of vectors A and B is the magnitude of A times the magnitude of B times the cosine of the angle formed between the vectors.

$$A \bullet B = |A||B|\cos\varnothing$$

Now, the more common interpretation of the dot-product used in machine learning is the Algebraic form. In this case, the dot product is the sum of the products of each of the elements of vectors of equal sizes.

$$A = \begin{bmatrix} a_1 \\ a_2 \\ \vdots \\ a_j \end{bmatrix} \quad B = \begin{bmatrix} b_1 \\ b_2 \\ \vdots \\ b_j \end{bmatrix} \quad A \cdot B = a_1b_1 + a_2b_2 + \cdots + a_jb_j$$

Both formulas shown above can be used to calculate the dot product of two vectors and will result in the same value, which will always be a scalar. One application of the dot product is shown here, where we can determine the type of angle formed by computation using the algebraic definition. For example, if we have two vectors whose dot product results in a positive value, we can conclude the vectors form an acute angle; that is, it is less than 90 degrees.

The following code block and console output provides an example of the algebraic dot product calculation with standard Python Lists and NumPy arrays.

```
1   #Algebraic Dot Product
2
3   import numpy as np
4
5   #Using Python Lists
6   A = [1, 2, 3]
7   B = [4, -5, 6]
8   C = 0
9   for j in range(len(A)):
10      C += A[j]*B[j]
11
12  #Using NumPy
13  A_np = np.array([1, 2, 3])
14  B_np = np.array([4, -5, 6])
15  C_np = np.dot(A_np, B_np)
16
17  print('Python list:', C)
18  print('Numpy array:', C_np)
```

```
Python list: 12
Numpy array: 12
```

MATRIX OPERATIONS

Next, we'll move on to matrix operations. Here we show a generic matrix of shape (j, i) comprised of j horizontal rows and i vertical columns, where the first subscript represents the row and the second subscript, the column. Note that except for the zero-based indexing scheme that Python data structures conform to, our notation adheres to the "row-major" format whereby accesses to the matrix would identify the row in the first array, followed by the column index in the second array.

$$W^{[1]} = \begin{bmatrix} w_{11}^{[1]} & w_{12}^{[1]} & \cdots & w_{1i}^{[1]} \\ w_{21}^{[1]} & w_{22}^{[1]} & \cdots & w_{2i}^{[1]} \\ \vdots & \vdots & & \vdots \\ w_{j1}^{[1]} & w_{j2}^{[1]} & \cdots & w_{ji}^{[1]} \end{bmatrix}$$

MATRIX OPERATIONS - ADDITION

Now, like vectors, matrices can be added, but they require that their shapes be equal. In this case, each element located at a specific row and column index in the resultant matrix is formed by summing the elements from each of the same row and column indices in the source matrices. The resultant matrix will therefore retain the same shape as each of the source matrices.

$$\begin{bmatrix} a_{11} & a_{12} & a_{13} \\ a_{21} & a_{22} & a_{23} \end{bmatrix} + \begin{bmatrix} b_{11} & b_{12} & b_{13} \\ b_{21} & b_{22} & b_{23} \end{bmatrix} = \begin{bmatrix} a_{11} + b_{11} & a_{12} + b_{12} & a_{13} + b_{13} \\ a_{21} + b_{21} & a_{22} + b_{22} & a_{23} + b_{23} \end{bmatrix}$$

Example:

$$\begin{bmatrix} 0 & -1 \\ 4 & -8 \\ -2 & 3 \end{bmatrix} + \begin{bmatrix} 5 & 1 \\ -3 & 2 \\ 9 & 4 \end{bmatrix} = \begin{bmatrix} 0+5 & -1+1 \\ 4+(-3) & -8+2 \\ -2+9 & 3+4 \end{bmatrix} = \begin{bmatrix} 5 & 0 \\ 1 & -6 \\ 7 & 7 \end{bmatrix}$$

The following code block and console output provides an example of *matrix* addition with standard Python Lists and NumPy arrays.

```
1    #Matrix Addition
2
3    import numpy as np
4
5    #Using Python Lists
6    Ma = [[0, -1],
7          [4, -8],
8          [-2, 3]]
9    Mb = [[5, 1],
10         [-3, 2],
11         [9, 4]]
12   Mc = []
13   for j in range(len(Ma)):        #rows
14       sub_list = []
15       for i in range(len(Ma[j])): #columns
16           sub_list.append(Ma[j][i] + Mb[j][i])
17       Mc.append(sub_list)
18
19   #Using NumPy
20   Ma_np = np.array([[3, -1],
21                     [4, -8],
22                     [-2, 3]])
23   Mb_np = np.array([[5, 1],
24                     [-3, 2],
25                     [9, 4]])
26   Mc_np = Ma_np + Mb_np
27
28   print('Python list:', Mc)
29   print('Numpy array:\n', Mc_np)
```

Python list: [[5, 0], [1, -6], [7, 7]]
Numpy array:
[[8 0]
 [1 -6]
 [7 7]]

MATRIX OPERATIONS - MULTIPLICATION (SCALAR)

Like vectors, a matrix of any shape can be multiplied by a scalar. In this case, each element of the matrix is multiplied by the scalar and the product is placed back at the same location in the matrix. The example shown here illustrates scalar multiplication.

$$2 * \begin{bmatrix} 1 & 2 & 3 \\ 4 & 5 & 6 \\ 7 & 8 & 9 \end{bmatrix} = \begin{bmatrix} 2*1 & 2*2 & 2*3 \\ 2*4 & 2*5 & 2*6 \\ 2*7 & 2*8 & 2*9 \end{bmatrix} = \begin{bmatrix} 2 & 4 & 6 \\ 8 & 10 & 12 \\ 14 & 16 & 18 \end{bmatrix}$$

The following code block and console output provides an example of matrix multiplication with standard Python Lists and NumPy arrays.

```
1    #Matrix Scalar Multiplication
2
3    import numpy as np
4
5
6    #Using Python Lists
7    Ma = [[1, 2, 3],
8         [4, 5, 6],
9         [7, 8, 9]]
10
11   Mc = []
12   for j in range(len(Ma)):          #rows
13       sub_list = []
14       for i in range(len(Ma[j])):   #columns
15           sub_list.append(2*Ma[j][i])
16       Mc.append(sub_list)
17
18   #Using NumPy
19   Ma_np = np.array([[1, 2, 3],
20                    [4, 5, 6],
21                    [7, 8, 9]])
22   Mc_np = 2*Ma_np
23
24   print('Python list:', Mc)
25   print('Numpy array:\n', Mc_np)
```

```
Python list: [[2, 4, 6], [8, 10, 12], [14, 16, 18]]
Numpy array:
[[ 2  4  6]
 [ 8 10 12]
 [14 16 18]]
```

MATRIX OPERATIONS - MULTIPLICATION

So far, the matrix operations have been straightforward to implement and consistent with vector operations, but matrix multiplication is a bit more complicated. First, some multiplication operations in machine learning algorithms implement element-by-element products where the multiplicand and multiplier matrices each have the same shape, for example (j, i), resulting in a matrix of the same shape, (j, i). Here the product matrix is formed by multiplying the elements from the multiplicand and multiplier matrices at each of the individual row and column indices and storing the result at the same row and column index. This type of matrix multiplication operation is most commonly known as "elementwise" or Hadamard products, and is used in Convolutional and Recurrent Neural Network implementations.

$$\begin{bmatrix} a_{11} & a_{12} & a_{13} \\ a_{21} & a_{22} & a_{23} \end{bmatrix} * \begin{bmatrix} b_{11} & b_{12} & b_{13} \\ b_{21} & b_{22} & b_{23} \end{bmatrix} = \begin{bmatrix} a_{11} * b_{11} & a_{12} * b_{12} & a_{13} * b_{13} \\ a_{21} * b_{21} & a_{22} * b_{22} & a_{23} * b_{23} \end{bmatrix}$$

$$(j, i) \qquad\qquad (j, i) \qquad\qquad\qquad (j, i)$$

The following code and console output provides an example of elementwise matrix multiplication with standard Python Lists and NumPy arrays. Note that with the NumPy library, we use either the asterisk symbol (*) or the function, *multiply*, to perform the operation.

```
1    #Matrix Multiplication - Elementwise (Hadamard)
2
3    #Using Python Lists
4    Ma = [[6, -2, 1],
5          [1, -1, 3]]
6    Mb = [[3, 5, -3],
7          [2, 1, 2]]
8    Mc = []
9
10   for j in range(len(Ma)):          #rows
11       sub_list = []
12       for i in range(len(Ma[j])):   #columns
13           sub_list.append(Ma[j][i] * Mb[j][i])
14       Mc.append(sub_list)
15
16   #Using NumPy
17   Ma_np = np.array([[6, -2, 1],
18                     [1, -1, 3]])
19   Mb_np = np.array([[3, 5, -3],
20                     [2, 1, 2]])
21   Mc_np = Ma_np * Mb_np
22   Md_np = np.multiply(Ma_np, Mb_np)
23
24   print('Python list:', Mc)
25   print('Numpy array using *:\n', Mc_np)
26   print('Numpy array using multiply:\n', Md_np)
```

→ Python list: [[18, -10, -3], [2, -1, 6]]
Numpy array using *:
[[18 -10 -3]
 [2 -1 6]]
Numpy array using multiply:
[[18 -10 -3]
 [2 -1 6]]

Now, the more traditional matrix multiplication is described using the dot product. For two matrices to be multiplied together, the number of columns in the first matrix must equal the number of rows in the second matrix, and results in a matrix with shape equal to the number of rows in the first matrix by the number of columns in a second. In other words, a matrix of shape (j, i) multiplied by another matrix with shape (i, k) will result in a matrix of shape (j, k). You can think of the product shape being constructed from the outer dimension of the two matrices j and k, with the inner dimension, i in this example, being omitted as shown in the following figure.

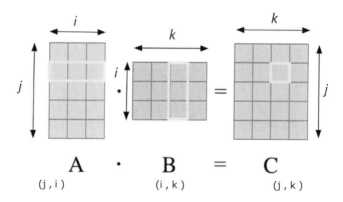

Each element in the nth row and m^{th} column in the result matrix is calculated from the dot product of the nth row of the first matrix, that is the nth row vector, and the mth column in the second matrix, the mth column vector. Recall that the dot-product for vectors is calculated as the sum of the products of each of the elements.

$$= \begin{bmatrix} row\ 1\ \cdot\ col\ 1 & row\ 1\ \cdot\ col\ 2 \\ row\ 2\ \cdot\ col\ 1 & row\ 2\ \cdot\ col\ 2 \end{bmatrix}$$

$$\begin{bmatrix} a_{11} & a_{12} & a_{13} \\ a_{21} & a_{22} & a_{23} \end{bmatrix} * \begin{bmatrix} b_{11} & b_{12} \\ b_{21} & b_{22} \\ b_{31} & b_{32} \end{bmatrix}$$

$$= \begin{bmatrix} a_{11}*b_{11} + a_{12}*b_{21} + a_{13}*b_{31} & a_{11}*b_{12} + a_{12}*b_{22} + a_{13}*b_{32} \\ a_{21}*b_{11} + a_{22}*b_{21} + a_{23}*b_{31} & a_{21}*b_{12} + a_{22}*b_{22} + a_{23}*b_{32} \end{bmatrix}$$

(2, 3)　　　(3, 2)　　　　　　　　　　　(2, 2)

The following example shows the steps in computing the product of a two-by-three matrix with a three by two matrix. We know that this will work since their inner dimensions, 3, in this case are the same. We also know that the resultant matrix will have a shape $(2, 2)$, since the number of rows in the first matrix is 2 and the number of columns and the second is also 2. In other words, we omit the inner dimension 3. Now for each element located at position rji, we compute the dot product of the corresponding j^{th} row and the ith column. We can see how each element is calculated in this example, which results in that final 2x2 matrix shown.

$$= \begin{bmatrix} row\ 1\ \cdot\ col\ 1 & row\ 1\ \cdot\ col\ 2 \\ row\ 2\ \cdot\ col\ 1 & row\ 2\ \cdot\ col\ 2 \end{bmatrix}$$

$$\begin{bmatrix} 6 & -2 & 1 \\ 1 & -1 & 3 \end{bmatrix} * \begin{bmatrix} 3 & 2 \\ 5 & 1 \\ -3 & 2 \end{bmatrix}$$

$$= \begin{bmatrix} (6*3) + (-2*5) + (1*-3) & (6*2) + (-2*1) + (1*2) \\ (1*3) + (-1*5) + (3*-3) & (1*2) + (-1*1) + (3*2) \end{bmatrix}$$

$$= \begin{bmatrix} 5 & 12 \\ -11 & 7 \end{bmatrix}$$

(2, 3)　　　(3, 2)　　　　　　　　　　　(2, 2)

The following code block and console output provides an example of dot-product matrix multiplication with standard Python Lists and NumPy arrays. Note that with the NumPy library, we can use either the "at" symbol, @ or the function, *dot*, to perform the operation.

```
1    #Matrix Multiplication - Dot product
2
3    #Using Python Lists
4    Ma = [[6, -2, 1],
5          [1, -1, 3]]
6    Mb = [[3, 2],
7          [5, 1],
8          [-3, 2]]
9    Mc = [[0, 0],
10         [0, 0]]
11
12   for j in range(len(Ma)):
13       for k in range(len(Mb[j])):
14           for i in range(len(Mb)):
15               Mc[j][k] += Ma[j][i] * Mb[i][k]
16
17   #Using NumPy
18   Ma_np = np.array([[6, -2, 1],
19                     [1, -1, 3]])
20   Mb_np = np.array([[3, 2],
21                     [5, 1],
22                     [-3, 2]])
23   Mc_np = Ma_np @ Mb_np
24   Md_np = np.dot(Ma_np, Mb_np)
25
26   print('Python list:', Mc)
27   print('Numpy array using @:\n', Mc_np)
28   print('Numpy array using dot:\n', Md_np)
```

```
Python list: [[5, 12], [-11, 7]]
Numpy array using @:
[[ 5 12]
 [-11 7]]
Numpy array using dot:
[[ 5 12]
 [-11 7]]
```

IDENTITY MATRIX

A useful but simple matrix used in Linear Algebra and machine learning is the *Identity* matrix. The Identity matrix is simply a square matrix where all elements on the diagonal from the upper left to the bottom right are 1's, and all other elements are 0. Various identity matrices of different dimensions are shown below.

$$\begin{bmatrix} 1 & 0 \\ 0 & 1 \end{bmatrix} \qquad \begin{bmatrix} 1 & 0 & 0 \\ 0 & 1 & 0 \\ 0 & 0 & 1 \end{bmatrix} \qquad \begin{bmatrix} 1 & 0 & \cdots & 0 \\ 0 & 1 & \cdots & 0 \\ \vdots & \vdots & \ddots & \vdots \\ 0 & 0 & \cdots & 1 \end{bmatrix}$$

$$(2,2) \qquad\qquad (3,3) \qquad\qquad (j,j)$$

The identity matrix is special because it plays a role in matrix operations similar to how the value 1 works with scalars. This matrix has the property that if we multiply it with any matrix A, the result will be matrix A. We show an example of this property below.

$$\begin{bmatrix} 1 & 0 \\ 0 & 1 \end{bmatrix} \cdot \begin{bmatrix} 1 & 2 & 3 \\ 4 & 5 & 6 \end{bmatrix} = \begin{bmatrix} (1*1)+(0*4) & (1*2)+(0*5) & (1*3)+(0*6) \\ (0*1)+(1*4) & (0*2)+(1*5) & (0*3)+(1*6) \end{bmatrix} = \begin{bmatrix} 1 & 2 & 3 \\ 4 & 5 & 6 \end{bmatrix}$$

MATRIX TRANSPOSE

Another important but simple operation is called the *transpose* of a matrix. The transpose operation simply means that we interchange all the rows and columns in the matrix; or in other words, we reflect the elements in the matrix across its main diagonal. This also means the shape of the transpose matrix is reversed. An example of a transpose matrix is shown below. Here we see the notation which represents the transpose operation is the superscript T. Now, why do we transpose operations? The transpose is often used to rearrange matrices into a form that will allow for dot products or matrix multiplications in machine learning algorithms, as we will see in the future courses of this series.

$$\begin{bmatrix} 6 & -2 & 1 \\ 1 & -1 & 3 \end{bmatrix}^T = \begin{bmatrix} 6 & 1 \\ -2 & -1 \\ 1 & 3 \end{bmatrix}$$

$$(2,3) \qquad\qquad (3,2)$$

MATRIX DETERMINANT

Yet another important matrix operation is the determinant. One of the most common uses of the determinant is calculating an inverse of a matrix. Now the determinant can be calculated for square matrices only and will result in a scalar. Examples of the generic calculation is shown here for a (2×2) and (3×3) matrix, and a specific example for a (4×4) matrix is also shown.

For example, when working with a two-by-two matrix, the determinant is simply calculated as the difference of the product of the cross terms.

Given:

$$A = \begin{bmatrix} a & b \\ c & d \end{bmatrix}$$

the determinant of
A is calculated as:

$$det(A) = |A| = \begin{vmatrix} a & b \\ c & d \end{vmatrix} = ad - bc$$

When working with a larger shape matrix, we need to break it down into successively smaller determinants until we end up with two-by-two determinants, which we can then compute directly with the difference of the cross-products. We do this by selecting a row in the original matrix then multiplying each term in the row by its matrix "minor", where the minor is defined as the determinant of the elements remaining when we omit all the elements in the row and the column belonging to that term. We see that illustrated here for a (3×3) matrix.

Given:

$$A = \begin{bmatrix} a & b & c \\ d & e & f \\ g & h & i \end{bmatrix}$$

the determinant of
A is calculated as:

$$= |A| = \begin{vmatrix} a & b & c \\ d & e & f \\ g & h & i \end{vmatrix} = a\begin{vmatrix} e & f \\ h & i \end{vmatrix} - b\begin{vmatrix} d & f \\ g & i \end{vmatrix} + c\begin{vmatrix} d & e \\ g & h \end{vmatrix}$$

$$= (aei + bfg + cdh) - (ceg + bdi + afh)$$

In this case, our three-by-three determinant breaks down into the terms in the first row multiplied by each term's minor. For instance, the term a has a minor constructed with the elements remaining after we cross out the elements in the row and the column that belong to a; that is, the first row and the first column in this case.

Now you may have noticed the alternating pattern of plus and minus signs as we multiply each term across a row with its minor, we call this the "array of signs", and is calculated as:

$(-1)^{(j+i)}$, where j and i are the matrix row and column index respectively.

Note that the row and column indices may use Python data structure zero-based indexing; for example, $[0][0]$ for the first row and first column or the scheme presented previously using subscripts "11" . We call the result of multiplying $(-1)^{(j+i)}$ by the minor a "cofactor", and we'll see how cofactors are useful when calculating the inverse of a matrix.

We show an example of how we can start the determinant calculation for a (4×4) matrix here.

$$\text{Example: } A = \begin{bmatrix} -1 & -2 & 3 & 2 \\ 0 & 1 & 4 & -2 \\ 3 & -1 & 4 & 0 \\ 2 & 1 & 0 & 3 \end{bmatrix} \rightarrow |A| = -2\begin{vmatrix} -2 & 3 & 2 \\ 1 & 4 & -2 \\ -1 & 4 & 0 \end{vmatrix} + 1\begin{vmatrix} -1 & 3 & 2 \\ 0 & 4 & -2 \\ 3 & 4 & 0 \end{vmatrix} - 0\begin{vmatrix} -1 & -2 & 2 \\ 0 & 1 & -2 \\ 3 & -1 & 0 \end{vmatrix} + 3\begin{vmatrix} -1 & -2 & 3 \\ 0 & 1 & 4 \\ 3 & -1 & 4 \end{vmatrix}$$

In this example, we select a row in the original matrix to expand about, then calculate the cofactors. Note that we selected the fourth row to expand about which is permissible, and we chose the fourth row to take advantage of the 0 in the third column, which will simplify the calculation since the product of 0 times the (3×3) minor attached to it will be 0, thus simplifying the calculation. The remaining steps of solving each of the (3×3) determinants as were described above.

While it is possible to compute the determinant of a matrix using standard Python Lists, it is not recommended due to the complexity. There are example implementations that utilize recursive routines to provide generic functionality for different sized matrices, but fortunately NumPy also provides a function in its linear algebra library, *numpy.linalg*. The following code and console output provides an example of matrix determinant calculations using NumPy.

```
1    #Matrix Determinant using NumPy
2
3    import numpy as np
4
5    A_np = np.array([[3, 7],
6                     [2, 1]])
7    B_np = np.array([[-1, -2, 3, 2],
8                     [ 0, 1, 4, -2],
9                     [ 3, -1, 4, 0],
10                    [ 2, 1, 0, 3]])
11
12   C_np = np.linalg.det(A_np)
13   D_np = np.linalg.det(B_np)
14
15   print('Numpy array using linalg library:\n', np.round(C_np,1))
16   print('Numpy array using linalg library:\n', np.round(D_np,1))
```

Numpy array using linalg library:
-11.0
Numpy array using linalg library:
-185.0

MATRIX COFACTOR AND ADJUGATE

We described the *cofactor* of a matrix as the product of $(-1)^{(j+i)}$ and the minor, where j and i are the row and column index respectively. To calculate the cofactor, we do the following. First, find the minor of each element of the matrix by excluding the row and column of that element, and then finding the determinant of the remaining elements of the matrix. Next, find the cofactor of the element by multiplying this value with -1 to the power of the position indices of that element: $(-1)^{(j+i)}$. Each of these cofactor elements are then arranged in a matrix at those j and i positions. Note that we show the element indexing as zero-based, but the procedure is the same if using our notation defining index "11" for the first row and first column.

For a (2 x 2) matrix, the cofactor matrix is straightforward to compute since excluding the row and column for a given element results in only one element remaining.

Given: $$A = \begin{bmatrix} a & b \\ c & d \end{bmatrix}$$

the Cofactor Matrix of A: $$= \begin{bmatrix} c_{00} & c_{01} \\ c_{10} & c_{11} \end{bmatrix} = \begin{bmatrix} d & -c \\ -b & a \end{bmatrix}$$

For a (3 x 3) matrix, the calculation is a bit more involved. To demonstrate this example, we write the A matrix with zero-based indices so that the: $(-1)^{(j+i)}$ factor will generate the correct sign.

Given: $$A = \begin{bmatrix} a_{00} & a_{01} & a_{02} \\ a_{10} & a_{11} & a_{12} \\ a_{20} & a_{21} & a_{22} \end{bmatrix}$$

where cji is the cofactor at (j, i)

the Cofactor Matrix of A: $$= \begin{bmatrix} c_{00} & c_{01} & c_{02} \\ c_{10} & c_{11} & c_{12} \\ c_{20} & c_{21} & c_{22} \end{bmatrix}$$

We show a few of the cofactor calculations as follows.

$$c_{00} = (-1)^{0+0} \cdot \begin{vmatrix} a_{11} & a_{12} \\ a_{21} & a_{22} \end{vmatrix} = +(a_{11} * a_{22} - a_{12} * a_{21})$$

$$c_{01} = (-1)^{0+1} \cdot \begin{vmatrix} a_{10} & a_{12} \\ a_{20} & a_{22} \end{vmatrix} = -(a_{10} * a_{22} - a_{12} * a_{20})$$

$$\vdots$$

$$c_{22} = (-1)^{2+2} \cdot \begin{vmatrix} a_{00} & a_{01} \\ a_{10} & a_{11} \end{vmatrix} = +(a_{00} * a_{11} - a_{01} * a_{10})$$

Now if we simply transpose the elements in a cofactor matrix, we end up with what is called an *adjugate* matrix. We will see how we can use the adjugate to compute the inverse of a matrix next.

Given:

$$A = \begin{bmatrix} a_{00} & a_{01} & a_{02} \\ a_{10} & a_{11} & a_{12} \\ a_{20} & a_{21} & a_{22} \end{bmatrix}$$

the Adjugate Matrix of A:

$$Adj(A) = \begin{bmatrix} c_{00} & c_{01} & c_{02} \\ c_{10} & c_{11} & c_{12} \\ c_{20} & c_{21} & c_{22} \end{bmatrix}^T = \begin{bmatrix} c_{00} & c_{10} & c_{20} \\ c_{01} & c_{11} & c_{21} \\ c_{02} & c_{12} & c_{22} \end{bmatrix}$$

where cji is the cofactor at (j, i)

MATRIX INVERSE

The final basic matrix operation we will consider is the matrix inverse. What we want to do is to find an inverse such that a matrix times its inverse is equal to the identity matrix,

$$M \bullet M^{-1} = I$$

The inverse of a matrix does not exist for all matrices. For a matrix to be invertible (meaning the inverse exists), it must be linearly independent. This means that each row in the matrix must not contain a combination of rows or columns that when added or subtracted together, or scaled and added or subtracted is equal to zero. We must also ensure that the matrix has a non-zero determinant.

Now, matrix inverses can be complex to calculate and there are many methods that can be used. We will look at two methods here, but also note that most machine learning algorithms that require a matrix inversion can be done through dedicated library functions. However, we will go through the procedure on inverting a matrix for completeness, then show an example using a function in the NumPy linear algebra library.

One of the more popular matrix inversion techniques used is a method called "Gauss-Jordan". In this method, we append the identity matrix of the same dimensions to the right of the main matrix, where the main matrix must be square. If the main matrix happens not to be square, then we can append zeros to the rows to make it square.

We then reduce the main matrix to a special case of what is called its row echelon form using elementary row operations. The row echelon form amounts to three basic requirements:

1. Rows of all zeros are located at the bottom

2. Nonzero rows have 1 for first nonzero entry

3. Successive rows have leading 1 to right of preceding row

First, we move all rows of zeros to the bottom of the matrix. Next, we use techniques such as elementary row operations to interchange rows or multiply one row by a non-zero constant and add or subtract it from another row to produce a one in the first non-zero entry of a row. We then arrange the rows so that successive rows have a leading "1" to the right of the preceding row. An example of a three-by-three matrix in row echelon form is shown.

$$\begin{bmatrix} 1 & 2 & -1 \\ 0 & 1 & 3 \\ 0 & 0 & 1 \end{bmatrix}$$

The identity matrix is a special form of row echelon form, called *reduced row echelon*. A matrix is in reduced row-echelon form if: in each row, the left-most nonzero entry is 1 (called the leading 1) and the column that contains this 1 has all other entries equal to 0. Then the leading 1 in the second row or beyond is to the right of the leading 1 in the row just above it. Note that there are cases where a reduced row echelon is not the identity matrix such as with non-square matrices (Identity matrices are always square), or with square matrices that have all-zero rows.

We covered properties of row echelon to provide some continuity with the description of the Gauss-Jordan matrix inversion method. As stated, we append the identity matrix of the same dimensions to the right of the main matrix, where the main matrix must be square. Then we perform elementary row operations including interchanging rows, scaling (multiplying) a row or column by a non-zero number and adding (or subtracting) a scaled row or column to another row or column, to transform the main matrix into its reduced row echelon form (or identity matrix), and at the point, the right side that was originally the appended identity matrix will be the main matrix inverse. Note, that if we are unable to transform the main matrix into the identity matrix, then the inverse does not exist.

Now the Gauss-Jordan matrix inversion method is popular but a another, simpler, method exists called the *matrix of minors* or *adjugate* method and involves the operations we have previously discussed; that is, the determinant and the adjugate. In this method, the inverse of a matrix can be computed by dividing the adjugate of the matrix by its determinant. Note that this is the reason the determinant of the matrix must be non-zero, because if it was not, then we would have a divide-by-zero condition.

Recall that the adjugate of a matrix can be computed as the transpose of the cofactor matrix. We described the cofactors as the product of $(-1)^{(j+i)}$ and the minor, where j and i are the row and column index, respectively.

Given:
$$A = \begin{bmatrix} a & b \\ c & d \end{bmatrix}$$

the inverse of A:
$$A^{-1} = \frac{1}{|A|} \cdot Adj(A) = \frac{1}{ad-bc}\begin{bmatrix} d & -b \\ -c & a \end{bmatrix}$$

For example, we show the inverse calculation for a (2×2) matrix below using the adjugate method:

Given:
$$A = \begin{bmatrix} 1 & 2 \\ -2 & 0 \end{bmatrix}$$

the inverse of A:
$$A^{-1} = \frac{1}{|A|} \cdot Adj(A) = \frac{1}{0-(-4)}\begin{bmatrix} 0 & -2 \\ 2 & 1 \end{bmatrix} = \begin{bmatrix} 0 & -0.5 \\ 0.5 & 0.25 \end{bmatrix}$$

For a (3×3) generic matrix, we set up the inverse calculation as shown.

Given:

$$A = \begin{bmatrix} a & b & c \\ d & e & f \\ g & h & j \end{bmatrix}$$

the inverse of A:

$$A^{-1} = \frac{1}{|A|} \cdot Adj(A) = \frac{1}{|A|} \cdot \begin{bmatrix} \begin{vmatrix} e & f \\ h & i \end{vmatrix} & \begin{vmatrix} c & b \\ i & h \end{vmatrix} & \begin{vmatrix} b & c \\ e & f \end{vmatrix} \\ \begin{vmatrix} f & d \\ i & g \end{vmatrix} & \begin{vmatrix} a & c \\ g & i \end{vmatrix} & \begin{vmatrix} c & a \\ f & d \end{vmatrix} \\ \begin{vmatrix} d & e \\ g & h \end{vmatrix} & \begin{vmatrix} b & a \\ h & g \end{vmatrix} & \begin{vmatrix} a & b \\ d & e \end{vmatrix} \end{bmatrix}$$

Finally, regarding our Python implementations, like with the determinant, NumPy supports a matrix inverse function in its linear algebra library, *numpy. linalg.* The following code block and console output provides an example of matrix inverse calculations using NumPy.

```
1   #Matrix Inverse using NumPy
2
3   import numpy as np
4
5
6   A_np = np.array([[1, 2],
7                    [-2, 0]])
8   B_np = np.array([[-1, -2, 3],
9                    [ 0, 1, 4],
10                   [ 3, -1, 4]])
11
12  C_np = np.linalg.inv(A_np)
13  D_np = np.linalg.inv(B_np)
14
15  print('Numpy array using linalg library:\n', np.round(C_np,2))
16  print('Numpy array using linalg library:\n', np.round(D_np,2))
```

```
Numpy array using linalg library:
[[-0. -0.5 ]
 [ 0.5 0.25]]
Numpy array using linalg library:
[[-0.2 -0.12 0.27]
 [-0.29 0.32 -0.1 ]
 [ 0.07 0.17 0.02]]
```

LINEAR ALGEBRA - SPECIAL VECTORS AND MATRICES

Next, will continue our discussion of linear algebra data structures and focus on the more advanced operations we use specifically in machine learning. This chapter, along with the topics covered in statistics, and calculus in this series form the fundamental mathematics that we will need to understand most of the concepts behind the traditional machine-learning algorithms such as regression, classification, feature reduction, recommender systems, and in neural network applications in deep learning.

DIAGONAL MATRIX

First, we'll look at a few special types of vectors and matrices that we use in machine learning and Data Science. Previously, we discussed the identity matrix as one example of a matrix in reduced row echelon form, but the identity matrix is also a special form of a *diagonal* matrix. A diagonal matrix contains non-zero entries along its main diagonal and zeros elsewhere. More formally, if M is a matrix, then its diagonal form is:

$$M_{ji} \neq 0 \text{ for } j = i \text{ and } M_{ji} = 0 \text{ for } j \neq i.$$

$$\text{Identity matrix } (j \times j): \begin{bmatrix} 1 & 0 & 0 & \cdots & 0 \\ 0 & 1 & 0 & \cdots & 0 \\ 0 & 0 & 1 & \cdots & 0 \\ \vdots & \vdots & \vdots & \ddots & \vdots \\ 0 & 0 & 0 & \cdots & 1 \end{bmatrix}$$

If we have a vector, v, we can form a square diagonal matrix called diag(v) if the entries along the diagonal are the entries of v and all the other entries are zero. This matrix, diag(v), has some nice properties that provide efficient computation, which can be helpful when implementing complex machine learning algorithms, one of which is the inverse. We saw the complexities in calculating a matrix inverse previously, but if every element in v is non-zero, then an inverse exists $diag^{-1}(v)$ and its inverse is simply the inverse of each of the elements along its diagonal. That is, we compute the inverse of each element along the diagonal such that:

$$diag^{-1}(v) = diag\left(\frac{1}{v_i}\right) \text{ if } v_i \neq 0$$

There are also efficiency gains with multiplication operations involving a diagonal matrix. Specifically, diag(v) • a = v * a ; that is, the dot product of the diagonal matrix and the vector a can be computed by taking the Hadamard (elementwise) product of the vectors, v and a. This provides memory efficiencies in that all the 0's in the matrix do not need to be stored. We will see this is a useful property when we discuss the gradient derivations used in backpropagation in the Deep Neural Networks course.

L1, L2, MAX NORM

The *norm* of a vector has the following generalized notation and is defined as the length or the magnitude of the vector.

$$\|v\|_p = \left(\sum_i |v_i|^p\right)^{\frac{1}{p}}$$

Because we're computing the magnitude, the norm is always greater than or equal to zero. In the generalized equation, p is the "level" of the norm we are taking, with the most common being L1 (level 1), L2 (level 2) and the max norm.

The L1 norm of a vector is also known as the Manhattan norm and is equal to the sum of the absolute values of each of the elements in the vector. You are likely familiar with L1 norm from a basic algebra class, this is also known as the Manhattan distance.

$$\|v\|_1 = |v_1| + |v_2| + \cdots + |v_n|$$

The L2 norm is known as the Euclidean norm and should be another familiar concept from basic algebra. The L2 norm is equal to the square root of the sum of the squares of each of the vector elements, also known as the Euclidean distance.

$$\|v\|_2 = \sqrt{v_1^2 + v_1^2 + \cdots + v_n^2}$$

Finally, the max norm is the maximum element in the vector.

$$\|v\|_\infty = max|v_i|$$

For example, we show the L1, L2, and max norm for the vector: v = [1, -2, 3]

L1 : $\|\boldsymbol{v}\|_1$	L2 : $\|\boldsymbol{v}\|_2$	Lmax : $\|\boldsymbol{v}\|_\infty$
$\|\boldsymbol{v}\|_1 = 1 + 2 + 3 = 6$	$\|\boldsymbol{v}\|_2 = \sqrt{1 + 4 + 9} = \sqrt{14}$	$\|\boldsymbol{v}\|_\infty = 3$

Now, why do we need the norm in machine learning? Norms are commonly used to scale a vector in the dataset, and this can be done by dividing each of the elements in the vector by its norm. The norm is also used in the error evaluation step of a machine learning model training sequence, which is commonly computed as the difference between the output predicted by the model and the expected output. The norm can further be used in regularization in machine learning regression models, for example with Lasso and Ridge Regression. We will learn about applications of the norm in machine learning models in the next course of this series.

UNIT NORM

Now that we have a grasp of the norm, we can define a few other types of vectors and matrices. The unit vector is one which has a unit norm. In other words, the L2 norm of vector v is 1. We will see how we use this in what is called Singular Value Decomposition and Eigenvalue decomposition.

$$\|\boldsymbol{v}\|_2 = 1$$

ORTHOGONAL VECTORS

Vectors are said to be orthogonal if the angle between them is 90 degrees, or in linear algebra terms at the dot product is zero.

$$v \cdot w = 0 \rightarrow v \perp w$$

ORTHONORMAL VECTORS AND MATRICES

Orthonormal vectors are ones which are both orthogonal and have unit norm. An orthonormal matrix, M, is a square matrix whose columns are orthonormal vectors. This means that an orthonormal matrix times its transpose is the identity matrix.

$$M \cdot M^T = I$$

Now, because we know that a matrix times its inverse is also identity, we can conclude that the inverse of an orthonormal matrix is its transpose, which, like the diagonal matrix discussed previously, is computationally efficient to calculate. Orthonormal matrices are also used in singular value decomposition, which we will briefly discuss next.

$$M \cdot M^{-1} = I \longrightarrow M^{-1} = M^T$$

The following code block shows an example orthonormal matrix, U, and the result of computing U • U^T as well as the result of comparing each of the elements of U^{-1} (inverse) and U^T (transpose).

```
1   #Orthonormal matrix
2
3   import numpy as np
4
5   U = np.array([[ 0.29194724, 0.48414319, 0.11214409, 0.01515674, 0.81704722],
6    [ 0.36153521, -0.4674602, 0.72261735, 0.3561343, 0.04202128],
7    [ 0.87205863, 0.0257873, -0.25278854, -0.30470362, -0.28653522],
8    [ 0.15252612, 0.11795344, -0.42842901, 0.8789565, -0.08189522],
9    [ 0.01756805, -0.72973169, -0.46668449, -0.08677452, 0.49179142]]
10  )
11
12  print(np.round(np.dot(U, U.T), 1))
13  print(np.round(np.linalg.inv(U), 2) == np.round(U.T, 2))
```

```
[[ 1. 0. -0. 0. 0.]
 [ 0. 1. -0. 0. 0.]
 [-0. -0. 1. 0. -0.]
 [ 0. 0. 0. 1. 0.]
 [ 0. 0. -0. 0. 1.]]
[[ True True True True True]
 [ True True True True True]
 [ True True True True True]
 [ True True True True True]
 [ True True True True True]]
```

COVARIANCE MATRIX

Next, we will discuss *covariance* and the *covariance matrix* which we'll use when performing Eigenvalue decomposition. The covariance is a measure of the direction of the relationship between two variables. The covariance measure is like correlation, where correlation can be thought of as a normalized version of covariance, where the correlation value is limited to between -1 and +1.

If a covariance measure is positive, the dependent variables increase or decrease together with the independent variables, whereas if it is negative, the variables increase or decrease inversely, meaning if one variable increases, the other decreases and vice versa. Further, if the covariance is zero, then the variables do not have any increasing or decreasing relationship.

The covariance matrix is an $(n \times n)$ square symmetric matrix, where n is the number of dimensions or independent variables (also known as features in machine learning) in the data. An example covariance matrix is as shown for n = 3 features or independent variables.

$$Cov = \sum = \begin{bmatrix} Cov(x,x) & Cov(x,y) & Cov(x,z) \\ Cov(y,x) & Cov(y,y) & Cov(y,z) \\ Cov(z,x) & Cov(z,y) & Cov(z,z) \end{bmatrix} = \begin{bmatrix} var(x) & Cov(x,y) & Cov(x,z) \\ Cov(y,x) & var(y) & Cov(y,z) \\ Cov(z,x) & Cov(z,y) & var(z) \end{bmatrix}$$

where,

$$Cov(x, y) = E[(x - E[x])(y - E[y])] = E[xy] - E[x]E[y]$$

That is, the covariance of features x, y is the product of the expectation of x minus the expectation of x and y minus the expectation of y, where *expectation* in the formula, E[ ], is defined as the arithmetic mean a random variable. Subtracting the expectation is also known as *centering* the data.

The covariance of a variable with itself is equal to the variance of the variable, and so the diagonal represents the feature or independent variables' variance; for example, $Cov(x, x) = var(x)$. The covariance of the feature combinations is then positioned in the off-diagonal elements. Since the matrix is symmetric, the covariance of the element at position (j, i) is the same as at position (i, j).

The following equation shows an estimate of the covariance matrix with n = 2 features along with the detailed calculations. Note here, we use the sample variance (divide by n - 1) and as a result it is technically an estimate of the true population variance.

$$Cov(x, y) = \begin{bmatrix} var(x) & Cov(x, y) \\ Cov(y, x) & var(y) \end{bmatrix} = \begin{bmatrix} \frac{\sum_{i=1}^{n}(x_i-\bar{x})^2}{n-1} & \frac{\sum_{i=1}^{n}(x_i-\bar{x})(y_i-\bar{y})}{n-1} \\ \frac{\sum_{i=1}^{n}(x_i-\bar{x})(y_i-\bar{y})}{n-1} & \frac{\sum_{i=1}^{n}(y_i-\bar{y})^2}{n-1} \end{bmatrix}$$

Alternatively, the covariance of a matrix, A, where A might represent a dataset of multiple examples, each with multiple features (independent variables) is the product of the transposed centered matrix Ac^T and Ac divided by the number of examples, n, for the population covariance, or (n - 1) for a sample covariance:

$$Cov(A) = \frac{A_c^T \cdot A_c}{n - 1}$$

Example: Consider a dataset, comprised of 6 patients of various ages and sleep profiles shown in the following table.

	Patient 1	Patient 2	Patient 3	Patient 4	Patient 5	Patient 6
Age	43	26	28	29	42	39
Avg Sleep	8.5	5.0	6.1	4.6	7.2	7.4

If we plotted the data on a 2-dimensional graph, we would observe a positive correlation between Age and Avg Sleep.

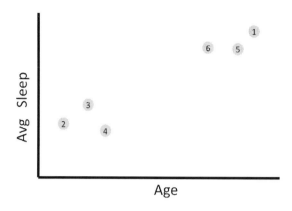

We can confirm a positive correlation observation by computing and inspecting the Covariance Matrix as shown in the following code block. The dataset is input as a NumPy array on lines 5-6, and the covariance is calculated using the NumPy *cov* function on line 8. Now the covariance calculation assumes a centered matrix and NumPy will do this for us in the function; that is, we do not have to center the dataset prior to calling the function. The hand calculated Covariance matrix is shown in lines 12-16, where centering of data is performed prior to calculating Cov(A).

We see both the NumPy and hand calculated Covariance matrices are computed using a sample population; that is, using the (n - 1) scale factor.

```
1    #Covariance matrix
2
3    import numpy as np
4
5    X = np.array([[43, 26, 28, 29, 42, 39],
6                  [8.5, 5.0, 6.1, 4.6, 7.2, 7.4]])
7
8    X_cov = np.cov(X)
9    print('Covariance NumPy:\n', np.round(X_cov, 1))
10
11   #Calc mean along axis=1 --> the axis ALONG the columns == ACROSS the row
12   X_mean = np.mean(X, axis=1)
13   #Center the data
14   Xc = X.T - X_mean
15   print('\nCentered data:\n', Xc)
16   X_cov2 = np.dot(Xc.T, Xc)/(len(Xc) - 1)
17   print('\nCovariance hand calc:\n', np.round(X_cov2,1))
```

Covariance NumPy:
[[58.7 10.4]
[10.4 2.3]]

Centered data:
[[8.5 2.03333333]
[-8.5 -1.46666667]
[-6.5 -0.36666667]
[-5.5 -1.86666667]
[7.5 0.73333333]
[4.5 0.93333333]]

Covariance hand calc:
[[58.7 10.4]
[10.4 2.3]]

We see in the console outputs that the covariances (the off-diagonal elements) are positive, indicating a positive correlation between the features in the dataset, thus confirming what we saw in the original graph.

SINGULAR VALUE DECOMPOSITION INTRODUCTION

One of the common operations performed in machine learning when implementing algorithms such as dimension reduction is called SVD (Singular Value Decomposition). SVD is a result of a fundamental theorem of linear algebra which states that every matrix can be factored into a product of 3 matrices, and we call this factorization process decomposition. We show an example in the following diagram where X is an (n x m) input matrix, and is typically comprised of several rows, where each row represents a data example, and the columns represent the independent variables or dimensions of our dataset, also known as features for each example. In SVD, X is factored into the following product of matrices: U which has shape (n x n), and contains orthonormal columns; S which contains singular values (non-negative real numbers), has shape (n x m), and is diagonal; and V^T which is (m x m) and contains both orthonormal rows and columns. Note that S could have more rows of 0's under the diagonal, with the diagonal portion shape being (m x m).

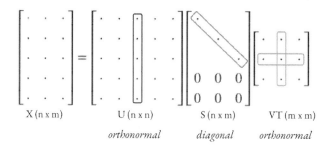

X (n x m)   U (n x n)   S (n x m)   VT (m x m)

orthonormal   *diagonal*   *orthonormal*

Now the matrix, U, has orthonormal columns, and from the previous discussion, we then know that $U^T \bullet U = I$. The V^T matrix is also orthonormal along its rows and columns, which means:

$$V^T \cdot V = I \text{ and } V \cdot V^T = I$$

The *S* matrix values along the (m x m) diagonal are the *singular* value part of the Singular Value Decomposition.

Now, we know that $X = USV^T$. Consider the product, X^TX. If we take the transpose of the product of matrices, the result is the transpose of each matrix that make up the product in reverse order; that is $X^T = VS^TU^T$. So,

$$X^TX = VS^TU^TUSV^T$$

Now, since U is orthornomal, then $U^T \bullet U = I$ resulting in:

$$X^TX = VS^TSV^T$$

Since S is a diagonal matrix, we can write $D = S^TS$ where D is a diagonal matrix comprised of the squares of the singular values in S. So now we have:

$$X^TX = VDV^T$$

Now, we can multiply both sides of the equation with V, resulting in:

$$X^TXV = VD$$

Note that the V^TV term on the right side of the equation cancels since V is orthonormal.

This equation provides some insight into what we'll look at next, called Eigenvalue decomposition. In the equation, it turns out that the columns of matrix V are the eigenvectors of X^TX, and the squared singular values along the diagonal of D are the eigenvalues. Further, the product X^TX was previously defined as a way to compute the covariance matrix of our dataset. Therefore, we can extract the eigenvectors and eigenvalues from the covariance matrix, which are computed by performing SVD on X^TX (the covariance matrix) $=VDV^T$, where the columns of V are the eigenvectors and the values along the diagonal of D are the eigenvalues.

The following example code shows how we can decompose an input matrix X using SVD. We set the input dataset on line 6, then run the NumPy linalg.svd function on line 9. The output provides X decomposed in U, S, and V^T matrices. The singular values are stored in a vector, s, and we need to convert it to a diagonal matrix, which we do using the NumPy diag method then modify the shape with padded zeros so that the multiplier shapes are valid.

```
1    #Singular Value Decomposition (SVD)
2
3    import numpy as np
4
5    #Input dataset
6    X = np.random.randn(5, 3)
7
8    #Run SVD
9    u, s, v_t = np.linalg.svd(X, full_matrices=True)
10   U = u
11   V_t = v_t
12   S = np.diag(s) #Map singular values into diag matrix
13
14   #Pad S with 0's at the bottom (so multiplication shapes are valid)
15   #np.pad(S, (top, bottom), (left, right)),
16   #          number = number of rows/cols, mode='constant' default 0
17   S_pad_zeros_rows = U.shape[1] - S.shape[0]
18   S_pad_zeros_cols = 0
19   S_pad = np.pad(S, ((0, S_pad_zeros_rows), (0, S_pad_zeros_cols)), mode='constant')
20
21   #Confirm the decomposed matrices product is the same as the original
22   X2 = np.dot(np.dot(U, S_pad), V_t)
23   print('\n', np.round(X2, 2) == np.round(X, 2))
24   print('X:\n', X)
25   print(X.shape)
26   print('\nU:\n', U)
27   print(U.shape)
28   print('\nS:\n', S)
29   print(S.shape)
30   print('\nV_t:\n', V_t)
31   print(V_t.shape)
32   print('\nS_pad:\n', S_pad)
33   print(S_pad.shape)
34   print('\nX2:\n', X2)
```

⊡→ [[True True True]
[True True True]
[True True True]
[True True True]
[True True True]]
X:
[[-1.05367002 -1.10712846 -0.04480669]
[0.66182724 0.77558002 -0.10696368]
[1.67486898 1.43375678 -1.04853192]
[-1.08890223 -0.44964874 -0.02821059]
[-0.26195733 0.5372516 -2.98388339]]
(5, 3)

U:
[[-0.27320524 0.43278856 -0.54202041 -0.0207231 -0.66621122]
[0.21155762 -0.25102963 0.42560374 -0.61497637 -0.57696882]
[0.62406812 -0.37731606 -0.20896894 0.55071999 -0.34815377]
[-0.18706888 0.34612358 0.69307427 0.53574692 -0.27897489]
[0.67538618 0.69821862 0.03248653 -0.17623094 0.15566487]]
(5, 5)

S:
[[3.56002713 0. 0.]
[0. 2.67157912 0.]
[0. 0. 0.43311314]]
(3, 3)

V_t:
[[0.4213149 0.50794069 -0.7513255]
[-0.67896464 -0.37256636 -0.63261467]
[-0.60124934 0.77665344 0.18790601]]
(3, 3)

S_pad:
[[3.56002713 0. 0.]
[0. 2.67157912 0.]
[0. 0. 0.43311314]
[0. 0. 0.]
[0. 0. 0.]]
(5, 3)

X2:
[[-1.05367002 -1.10712846 -0.04480669]
[0.66182724 0.77558002 -0.10696368]
[1.67486898 1.43375678 -1.04853192]
[-1.08890223 -0.44964874 -0.02821059]
[-0.26195733 0.5372516 -2.98388339]]

We will see that the eigenvectors and eigenvalues provide a way to transform our dataset by projecting it onto another set of axes, which is the foundation of dimension reduction techniques in machine learning. In other words, SVD generalizes Eigenvalue decomposition, which we will discuss next.

6.2:
EIGENVALUE DECOMPOSITION

Now we will describe an important linear algebra technique called *Eigenvalue Decomposition*. Before we get into the details, we will introduce the *eigenvalue* and *eigenvector*.

The following equation here shows the relationship between a square matrix A, its eigenvector (a vector), e, and eigenvalue (a scalar), λ:

$$Ae = \lambda e$$

We show a simple example where e is an eigenvector of the matrix A.

Given:
$$A = \begin{bmatrix} 4 & 0 & 1 \\ 2 & -2 & 3 \\ 7 & 5 & 0 \end{bmatrix}, \quad e = \begin{bmatrix} 1 \\ 1 \\ 2 \end{bmatrix}$$

$$Ae = \lambda e \rightarrow \quad \begin{bmatrix} 4 & 0 & 1 \\ 2 & -2 & 3 \\ 7 & 5 & 0 \end{bmatrix} \cdot \begin{bmatrix} 1 \\ 1 \\ 2 \end{bmatrix} = \begin{bmatrix} 6 \\ 6 \\ 12 \end{bmatrix} = 6e \rightarrow \lambda = 6$$

In many machine learning applications, however, λ may not be as easy to factor out as in the previous example, or we may need to find both the eigenvectors and eigenvalues. In that case, we would start by solving what is called the *characteristic equation*:

$$\lambda = \det(A - \lambda I) = 0$$

which provides the eigenvalues, and then substitute back into the equation:

$$Ae = \lambda e$$

to find the eigenvectors.

Example: Now we can apply Eigenvalue Decomposition to a real example application in machine learning. We can apply the process of factoring a Covariance matrix into a standard form that consists of its Eigenvalues and Eigenvectors using Singular Value Decomposition (SVD), and this can be used to transform a dataset into components which maximize the amount of variance between the data points. The process of maximizing the variance among the data points is the primary goal in the dimension reduction algorithm called Principal Component Analysis (PCA). Specifically, the eigenvectors define the data's direction with the most variance, and the eigenvalues, the amount of variance. We show the preliminary steps in preparing the dataset by performing Eigenvalue Decomposition, and when complete, we will have calculated an eigenvector and its associated eigenvalue for each of the independent variables or features in our dataset.

We will use the same dataset as was used with the Covariance example as shown.

	Patient 1	Patient 2	Patient 3	Patient 4	Patient 5	Patient 6
Age	43	26	28	29	42	39
Avg Sleep	8.5	5.0	6.1	4.6	7.2	7.4

In the first step, we'll call step 0, we preprocess the data to normalize or fill in missing values or to rearrange the data to make it more convenient for the matrix operations. Next, in step 1 we calculate the means of each independent variable or feature of the dataset. Then in step two, we center the data by subtracting the mean from each of its feature column. This serves to shift the data to the origin of its axes. Next, in step 3, we calculate the covariance matrix, which then creates an (n x n) square matrix. Note that if we called the NumPy *cov* function, we would not have had to center the data.

```
Data: [[43.    8.5]   Data_centered:   [[ 8.5    2.03333333]   Cov:   [[58.7   10.4]
       [26.    5. ]                     [-8.5   -1.46666667]            [10.4    2.3]]
       [28.    6.1]                     [-6.5   -0.36666667]
       [29.    4.6]                     [-5.5   -1.86666667]
       [42.    7.2]                     [ 7.5    0.73333333]
       [39.    7.4]]                    [ 4.5    0.93333333]]
```

Finally, in step 4, we calculate the eigenvectors and eigenvalues of the covariance matrix, where the eigenvalues are calculated by solving for the roots of the characteristic polynomial.

$$\lambda = \det(A - \lambda I) = 0 \rightarrow \lambda = \det(Cov - \lambda I) = 0$$

Since we have 2 independent variables (features), we will have 2 eigenvalues:

$$\{\lambda_1, \lambda_2\}$$

$$det(Cov - \lambda I) = 0: \quad \begin{bmatrix} 58.7 - \lambda & 10.4 \\ 10.4 & 2.3 - \lambda \end{bmatrix} = (58.7 - \lambda)(2.3 - \lambda) - (10.4)(10.4) = 0$$

which yields the characteristic polynomial with roots equal to the eigenvalues:

$$\lambda^2 - 61\lambda + 27 = 0 \quad \rightarrow \quad \{\lambda_1, \lambda_2\} = \{60.6, 0.4\}$$

Then the eigenvectors are calculated by substituting the eigenvalues into:

$$Ae = \lambda e \rightarrow Cov \cdot e = \lambda e$$

Again, since we have 2 features, we will have 2 eigenvectors, {e1, e2}. Solving for each of the eigenvectors:

$$Cov \cdot e_1 = \lambda_1 e_1 \quad \rightarrow \quad \begin{bmatrix} 58.7 & 10.4 \\ 10.4 & 2.3 \end{bmatrix} \begin{bmatrix} e_{11} \\ e_{12} \end{bmatrix} = 60.6 \begin{bmatrix} e_{11} \\ e_{12} \end{bmatrix}$$

produces two equations:

(1) $58.7 e_{11} + 10.4 e_{12} = 60.6 e_{11}$
(2) $10.4 e_{11} + 2.3 e_{12} = 60.6 e_{12}$

Solving equation (1) yields:

$$e_{11} = 5.6e_{12} \rightarrow e_1 = \begin{bmatrix} 5.6 \\ 1 \end{bmatrix}$$

Similarly, solving for eigenvector e2:

$$Cov \cdot e_2 = \lambda_2 e_2 \rightarrow Cov \cdot e_2 = 0.4 \begin{bmatrix} e_{21} \\ e_{22} \end{bmatrix} \rightarrow e_2 = \begin{bmatrix} -0.17 \\ 1 \end{bmatrix}$$

To summarize this example, we applied Singular Value Decomposition to an example dataset to find the Eigenvalues and Eigenvectors of the Covariance matrix. The Eigenvectors represented the directions of the axes in our dataset with the most variance, while the Eigenvalues were coefficients that define the amount of variance attached to each Eigenvector. We will see how this can be advanced to project our dataset onto a new set of axes, and allow us to perform machine learning modeling with a reduced feature set and improve performance of our model.

CHAPTER 7:
Calculus Introduction
for Machine Learning

In this chapter, we will introduce a subset of Calculus, namely the derivative and its use in machine learning.

LEARNING OBJECTIVES

By the end of this chapter, you will be able to do the following:

- Describe the basic function of a derivative
- Calculate a derivative of a function using the power and chain rules
- Calculate a partial derivative of a function of several variables
- Describe a gradient and how it is used to find a minimum of a function
- Define a cost function and provide an example
- Describe the steps in the gradient descent algorithm
- Define the learning rate as it applied to gradient descent

7.1:
INTRODUCTION TO CALCULUS FOR MACHINE LEARNING

Calculus is a vast subject, and one which forms a base for many of the algorithms implemented in Data Science and Machine Learning. Calculus can be boiled down to two main concepts: differentiation (or derivative) and integration (or integral), and fortunately in machine learning differentiation plays a larger role. Therefore, we will limit out discussions to differentiation, and more specifically techniques on how to compute the derivative for single and multivariate (multiple variables); functions that is the full and partial derivative, then apply this to the most common optimization technique used in machine learning, called Gradient Descent.

Next, we will cover the physical meaning of the derivative as it relates to slope and describe how to compute derivatives using the power rule, the chain rule, and via partial differentiation.

From a historical perspective, Sir Isaac Newton and Gottfried Leibniz are both credited with inventing Calculus in the 17th century.

Sir Isaac Newton   Gottfried Leibniz

Attribution for images: Wikipedia Creative Commons
https://creativecommons.org/licenses/by/2.5
File: Portrait of Sir Isaac Newton, 1689.jpg from
https://exhibitions.lib.cam.ac.uk/linesofthought/artifacts
File: Fottfried_Wilhelm_Leibniz_c1700.jpg from
https://commons.wikimedia.org/wiki/File:Gottfried_Wilhelm_Leibniz_c1700.jpg

DERIVATIVES OF LINEAR FUNCTIONS

The term *derivative* is one of the two major concepts covered in an introductory course in Calculus and whole books have been written on this subject which we will not go into in this chapter, but we'll provide the basics that you will need to understand for machine learning, specifically for the cost minimization algorithm Gradient descent.

The derivative of a function in the simplest terms is the slope of a line which is tangent (or just touches) a function curve at a point. Now you've likely already computed derivatives in your algebra classes when you calculated the slope of a linear function, or straight line, which we know is the change in the dependent variable, Y divided by the change in the independent variable, X.

For example, the following graph shows a line which has the generic equation, y = mx + b where y is the dependent variable, x is the independent variable, m is the slope and b is the y-intercept.

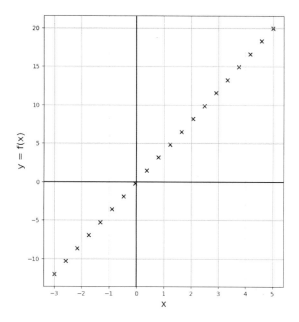

Note that we also refer to our independent variable, y as f(x). In this case our function can then be represented by the equation f(x) = 4x. Now the derivative of the function, per its definition, is the same as the slope at a point on the line. The slope here is constant (4 in this example) at any point on the line. So, we can then say that the derivative of a straight-line (or linear) function is a constant, and we denote the derivative using the notation:

$$\frac{df(x)}{dx}$$

which we describe as the derivative of f(x) with respect to x. Thus, for the function f(x) = 4x we can write:

$$\frac{df(x)}{dx} = 4$$

In other words, for every increase in x by 1, f(x) increases by 4. Note that this is consistent with the definition of the slope of a function.

Similarly, the following graph is a line with the equation: f(x) = 2.

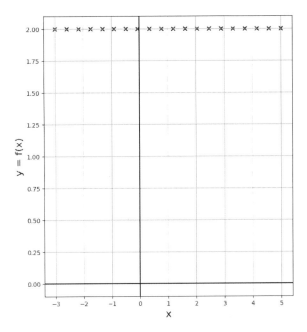

The derivative in this case is the slope at a point on the line or in this case, 0, so we can say the derivative of f(x) with respect to x is 0 for this function; that is,

$$\frac{df(x)}{dx} = 0$$

Interpreting this again, we can say that for every increase in x by 1, f(x) increases by 0, which makes sense given the graph.

Note that this property holds true for any horizontal line which would be represented in our equations as f(x) equal to a constant, and therefore, the derivative of any constant value is 0. This property is important and will be revisited when we discuss partial differentiation. Also notice from these graphs that if we have a line with a steep slope, the magnitude of the derivative will be large. As the slope decreases, the derivative's magnitude will also decrease and approach 0 when the point on the graph approaches a horizontal line. This will be a key point when we discuss the gradient descent algorithm. And finally, we can have negative derivatives which would correspond to negative slopes in our functions.

DERIVATIVES OF NONLINEAR FUNCTIONS

Now, we looked at the simplest case in finding the derivative or slope for a linear function (or straight line), but what if our function is not linear? For example, how would we calculate the slopes for the graphs shown here implementing the function $y = f(x) = x^2$ at the points marked?

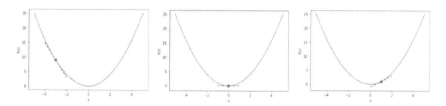

In these cases, we cannot simply calculate the change in $f(x)$ over the change in x; that is, the slope, as we do for straight lines since it varies at different points on the function as shown on the graphs. Here we need to find the slope at a specific point on the curve.

Now recall the derivative was defined previously as the slope of a line which is tangent (or just touches) a function curve at a point. You may have noticed that the graphs shown are all the same quadratic function, but as pointed out, we see each of the points highlighted on the graph have a different slope when we construct a line at the point which is tangent to (or touching) the graph. For example, if we want to find the derivative (or slope) of $f(x)$ on the left-most graph at the point $x = -3$, denoted as:

$$slope|_{x=-3} = \frac{df(x)}{dx}\bigg|_{x=-3}$$

we need to find the slope of the curve at that point, which we can see is negative and, in this case, happens to be equal to -6. We will learn how to calculate this value next.

Similarly, for the middle graph, if we want to find the derivative of $f(x)$ at the point $x = 0$, we need to find the slope of the curve at that point, which we can see is equal to 0.

$$slope|_{x=0} = \frac{df(x)}{dx}\bigg|_{x=0} = 0$$

And finally, for the right-most graph, the derivative of f(x) on this graph at the point x = 1, is 2.

$$slope|_{x=1} = \frac{df(x)}{dx}\bigg|_{x=1} = 2$$

DERIVATIVE CHAIN AND POWER RULES

Previously, we evaluated the derivative (or slope) of a function at a point on a curve, but we didn't describe how we actually calculated the slopes at the points. This is an involved process using what is called a *limit* that is covered in an introductory course in Calculus, but fortunately, the resultant formula for calculating derivatives of polynomial functions is straightforward using what is called the *power rule*. Specifically, we can calculate the derivative of x^r using the formula:

$$f(x) = x^r \quad \rightarrow \quad \frac{df(x)}{dx} = rx^{r-1}$$

which basically multiplies the coefficient of the independent variable, x, by its exponent and then subtracts 1 from the exponent. For example, from our previous function:

$$y = f(x) = x^2 \quad \rightarrow \quad \frac{df(x)}{dx} = 2x$$

that is, we multiply the coefficient of x which is 1 by the exponent 2 then subtract 1 from the exponent of x $(2 - 1 = 1)$.

Then if we want to evaluate the derivative (that is find the slope) at any point on this graph, for example, x = 1 as shown in the following graph, we can do so by simply plugging in the x value into the derivative, 2x, and in the example see that the slope of the function x squared at the point x = 1 is 2.

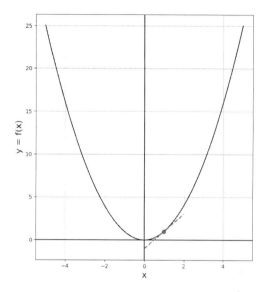

$$slope|_{x=1} = \left.\frac{df(x)}{dx}\right|_{x=1} = 2$$

Now, we can extend this procedure to the more complicated polynomial function:

$$f(x) = x^3 + 4x^2 - 10x - 2$$

at the point x = -3 as shown in the following graph.

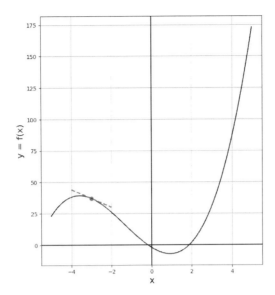

In this case the derivative of f(x):

$$\frac{df(x)}{dx} = 3x^2 + 2 \cdot 4x - 10$$

Here we take the exponent of each of the x variables, multiply it by their coefficient then subtract one from the exponent. Note that in our original equation we had a constant term −2 at the end of the equation which disappeared from the derivative. This is because -2 can be interpreted as negative 2 times x to the power 0, which when we multiply the exponent 0 times the coefficient -2, we get 0. It is also consistent with the statement made previously related to taking the derivative of a constant would result in 0 (the slope of a constant is 0), so taking the derivative of the constant −10 would therefore be 0.

Like the previous example, we can evaluate the slope at any point on the graph by plugging in the x value of the point we want to evaluate into our derivative. In this case, we see that the slope at the point -3 is -7.

$$\left.\frac{df(x)}{dx}\right|_{x=-3} = \left. 3x^2 + 8x - 10 \right|_{x=-3} = -7$$

Next let's extend the power rule to more complex polynomial functions. For example, consider the following polynomial function:

$$f(x) = (x^2 - 4x)^3$$

To compute the derivative, we could work out the algebra to calculate all the terms associated with multiplying $(x^2 - 4x)$ by itself 3 times, then apply the power rule described previously to each of the terms, or we can use what is called the *chain rule*. In this case we work inward from the outer most exponent, repeating the power rule operation for each pair of parentheses in the function and then multiplying the values together.

For example, to compute the derivative of $f(x) = (x^2 - 4x)^3$, we take the exponent outside the parentheses, 3, and multiply it with the coefficient in front of the parentheses (which is 1 in this case), then reduce the exponent by 1 ($3 - 1 = 2$), which gives us $3 \bullet (x^2 - 4x)^2$. Then we implement the chain rule on the terms inside the parentheses, which means we repeat the power rule for the individual terms, giving us $2x - 4$ for the inner derivative. We then multiply the two derivatives together, resulting in:

$$f(x) = (x^2 - 4x)^3 \rightarrow \frac{df(x)}{dx} = 3 \cdot (x^2 - 4x)^2 \cdot (2x - 4)$$

Now just like we did with our previous examples, we can compute the slope of the function at a point by plugging in an x value into our derivative.

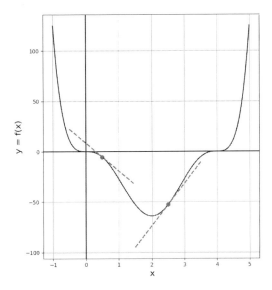

In the examples shown in the graph we evaluate the derivative at the points $x = 0.5$ and $x = 2.5$, which again represents the slopes of the line which is tangent to the curve at those points.

$$\frac{df(x)}{dx}\bigg|_{x=0.5} = 3 \cdot (x^2 - 4x)^2 \cdot (2x - 4) \big|_{x=0.5} = -27.6$$

and

$$\frac{df(x)}{dx}\bigg|_{x=2.5} = 3 \cdot (x^2 - 4x)^2 \cdot (2x - 4) \big|_{x=2.5} = 42.2$$

A variant of the chain rule can be applied to simplify multivariate functions with what are called "intermediate variables". This property is valuable when solving the parameter equations in the Neural networks, as we will see with Deep Neural Networks. Here we show an example to get a feel for how it works.

Say we want to calculate the derivative of z with respect to x, but are provided the functions z(w) and w(x), where z is a function of w and w is a function of x. We can calculate the derivative by breaking it into the product (or chain) of derivatives:

$$\frac{dz}{dx} = \frac{dz}{dw}\frac{dw}{dx}$$

which allows us to effectively cancel the common dw terms. You can think of this as cancelling the denominator dw term in dz/dw with the numerator term dw in dw/dx.

For example, find dz/dx given:

$$z = \frac{1}{2}(w^2 - 2)^2 \text{ and } w = \pi x^2$$

First, we separately compute dz/dw and dw/dx, then simplify the product of derivatives.

$$\frac{dz}{dw} = 2 \cdot \frac{1}{2}(w^2 - 2)^1 \cdot 2w = 2w(w^2 - 2)$$

$$\frac{dw}{dx} = 2\pi x$$

therefore,

$$\frac{dz}{dx} = \frac{dz}{dw}\frac{dw}{dx} = 2w(w^2 - 2) \cdot 2\pi x = 4w\pi x(w^2 - 2)$$

PARTIAL DERIVATIVES

Next, we'll discuss the *partial derivative* which we will apply to multivariate functions, and more specifically to the minimization method we'll use when calculating equations used in Deep Neural Network training. Note that up to this point, we have taken derivatives of functions with a single independent variable, x in this case. A partial derivative is used to calculate the derivative of a function of several variables such as with a dataset containing several features where each feature represents an independent variable. Say we want to calculate the derivative of y with respect to x, where y depends on variables x, a, and b. We can calculate this derivative by simply treating the variables a and b as constants, and we will demonstrate this in a similar example below.

As shown here we have a function, z, defined in terms of variables x and y:

$$z = f(x, y) = x^2 + yx + y^2$$

Now the partial derivative notation is similar to what was shown in our previous notation except that we use the Greek symbol delta, ∂, to indicate we are taking a partial derivative, and define in the denominator which variable we are taking the derivative with respect to. The process in taking the derivative is the same as previously described with the power and chain rules, except now we need to be careful to make sure we keep track of which variables are treated as constants.

For our function z, we want to compute $\partial z/\partial x$ and since we are taking the derivative with respect to x, we treat y as a constant. Let's look at the derivative of each term separately.

- $\frac{\partial(x^2)}{\partial x} = 2x$ The x^2 term is computed the same as described previously since we are taking the derivative with respect to x.

- $\frac{\partial(xy)}{\partial x} = y(1)$ The derivative of xy becomes simply y since the power rule procedure says to multiply the coefficient of the term (where the coefficient is y in this case since it's treated as a constant) by the exponent of the x term (1 in this case) and then the x term exponent is reduce by 1 which makes it x to the power 0, and we know that any value raised to the 0 power is 1. So, in this case we are left with the constant coefficient y times 1. Thinking about this intuitively, this is saying that for every increase in x by 1, xy increases by y, which makes sense logically.

- $\dfrac{\partial(y^2)}{\partial x} = 0$ Since we are taking the derivative of y^2 with respect to x, we treat it as a constant. Recall in the previous example, y = f(x) = 2, we observed that the slope of any horizontal line (which is a constant in this case) is 0 and then concluded that the derivative of any constant is simply 0. So, since we are taking the partial derivative with respect to x, then y^2 is treated as a constant, and its derivative will likewise be 0. This also makes sense logically because increasing x will not result in any changes in the y^2 term.

Therefore,

$$\frac{\partial z}{\partial x} = 2x + y(1) \cdot x^0 + 0 = 2x + y$$

Finally, we'll conclude our crash course in derivatives by walking through the calculation of the derivative of a common function used in machine learning models called the sigmoid function.

Now the sigmoid is what is called a logistic function and is used in many machine learning Algorithms. Not only we will use this function in an algorithm called *logistic regression*, but we'll also use it when training deep neural networks. So, it is important to introduce this function and know its derivative.

The sigmoid is basically used as a thresholding function to map values of independent variables onto a characteristic "S-shaped" curve as shown in the following figure.

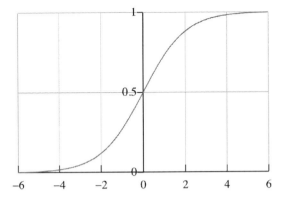

In the graph we see that values close to 0 are mapped to an output corresponding to a linear region centered around 0.5, and as we get further away from 0 in either negative or positive direction, the output is compressed to either 0 or 1. The equation of the function is:

$$\sigma(x) = \frac{1}{1 + e^{-x}}$$

which is a non-linear or more specifically, an exponential function.

Now let's walk through the calculation of the derivative of the sigmoid function. We can use what we have learned so far with the power and chain rules and apply it here.

First, we define the derivative of the exponential function d(e^u)/dx; that is, the derivative of e to the power u with respect to x as:

$$\frac{d(e^u)}{dx} = e^u \cdot \frac{du}{dx}$$

This is generally saying that the derivative of e^u is also e^u, but we need to apply the chain rule to the exponent which is why we include du/dx term.

Next, we can rewrite the original sigmoid function to get rid of the fractional representation.

$$\frac{d\sigma(x)}{dx} = \frac{d}{dx}\left(\frac{1}{1 + e^{-x}}\right) = \frac{d}{dx}(1 + e^{-x})^{-1}$$

Then we take the derivative using the power and chain rules. Here we multiply the function inside the parentheses by the exponent, -1, and reduce the term by 1 resulting in, $-(1+e^{-x})^{-2}$. Then using the chain rule, we take the derivative of what's inside the parentheses which, using the formula above, gives us $e^{-x}(-1)$, and multiplying them together gets us:

$$= -(1 + e^{-x})^{-2}(-e^{-x})$$

Now the rest is just algebraic manipulation of the derivative to get the equation into a form that is easier to work with and implement in code.

$$= \frac{e^{-x}}{(1 + e^{-x})^2}$$

$$= \frac{1}{(1 + e^{-x})} \cdot \frac{e^{-x}}{(1 + e^{-x})}$$

$$= \frac{1}{(1 + e^{-x})} \cdot \frac{(1 + e^{-x}) - 1}{(1 + e^{-x})}$$

$$= \left(\frac{1}{(1 + e^{-x})}\right) \cdot \left(\frac{(1 + e^{-x})}{(1 + e^{-x})} - \frac{1}{(1 + e^{-x})}\right)$$

Now remember that our original equation was:

$$\sigma(x) = \frac{1}{1 + e^{-x}}$$

so substituting we get our final derivative equation:

$$\frac{d}{dx}\sigma(x) = \sigma(x) \cdot \left(1 - \sigma(x)\right)$$

7.2:

CALCULUS APPLICATION IN MACHINE LEARNING - GRADIENT DESCENT

Next, we will discuss the *Gradient Descent* algorithm. Gradient Descent is probably the most widely used algorithm in machine learning model training. This is done through an iterative process which updates model parameters based on minimizing the error between a model prediction output and the known answer or *label* provided with the training features.

The gradient descent algorithm has been around for a while - it was first suggested by French mathematician Augustin-Louis Cauchy in 1847, then was more formally applied to non-linear optimization by Haskell Curry in 1944.

Augustin-Louis Cauchy   Haskell Curry

First, let's take a non-technical look at describing gradient descent. As an analogy to understand the algorithm procedure, imagine an area of hilly terrain as shown in the following image.

We can describe the terrain in the image geometrically with three dimensions: x, y, and z using the axes shown on the image. The contours of the terrain are described by the relationship between each of the x, y, and z axes; where the (x, y) coordinates define the position in a 2-D coordinate system and z represents the terrain height. Imagine you are standing at the top of the hill and assume that you want to get down to the lowest point in the terrain. If you are currently at the highest point, which direction should you go? Your objective is to reduce the height, z, of your (x, y) position as fast as possible. The quickest way to do this is to take steps downwards in the direction of the steepest slope; that is, you should take a step in the xy direction, modifying your x and y values) which most quickly decreases z. After your step, you should reevaluate which direction the steepest slope is in, and then take another step downwards in that direction. You should continue to do this until you reach the lowest possible z value at the bottom of the valley, where your height z is at a minimum.

Now, let's extend the analogy to gradient descent's use in machine learning. In creating a machine learning algorithm or *model*, the goal is to define a set of parameters which are used to try to predict output values. For example, the pixels of an image may be input to a machine learning model which tries to predict whether the image is a cat or a dog. Finding the set of parameters for the model is done through a process called *training* in which dataset examples, comprised of one or more independent variables (called features) are input to the model along with a known answer or *label*. Providing dataset labels along with the examples during training is called *supervised learning* and involves comparing the predicted outputs from the model with the labels to generate a *cost function* (also known as an *error function*), which provides a measure of how close the predictions are to the labels. If we set our model parameters to random values and get a large cost (large error), it means our predicted outputs do not compare well with the labels, and as a result the model is performing poorly. Conversely, if the model parameters are set such that we get a small cost, it means the predictions compare well with the labels, and our model is performing well.

Thus, it would be advantageous to find a set of model parameters which result in prediction output values that are close to the labels, resulting in as small a cost as possible. In other words, if we can minimize the cost function, we should attain the best predictions (and performance) from the model. We will see next how we can use the Gradient Descent algorithm to minimize the cost function during model training.

GRADIENT DESCENT APPLICATION

Here we show how Gradient Descent works by way of an example and apply it to the common machine learning algorithm, Simple Linear Regression. Suppose we start with an unknown function, in this case the line, $f(x) = 0.5x$, as shown in the following figure. Now, say we want to estimate a point on the function line by randomly guessing a point somewhere in the x, y coordinate system, for example the point $(0.5, 0)$ as shown in the figure.

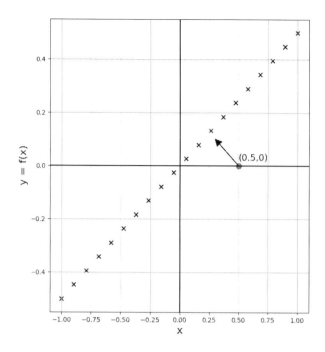

If we knew how far our guess was from the points on the line, we could use that information to help guess a new point that is closer to the curve. By comparing the guesses with actual points on the function (the labels), we can generate a cost (or error) function.

Now assume we knew the function was a line and we wanted to find its equation. We could try to guess the function by placing lines with different slopes and y-intercepts to try to predict the labels, comparing the guesses against the original line (labels) and calculate a cost function (error between the guess and the labels), then changing the slope and y-intercept of our guess and repeating the process until the cost is minimized. The following graph shows several lines with different slopes, and we see that the line highlighted as "Best fit" represents the closest estimate to the original (labels), where the original is called the *Truth* equation of the line.

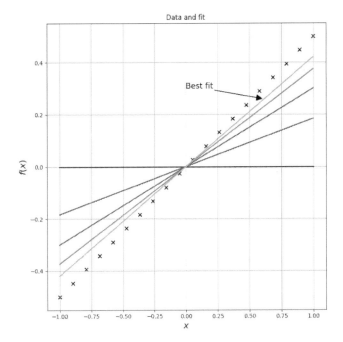

Now you may ask, how is the cost computed such that we can minimize it. Many different cost functions exist, but one of the more common cost functions is the *mean square error* which is defined as the sum of the squared differences between our Truth or the line we are trying to estimate and the estimates themselves summed over n examples.

$$MSE = \frac{1}{n}\sum_{i=1}^{n}(y_i - \hat{y}_i)^2$$

where y_i are the truth values and $\hat{y}_i$ are the estimates or predictions.

Intuitively, if the estimates (predictions) are very far off from the truth values, the terms will grow very large, making the MSE very high, but if the estimates and Truth values are close to identical, the MSE will approach 0. The following graph shows the cost function for various slopes of the lines used to estimate the Truth equation. Note that for this example, we assume the lines tested all have a y-intercept = 0. As we get close to a slope of approximately m = 0.5, the cost function, which we call J(m) in the graph, approaches 0. This would be the case for an estimated line that falls exactly on top of the Truth line in the previous graph. Also note that the further away our line's slope is from m = 0.5, the further up the Cost curve the point would be located. For example, a slope of m = 0 would result in a cost or error of approximately 0.092.

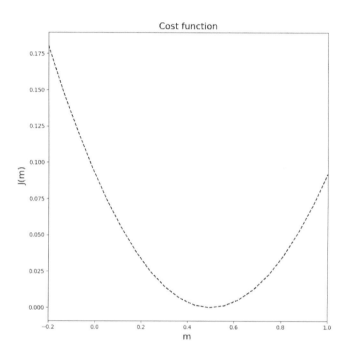

Now we are finally ready to introduce the basics of the Gradient Descent algorithm, which we will use to find the minimum cost. Formally speaking, Gradient Descent is an iterative optimization algorithm used to find the minimum of a function. In our case, we want to use it to find the minimum of our cost function(s) because we want the error in our model to be as close to 0 as possible. Note, we may have more than one cost function depending on the number of model parameters we are estimating. For example, the function $f(x) = mx + b$ has 2 parameters which define the function: m, b. We can generalize the equation as $f(x) = b_1x + b_0$, where the coefficients, b_1, b_0 are the model parameters we need to estimate.

We start at some initial point on the cost function curve and take steps proportional to the negative of the *gradient*, where the gradient is defined as the slope of a line tangent to the function at the current point, or as discussed previously, the derivative. More specifically, we need to compute the partial derivative of the cost function with respect to each of the model parameters. We summarize the calculations for our example function in the following table.

The function we are estimating:		$f(x) = mx + b \rightarrow f(x) = b_1 x + b_0$
The model parameters we are training: (i.e. parameters that generate cost functions):		$b, m \rightarrow b_0, b_1$
The cost function (mean square error), where n = number of examples in the dataset:		$MSE = \frac{1}{n}\sum_{i=1}^{n}(y_i - \hat{y}_i)^2 = \frac{1}{n}\sum_{i=1}^{n}\left(y_i - (b_0 + b_1 x_i)\right)^2$
The gradients:	$\dfrac{\partial(Cost)}{\partial b_1}$	$\dfrac{\partial(MSE)}{\partial b_1} = \dfrac{2}{n}\sum_{i=1}^{n}\left(y_i - (b_0 + b_1 x_i)\right) \cdot (-x_i)$
	$\dfrac{\partial(Cost)}{\partial b_0}$	$\dfrac{\partial(MSE)}{\partial b_0} = \dfrac{2}{n}\sum_{i=1}^{n}\left(y_i - (b_0 + b_1 x_i)\right) \cdot (-1)$
The update equations: (μ = step size)	b_1	$b_1 = b_1 - \mu\dfrac{\partial(MSE)}{\partial b_1}$
	b_0	$b_0 = b_0 - \mu\dfrac{\partial(MSE)}{\partial b_0}$

The magnitude of the steps taken along the cost function curve is controlled by a parameter called the *learning rate*, μ, where large learning rates result in bigger steps, and smaller learning rates result in smaller steps. The algorithm repeats (or iterates), taking steps until the cost is minimized, ideally to 0. At that point, we can say we have found the minimum of the cost function.

Let's look at an example of Gradient descent in action. In the following figures we repeat the example function shown previously; this is our truth function, f(x) = 0.5x, which is the line formed by the 20 'x' markers on the plot (n = 20). We show several estimates consisting of lines with different slopes, all with y-intercepts =

0. The graph is the same as was shown previously, with annotations denoting the line slopes for each training iteration. We also show the cost function and individually calculated costs (denoted with the dots along the cost function) for each of the slope values, b1, computed with the mean square error equation. Note, if our y-intercept was non-zero, we'd have a cost function for b0 as well. Our goal is to use the cost function to find the slope of the line that best estimates the Truth function by traversing down the cost curve in the path shown with the arrowed lines until the gradient (derivative) is as close to 0 as possible since this will represent the minimum of the cost function (and recall we are ultimately trying to minimize these cost functions).

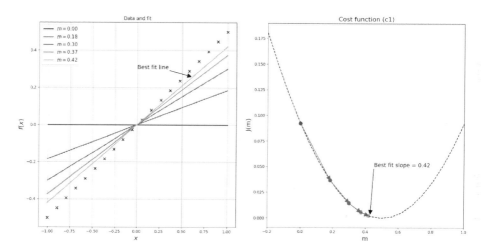

The algorithm starts at iteration 1 where the estimated line is horizontal (blue) with a slope, b1 = 0, and y-intercept, b0 = 0, and this results in the following MSE:

$$MSE = \frac{1}{n}\sum_{i=1}^{n}(y_i - \hat{y}_i)^2 = \frac{1}{n}\sum_{i=1}^{n}(y_i - (b_0 + b_1 x_i))^2$$

$$= \frac{1}{20}[(-0.5 - 0)^2 + (-0.45 - 0)^2 + \cdots + (0.5 - 0)^2] = 0.092$$

The step taken is proportional to the negative of the gradient (that is the negative of the derivative at the point m= 0) so we take a large step. We show the gradient calculation for b1 here.

$$\frac{\partial(MSE)}{\partial b_1} = \frac{2}{n}\sum_{i=1}^{n}(y_i - (b_0 + b_1 x_i)) \cdot (-x_i)$$

$$= \frac{2}{20}[(-0.5 - 0)\cdot(1) + (-0.45 - 0)\cdot(0.9) + \cdots + (0.5 - 0)\cdot(-1)]$$

$$= -0.368$$

Note that we should also calculate the b0 gradient, but since we constrained the example with y-intercept = 0, we omit that calculation here.

Next, we update the model parameters; that is, our coefficients, $b1, b0$. Now we must be careful about how we actually step the algorithm. Note that as we approach the minimum of the cost curve, the steps get smaller and this serves to slow down the algorithm such that we do not overshoot (or go past) the minimum as might happen if we took too large of steps. Accordingly, there are some tradeoffs to consider as it relates to the step size. First, a larger step would move quickly down the curve but may overshoot the minimum. Alternatively, a smaller step would move slowly down the curve increasing the processing time which may be prohibitive especially if we are training a complicated model with a large amount of data. In reality, we control the step size with a parameter called the learning rate in what is called the *update equation*. Here we show the update calculation for b1, where the learning rate, $\mu = 0.5$. Note, as before, we should also update b0 (the y-intercept) but since we constrained this example to 0, we omit the calculation here.

$$b_1 = b_1 - \mu\frac{\partial(MSE)}{\partial b_1} = 0 - 0.05(-0.368) = 0.184$$

The algorithm then repeats the process for iteration 2; that is, we compute the derivative of the curve at the point corresponding to m = b1 =0.184 and take a step proportional to it, which in this case will be a smaller step because the slope of the curve at m =0.184 is less steep than at m = 0.

The algorithm then repeats for iteration 3, 4, and 5 as shown in the above figure where each step is smaller than the previous due to the slope of the error function becoming less steep as we progress down the curve. This process repeats until we either have an error or cost of 0 or when it falls below some threshold or exceed a maximum number of iterations. This is shown in the graphs as the "Best fit line" and "Best fit slope".

So, to summarize the steps for each iteration, we compute the cost associated with the value of m = b1, take the derivative with respect to b1 then update a new b1. When J(m), which is the error or cost value for the model parameters we are considering (slope and y-intercept in this case), is either 0, or falls below a threshold, or we exhaust the number of iterations, we declare that value to be the best estimate of our function. For the cost graph shown, the simulation was run for 5 iterations resulting in a best fit slope, b = 0.42.

One final note, regarding gradient descent is that there are lots of variations to the algorithm, and we have only presented the base case here. For example, much research has been applied to finding the optimum learning rates but as a rule of thumb, one should use a fractional value between 0 and 1.0, with common example learning rates are 0.1 or 0.01. Adaptive learning rates are also quite common, and we will study in the future.

SUMMARY

Whether we realize it or not, machine learning has likely touched the lives of anyone who has browsed the internet, shopped either online or in a brick-and-mortar store, answered a survey, or interacted with almost anything in which data can be collected.

If you made it through "Python and Math Essentials for Machine Learning: A Beginner's Guide" you have experienced a comprehensive exploration of the foundational components necessary to understand and implement machine learning algorithms. As we conclude this this part of the journey, it is fitting to reflect on the knowledge gained and the pathways paved for future exploration.

We embarked on a comprehensive exploration of Python programming essentials tailored specifically for machine learning enthusiasts. From mastering the fundamentals of Python syntax to delving into advanced topics such as recursion and object-oriented programming, you have acquired the foundational skills necessary to navigate the intricate landscape of machine learning algorithms with confidence.

We then explored Python data analytics and machine learning libraries, introducing the tools and techniques required to manipulate, visualize, and analyze data effectively. With a deep dive into the NumPy, Pandas, and Matplotlib libraries, you have honed your ability to leverage these powerful resources to tackle real-world machine learning challenges.

We then switched gears and ventured into the realm of mathematics, where statistics, linear algebra, and calculus converge to form the bedrock of machine learning. Through these chapters, you were equipped with the mathematical tools necessary to understand the underlying principles of machine learning algorithms, from interpreting data and analyzing patterns to optimizing models through gradient descent.

The knowledge imparted in this book serves as the launchpad for deeper exploration and innovation in the field of machine learning. Armed with a solid understanding of Python programming, data analytics, and mathematical foundations, you are primed to embark on the subsequent books in this series "Machine Learning Algorithms: A Beginner's Guide" and "Artificial Neural Networks: A Beginner's Guide".

In conclusion, "Python and Math Essentials for Machine Learning: A Beginner's Guide " is not merely a textbook; it is a roadmap towards mastery in the dynamic and ever-evolving field of machine learning. As we turn the final page, let us remember that the journey does not end here; rather, it is just the beginning of a lifelong pursuit of knowledge and discovery in the fascinating world of machine learning.